FOR
REASONS
OF STATE

FOR REASONS OF STATE

Delhi under Emergency

JOHN DAYAL | AJOY BOSE

Foreword by Mark Tully

PENGUIN
VIKING
An imprint of Penguin Random House

VIKING

USA | Canada | UK | Ireland | Australia
New Zealand | India | South Africa | China | Singapore

Viking is part of the Penguin Random House group of companies
whose addresses can be found at global.penguinrandomhouse.com

Published by Penguin Random House India Pvt. Ltd
7th Floor, Infinity Tower C, DLF Cyber City,
Gurgaon 122 002, Haryana, India

First published by Orient Paperbacks, New Delhi 1977
Published in Viking by Penguin Random House India 2018

Copyright © Ajoy Bose and John Dayal 2018
Foreword copyright © Mark Tully 2018

10 9 8 7 6 5 4 3 2

The views and opinions expressed in this book are the authors' own and the facts are as
reported by them which have been verified to the extent possible, and the publishers are
not in any way liable for the same.

ISBN 9780670090808

Typeset in Bembo Std by Manipal Digital Systems, Manipal
Printed at Replika Press Pvt. Ltd, India

www.penguin.co.in

'The State seeks to hinder every free activity by its censorship, its supervision, its police, and holds the hindering to be its duty, because it is in truth a duty of self-preservation. The State wants to make something out of man, therefore there lives in it only made men; everyone who wants to be his own self is its opponent.'

—*Max Stirner, Der Einzige und sein Eigentum*
(The Ego and His Own)

CONTENTS

~

Foreword

IX

Introduction to the 2018 Edition

XIII

Introduction

XXI

PROLOGUE
Bioscope

1

CHAPTER ONE
The Story of Turkman Gate

33

CHAPTER TWO
The Bulldozers
66

CHAPTER THREE
Out in the Wilderness
101

CONTENTS

CHAPTER FOUR

The Days of the Long Knives

127

CHAPTER FIVE

The Dinosaurs . . .

170

CHAPTER SIX

. . . And the Primeval Slush

190

CHAPTER SEVEN

The Denouement

209

Aftermath

219

Glossary

225

Appendix I

227

Appendix II

233

Appendix III

235

Appendix IV

239

Notes

241

FOREWORD

~

A few years ago, I was at a conference in London marking the fortieth anniversary of the Emergency. Looking back at that time, it seemed the chief significance of the Emergency was that it could never be repeated. Two years later, I am not so certain about this any more.

The international reaction to the Emergency, I remember, was anger and disappointment. This undoubtedly had an impact on Indira Gandhi. She did not like being described as a tyrant, as someone who had murdered democracy. There was a fear internationally that the Emergency might be the end of democracy in India. There is a theory that Mrs Gandhi was affected by this international reaction and therefore called an election to demonstrate her democratic credentials. I don't believe this myself. I think she called an election because she was misinformed. She was completely out of touch because of the sycophants surrounding her and misled to believe that she would win the elections. This was told to me by none other than Dev Kant Barooah, the president of the Congress party. If she had won the election, I have no doubt she would have said that this was a sign that people liked the Emergency and approved of what she had done, and so maintained it. It is very important to remember that although she had called an election, she did not actually lift the Emergency till it became clear that she had been defeated.

There are several possible explanations for a democracy like India turning into a dictatorship overnight. The first and most important one is the collapse of institutions. The institutions were so feeble—the judiciary, police, administration, the Congress party and even the President himself—they simply accepted this illegal act. Thereafter there was no real resistance to it. However, it must be borne in mind that the entire Opposition was in jail. There was an atmosphere of fear because of these arrests and because the police were taking advantage of the situation by making random arrests and demanding money to release the arrested. The powerful business community, from what I remember, did absolutely zero to oppose the Emergency. Yet there was underground resistance to the Emergency, the most famous example being George Fernandes.

Today, once again, there is a government with an absolute majority and a very powerful prime minister dominating his party. This has created an atmosphere of fear. This atmosphere of fear is heightened among certain communities, particularly the Muslims, by the ideology of Hindu extremist groups that appear to have powerful influence on the government. It is fundamentally anti-Muslim and sets that community up as the other to create fear within the Hindu community and try to unite it on the basis of this fear. Fear is also created by the actions of groups like *gau rakshak*s or cow defenders.

However, it would be incorrect to say this is like the Emergency. The Constitution has not been suspended and all the fundamental rights still remain in place. The press has not been censored and Opposition leaders have not been arrested. Democracy is continuing, in the sense that we are having all these elections. The BJP may be winning most of them but they are accepting defeats too, like they did in Bihar. So on the surface democracy is still in place. Underneath, though, there is undoubtedly an atmosphere of fear. There is fear that if the BJP is re-elected with a firm majority, this could be taken as an endorsement of its policy and its ideology. Attempts could then be made to alter the Constitution, making it more presidential than parliamentary and therefore giving more power to the chief executive.

As far as the media is concerned, it would be wrong to compare the present situation to the Emergency. My own experience of the press was that while not all of them bowed to the Emergency regime, most of them did. There is no doubt that the press on the whole did collapse. We in the foreign press protested against the censorship. We had negotiations with the government for a month or so on how we could operate but in the end most of us, including the BBC, felt that the terms of censorship we were asked to sign were so absurd that we could not do so without signing away all our journalistic independence and integrity.

Today there is no censorship but there may be self-censorship out of fear or pressures. It has to be said that television channels like NDTV and newspapers I read every day like the *Indian Express*, *The Hindu* and *Business Standard* have not collapsed. I am also very impressed with media outfits on the Internet like the Wire which certainly have not collapsed. It is true that some of the print media and television channels have become either blatantly pro-government or at least very reluctant to criticize it. Those that are owned by business groups have other business interests and fear that they will be harmed if they oppose the government. Yet there is no parallel today with what happened during the Emergency. What is, however, distressing is the misuse of investigative agencies and that is common to the Emergency and the run-up to it.

When Indira Gandhi lost the elections because of the Emergency, it did not come as a surprise to me. I had travelled widely across the country and could sense a mood of real anger in the countryside at the Emergency. *Nasbandi* (forcible sterilization programme) for instance was a disastrous experiment. Frankly, I do not see today any such widespread anger but I do notice increasing signs of disappointment. I think if this disappointment is powerfully expressed by the Opposition and by sections of the press, people will ask, 'Narendra Modi promised so much but what has he done, where are the *achhe din* that were supposed to come?'

There is also anger in the farming community and one of the causes is the ruination of the cattle economy which is so crucial to farmers. There has also been resistance from Dalit groups and some other castes, and very strong resistance from student groups. This is significant because the great resistance movement of independent India was the Jayaprakash Narayan movement which grew out of student agitations. I think the student movement may get stronger because of the way some universities are behaving, imposing control on the students and changing their curriculum. If any major corruption scandal erupts, it could also derail the government.

In the end I would like to point to a book I wrote some years ago called *No Full Stops in India*. For all the perceived threats today, I still believe that there will be no full stops to Indian democracy. After all, the Emergency proved to be only a comma.

New Delhi   **Mark Tully**
April 2018

INTRODUCTION TO THE
2018 EDITION

~

Forty-one years ago, we had warned in the introduction to our book, 'the myriad beasts that had prowled the jungle so menacingly for twenty months may well be there still, albeit in an enforced hibernation, hoping for more suitable climes before they flex their muscles again'. This may have seemed unduly alarmist in the immediate aftermath of the crushing defeat of the Emergency regime but has once again become relevant in the present political context.

Significantly, even when the Gandhi dynasty regained power in the 1980s to rule the political roost, Indian democracy appeared safe. Buoyed by her triumphant comeback over the corpse of the Janata Party, Indira Gandhi showed no interest in returning to authoritarian ways although in Punjab brutal state repression was unleashed against the citizenry after Operation Blue Star. Her son Rajiv, despite winning a massive electoral mandate after Mrs Gandhi's assassination, too remained a democrat and a back-door attempt to muzzle the media through a defamation bill spectacularly failed.

Even after the trauma of the successive assassinations of two leaders of the Gandhi dynasty, democracy continued to flourish. In any case, a series of coalition governments at the Centre for over two decades provided no opportunity for a national despot. The Emergency slowly became a distant memory of a faded nightmare ritually recalled every year in June at anniversary functions. Our book, although treasured for its rare account of the travails of ordinary folk in the country's capital under the Emergency, had historical value no doubt, but appeared to have no immediate relevance.

All this appears to have changed over the past few years after the advent of Narendra Modi heading a majority BJP government in New Delhi. Suddenly, Opposition leaders have started lamenting about an undeclared Emergency, the media is seen to have gagged itself and the civil liberties of the citizenry are feared to be once again under threat. These alarm bells have been persistently ringing despite the absence of some of the more notorious features of the Emergency—the entire Opposition put behind bars, formal press censorship and a mauled Constitution. Interestingly, there has also been a growing demand for a fresh edition of *For Reasons of State*, long out of print, to reread the lessons of the Emergency.

There are indeed clear parallels between Indira Gandhi and Narendra Modi—two extremely powerful figures who dominate their respective eras. Both reduced their respective cabinets to no more than rubber stamps, and ran the government through supine bureaucrats. Both encouraged a band of extra-constitutional authorities. Mrs Gandhi had her son Sanjay and his cohorts in the Youth Congress, if not running the government, at least dominating it and the party. Modi maintains his superiority and has allowed the surrogacy of hate campaigns like Ghar Wapsi to sundry groups spouting extreme prejudice.

On the other hand, Mrs Gandhi's Deb Kant Barooah as party chief did not enjoy the same place as Amit Shah occupies in Modi's heart not just as a trusted old companion, major-domo, keeper of secrets, but also for keeping a tight rein on the party apparatus and the electoral process. Barooah, with his 'Indira is

India' catchline, appears a farcical character compared to the far more formidable figure of Shah.

In the bureaucracy, a coterie of loyalist officers runs the country today according to the prime minister's bidding, much as they did for Indira Gandhi. But there is no equivalent of R.K. Dhawan and the extraordinary clout he wielded during the Emergency in the current Prime Minister's Office despite the wide-ranging powers of Modi aides Nripen Misra and Ajit Doval. The President and other constitutional offices, including even the judiciary, today have the same, if not lesser, power than they did in 1975.

There is also a striking similarity in the psyches of Indira Gandhi and Narendra Modi battling their inner demons, inadequacies and insecurities. Both consummate politicians in the rough and tumble of Indian politics, they have not cared much for constitutional niceties and liberal principles, notwithstanding the contrast between Modi's self-proclaimed *chaiwala* background and Mrs Gandhi's patrician lineage.

Indira Gandhi was never in doubt of her own superior status within her party, especially after vanquishing the syndicate of the Congress old guard. Indeed, after her stupendous victory over Pakistan, truncating it to form Bangladesh, her megalomania reached humongous proportions. She quite believed in Atal Behari Vajpayee's supposed description of her as Durga, although he would later deny having described her in so many words.

Modi has in his prime-ministerial avatar modelled himself on Narendra Dev, Swami Vivekananda in posture if not in spirit. Twice as old as the swami, Modi still crosses his arms over his chest, wears turbans wherever he can, though he has continued to sport a beard. His public photographs, both as BJP candidate and political election leader, and as head of government, have copied the steely gaze into the distant future. The countryside is plastered with facsimiles of that face, beard and gaze, as images of Mrs Gandhi with her hooked nose and silver-framed coiffure once stared out at the landscape four decades ago.

Significantly, non-governmental organizations (NGOs) and civil society movements have been prime targets of both the Emergency regime and the current dispensation. It was Mrs Gandhi who brought in the Foreign Contribution Regulation Act (FCRA) to harass them, taking particular delight in hounding the Gandhi Peace Foundation. Modi has gone even further, using the FCRA to control the voluntary sector across the country. Many NGOs have been forced to close down or shift to programmes that depend on the crumbs his government throws at them.

Both leaders have used an elaborate propaganda campaign to project themselves as champions of the poor and downtrodden fighting the rich and corrupt. Indira Gandhi's twenty-point economic programme and Narendra Modi's various schemes, including his dramatic demonetization caper, share a pious zeal and moral one-upmanship designed to gain maximum public support. Ironically, the poor and marginalized have actually suffered the most under both regimes. During the Emergency, the real victims of forcible sterilizations and arbitrary demolition were Dalits and Muslims at the bottom of the social heap, most vulnerable to the depredations of the State. Indeed, the atrocities suffered, particularly across north India, by these previous vote banks of the Congress during the Emergency turned them against the party, which was a major reason why it was wiped out in the region in the 1977 Lok Sabha polls. Today Dalits and Muslims are once again the worst sufferers of a breakdown in law and order.

We feel that the plight of Muslims during the Emergency and the ordeal they face in today's highly charged communal atmosphere make for an interesting comparison. It is true that neither Indira Gandhi nor her son Sanjay was burdened by the ideological baggage that Modi and Shah, in our opinion, carry because of their long and close association with the Sangh Parivar, with its overt anti-Muslim agenda. However, there are good reasons to believe that the Emergency regime did target Muslims as a community.

While researching the Turkman Gate story which is one of the highlights of our book, we were told by several leaders of the walled city that there appeared to be a concerted bid by the Emergency administration to scatter the concentration of Muslim residents and businessmen around Jama Masjid. Chowdhry Kaimuddin, a Muslim resident of the area, went to the extent of quoting the then Delhi Development Authority (DDA) vice chairman, Jagmohan, that he would not allow a Pakistan to be formed in the heart of the capital city.

Although the DDA vice chairman would later vehemently deny that he made any such threat, confirmation of a certain slant in the demolition drive around Jama Masjid came from his successor, M.N. Buch, who quoted Sanjay Gandhi in an opinion piece many years later. In the article 'The Dharmic State' published in Boloji.com on 6 October 2002, Buch wrote:

> I still remember my days with the Delhi Development Authority shortly after the Emergency was lifted and the Janata government came to power. We had constructed shops in the Meena Bazar area of Jama Masjid and the Payenwala area of Dariba in Delhi to rehabilitate the shopkeepers who had been uprooted from there during the Emergency. The majority of them were Muslims. Sanjay Gandhi told me that we were making a mistake because removal of the shopkeepers during the Emergency had eradicated a potential nest of Pakistani supporters. I was horrified to hear this from the mouth of Jawaharlal Nehru's grandson . . .

However, there is a vast gap between the thinly veiled prejudices against Muslims displayed by a variety of officials, including the city constabulary, during the Emergency and the systematic persecution of the minority community today. No minister in Indira Gandhi's cabinet would have dared to make such openly offensive remarks about Muslims that have now become routine, accusing virtually the entire community or anyone who presumed to speak up on its behalf of being anti-nationals who should be sent to Pakistan. Yet the concerted attempt during the Emergency to contain the minority population by targeting Muslim ghettos for forcible sterilizations or dispersing their inhabitants by bulldozing their dwellings did reflect a mindset not so different from the rulers of today. Significantly, one of the principal movers and shakers of Delhi under the Emergency, Jagmohan, joined the BJP and became a minister and so did Sanjay's widow, Maneka, carrying along her son, Varun.

Looking beyond ideological nuances between the Emergency regime and the present one, the stark similarity between the two is the kind of fear both spread among citizenry and the arbitrary nature of repression by the State and its cohorts. Once Indira Gandhi's election was overturned, and she declared the Emergency on the advice of the lawyer-politician Siddhartha Shankar Ray, the savagery with which the provisions of the Emergency were rammed through made it clear she would brook no opposition. The sheer number of people who were arrested in the initial phase—many of them kept in confinement till she decided to lift the Emergency and call for elections—is unprecedented in modern political history in the democratic world.

Today's undeclared Emergency is felt most in the environment of fear that pervades the country. The police are once again an authority unto themselves and the Intelligence Bureau, now abetted by the National Investigation Agency, is working in a grey zone of opaqueness that has never been the case since the Emergency, or even perhaps during it. Fake encounters or extrajudicial executions are reported to be on the rise again, most notably in Uttar Pradesh where nearly fifty people have been killed and several hundred injured by the police in over 1000 encounters[1] with alleged criminals in just one year after the BJP government assumed power in the state in March 2017. Opposition parties in the state have condemned many of them as fake, the National Human Rights Commission has issued notices on several of these encounters and the news website Wire documented fourteen cases of alleged extrajudicial executions by the police.

Much like what they did during the Emergency, the income tax authorities and the Enforcement Directorate have unleashed a reign of terror against the small businessman and trader even as the big boys of corporate India laugh their way to the bank.

The media is the more blatant case of being in a state of undeclared Emergency, differing with the one forty years ago in that some of the biggest conglomerates have now willingly offered themselves to serve as handmaidens and propaganda agents of the regime. Although there are myriad private channels today to counter the Goebbelsian propaganda spouted by the sole Doordarshan channel during the Emergency, few dare to do so, such is the dread of the powers that be. Yet social media, completely missing in the 1970s, allows dissidence and opinion to bloom today in a manner unimaginable when Mrs Gandhi suspended democracy.

Ultimately, regardless of the similarities and differences between then and now and whether one is worse than the other, the time has come once again to recall the assault on the democratic rights of people more than four decades ago. Because even though no Emergency has been declared today, its presence is palpable—felt by the rich and the poor, in the universities and the factories.

New Delhi
2018

INTRODUCTION

~

The trouble with the post-election situation in India in 1977 is that the tiny bushes in the foreground have hidden the forest behind. Also hidden, from the less probing eyes, are the myriad beasts that had prowled the jungle so menacingly for twenty months and may well be there still, albeit in an enforced hibernation, hoping for more suitable climes before they flex their muscles again. After the Emergency was relaxed just before the elections to the Lok Sabha, information had trickled down about cases of police brutality in Delhi and the states.

After the new Janata Party government was formed at the Centre, a large volume of reports has appeared on corruption, specially favours shown with or without political duress to companies associated with Sanjay Gandhi and his friends. The Maruti scandal has been hogging newspaper headlines and public discussions and, for the time being, till perhaps the various commissions start their proceedings, even the reports of excesses during the Emergency have tended to take a back seat.

Formidable as it is, Maruti is not the final personification, nor even the most characteristic symbol, of despotic rule under the Emergency. At best it betrays only the logical extension of the happenings that had taken place and in which the principals had acted by the rule of the bazaar to make cash capital out of the political and administrative situation they had so successfully managed to create. This has been brought about by the total depoliticization of society and by the perversion of the administrative system which had indeed for quite some time before the Emergency become ripe for being taken over by upstarts.

Officials and politicians of even the petty variety are explaining their activities during the Emergency as being born out of fear. But it is worth remembering that fear was only one, and in fact for the senior officers and politicians, almost the least important, of the factors responsible for the situation. Those who have closely watched the administrative process of the Union Territory of Delhi just before, during, and after the months of Emergency would know that the diabolical plan was not just a case of Sanjay Gandhi or his friends creating people who would do their bidding. It was a case of such people existing within the administration, simultaneously finding an extra-constitutional centre of authority and recognizing in it the powerhead that would help them in their own respective ambitions. The ambitions of the politician, the official and the bosses of the youth wing of the ruling party had become coterminous, so identical as to be indistinguishable from one another.

At a general level, it now is easy to see the strategy that had been adopted to utilize the situation. In the political institution of the Delhi Pradesh Congress Committee (DPCC), the Congress-run Delhi Administration controlled eventually by a nominated lieutenant governor, the superseded municipal corporation run by an official of the DDA, the Delhi State Industrial Development Corporation (DSIDC) for industries, the New Delhi Municipal Council (NDMC), the subordinate electricity producer and distributor Delhi Electricity Supply Undertaking (DESU), Delhi University (DU) and in Delhi Police which is controlled simultaneously by the lieutenant governor and the central government, there had existed a situation just before the Emergency which had created a coterie of officials bent on consolidating individual power. Internal rivalries and power grouping had reduced most of these institutions which ostensibly had a democratic functioning but in reality were administered on factors more personal to a state where they lacked the internal strength to resist any attempt at their perversion by outside forces.

The 'extra-constitutional source of power' recognized this factor and played on it skilfully. These forces in turn had recognized in the concept of Sanjay Gandhi just the additional impetus they needed for themselves. The implementation of the five-point programme became the yardstick of the competition between the various power groups. The number of trees planted, houses demolished and sterilizations done became the measure of closeness of these various groups to Sanjay Gandhi.

In such a scheme of things, normal channels of administration had perforce to be bypassed. Initially they were bypassed but later they were abolished altogether because they tended to cause the minutest of delays. Not only did this make the man at the top an absolute master of his domain, it also, more dangerously, tended to create smaller replicas of him in subordinate departments, to whom their immediate boss looked as the local 'avatar' of Sanjay Gandhi. The common man ceased to matter in this scheme of things. Whether his house was being bulldozed with only forty minutes' notice or whether his vas deferens was being cut by inexperienced doctors in dingy rooms doubling up as operation theatres, the common man had become the inanimate object whose main value was in his contribution to better statistics about the successful implementation of programmes. The officials went about the job willingly, enthusiastically, brutally. The administrative agencies and the political groups had logically welded themselves into a machine that reasoned only mathematically, saw only figures, and did what fitted into its concept of reducing men, women and children into a mass that could be used for political and financial exploitation.

The book has concerned itself primarily with an investigation into the workings of this monstrous administrative machine during the Emergency and the devastation it has left behind. It does not touch on the myriad corruption scandals and underhand deals that had flourished under the aegis of the Emergency, for the uniqueness of the Emergency does not lie in this direction. Corruption has for years infested the social and political life of India and can at best be termed as one of the factors that made the imposition of the Emergency so seemingly easy.

The uniqueness of the Emergency lies in the tremendous powers that the State wielded over society without any moral will behind it. Despite popular confusion, the Emergency did not bring in a fascist regime. At no stage in the nineteen months were there any signs of political fanaticism, nor were there any attempts to whip up popular frenzy. The State neither sought to create nor had it any mass psychology to prop it up. On the contrary, the imposition of Emergency was a coup d'état—a virtual takeover of a bankrupt civil society by a coterie of individuals who cornered tremendous power by being able to represent the State.

The details and the immediate and long-term causes of the coup on 25 June 1975 lie beyond the scope of this book. It attempts merely to deal with Delhi under Emergency. Nevertheless, through analysis of the various administrative departments and their functioning, both immediately before and after the Emergency, a broad picture emerges of how and why the State developed such arbitrary powers.

The book has attempted to fuse a journalistic methodology with a literary flavour. Hours of tape-recorded interviews and secret official documents have provided the main skeleton of the book. The authors have fleshed the skeleton with many fictional details, but the fictionalization has been only of real situations, taking care that historical accuracy is adhered to. Any postmortem report which attempts to recreate an immediate image of the traumatic happenings in the capital under the Emergency encounters two main problems. The first is that one has to depend largely on eyewitness accounts of the incidents without any means of corroborating them. The second is the risk of running into the draconian libel laws of the country when investigating contemporary history. We have tried our best to check and recheck the same incident from three and sometimes four different sources and then used the one that seemed most credible and coherent. For controversial situations involving the reputation of high officials, we have banked largely on documented evidence. For the sake of authenticity, we have in many cases had to leave out vital incidents during the Emergency. One of these is the relevant question: Who ordered the firing in Turkman Gate? (There were four different high officials who could have ordered it.) We chose to be accurate rather than sensational. The book not only describes the happenings in the capital during those nineteen months but also juxtaposes high drama with an analysis of the causes behind it. Often the two have complemented each other.

The book starts with a Prologue titled 'Bioscope', because it presents an almost unending strip of cameos and images which go to build the surreal nightmare that the Emergency was. The 'Story of Turkman Gate' has been written as a narrative, with the characters of the piece living and acting out the story. And if any hitherto unknown incidents in the Turkman Gate massacre have been described in graphic detail, it is not because the authors possess a high degree of imagination but because two months of tough and continuous investigation at Turkman Gate yielded results.

The chapter called 'The Bulldozers' places the demolition at Turkman Gate in the context of the eighteen months of the campaign in almost all quarters of the capital by DDA bulldozers.

'Out in the Wilderness' builds up the misery and squalor of life in the resettlement colonies. The brutalization of Dwarka Prasad and his family in Mangolpuri is a real story. The vast vasectomy dragnet which was spread far and wide over Delhi has been described in 'The Days of the Long Knives'. It tries to picture not only the trauma of the threat to the individual's most intimate privacy but also shows how officials fought with each other to get their quotas increased. The 'Dinosaurs' and the 'Primeval Slush' are two complementary chapters which describe the arbitrary police terror that raged day and night in the capital and the slime and muck it thrived in. The Epilogue is a record of the people's final reply.

The authors record their thanks to W. Afroz, Madhu, T.V. Kunhi Krishanan, Dr Aurobindo Ghosh, Amitabh Mukhopadhyay, Sanjeev Aggarwal, Vinod Dayal, Raaj Kumar, many colleagues and Mrs Mercy M. John. The authors thank all the people who have helped garner information, especially the people of Turkman Gate.

PROLOGUE

BIOSCOPE

~

Town Hall, New Year, 1976, 'MOST IMPORTANT OUT TODAY'[1]

Office Order No. P 4 (30-II) 75-JSV:

> In exercise of the powers vested in me under section 491
> of the DMC Act, 1957, I hereby direct that all the powers
> conferred on me under the various sections of the said act
> for conversion of dry latrines into water-borne or flush-type
> latrines to implement effectual drainage systems within 10
> days of the notice issued to close or demolish the dry latrines
> at the risk and cost of the owner/occupant shall, subject to my
> overall supervision, control and review be also exercised by all
> the zonal engineers (drainage) of the municipal corporation
> w.e.f. the forenoon of 2-1-1976. Signed B.R. Tamta, IAS,
> Commissioner, The Municipal Corporation of Delhi.[2]

Shahdara, 9 September 1975. Eighty-year-old Premlata Devi was
in the latrine when the bulldozers came. 'Come out, you old
hag, we have to bulldoze the latrine,' said the demolition men
laughing outside. 'Just a minute, I am coming, I am coming,'

I

cried the old woman nervously. 'Come out this minute or we will run the bulldozer over the latrine with you in it,' shouted the demolition men. Shaking with fear, Premlata Devi emerged from the latrine and tottered away from the spot to the jeers and laughter of the demolition men.

Town Hall. A press note issued by the municipal corporation to be published in newspapers on 10 December 1975:

> The people living in several localities of the walled city (of Delhi) were taken by pleasant surprise when they saw Mr. Sanjay Gandhi accompanied by several civic officials inspecting their area this morning. Mr. Gandhi was accompanied by Mr. B.R. Tamta, Municipal Commissioner, Sardar Beant Singh, Zonal Assistant Commissioner of the city zone, besides some other officers.
>
> Mr. Gandhi visited Shardanand Marg, Lal Quan, Farash Khana, Ajmeri Gate and the interior lanes of Phatak Namak, Mohalla Rodagaran and Excelisor Road Sirki Walan. The residents of these colonies and voluntary organizations gave him a rousing reception at various places and told him about their civic problems. The civic officials made a note of these problems.
>
> Mr. Gandhi was specially shown the areas where the unauthorized encroachments were peacefully removed and nuisance of stray cattle was solved. He was very happy and congratulated the civic officials for their good work. He also noted of the highest standard of sanitation maintained by the civic officials in the congested and populated localities.

Early on 22 November 1975, the people living in and around Jama Masjid woke up to find a sea of khaki advancing towards them. First came the men of Central District Police marching in formation, carrying wide-bore guns that fire tear-gas shells. Behind them came the Delhi Armed Police (DAP), an ugly musket chained to each constable's belt. Bringing up the rear was a huge contingent of Central Reserve Police. Mounted policemen on frisky stallions moved in arrogantly ahead.

There was a hush in Jama Masjid marketplace as shopkeepers watched in stunned silence. The traffic police had already stopped all vehicles and pedestrians from approaching the market, and the normal bustle of the bazaar had been replaced by an electric atmosphere of tension.

At 10 a.m., from within the vast body of khaki, emerged an army of 1000 labourers and sixty trucks. As Commissioner B.R. Tamta, Deputy Commissioner K.N. Sharma and other municipal officers directed them, the workers moved in with pick and rod. Even as the first announcement on the loudspeakers told the shopkeepers that they should remove their belongings before their shops were demolished, the first row of shops fell under the onslaught of the demolition squad. Four hundred shops fell that day—400 shops that were doing business in anything from biryani to spare parts, from transistor radios to pigeons; 400 shops that had been plying their trade for generations.

And all the while the police kept vigil, occasionally moving in to drag aside the odd shopkeeper who tried to save his wares from becoming rubble. At a distance sat a DDA official. The queue in front of him was of the shopkeepers who did not own shops any more. The official gave them slips of paper. Then, as the municipal trucks took away the debris, the shopkeepers climbed on other trucks for the long drive to distant Mayapuri, across the width of Delhi where they were told to set up their business anew. Three days later, Superintendent of Police R.K. Ohri and Commissioner Tamta were again at the spot when the men moved in for a fresh wave of demolition that left 250 more shops in a heap of rubble.

4 FOR REASONS OF STATE

A senior officer who was busy with the exceptional chore of overseeing the Emergency operations in the city, one day received an important call. The voice at the other end had a disquieting message. Even as the pickaxes struck at the shops behind Jama Masjid, the old masonry of the masjid had disgorged a few stones and bricks. Work had ceased at once as the masjid caretakers brought divine imprecations on the heads of the officials. 'Come quickly,' the voice said, 'the masjid wall threatens to fall.'

Minutes later, senior engineers had chalked out a plan of action. An eighteen-inch-thick wall was to be constructed to buttress the old masjid masonry. At breakneck speed the masons fitted the bricks and, within hours, the wall was ready.

The Masjid, Turkman Gate, 19 April 1976. The labourers' picks dislodge a key stone in the masjid edifice. As mortar and dust collapse in a noisy cloud, the engineers decide to raise the wall, fast and quick. The wall is nearing completion when the bricks at the bottom, loosely set in soggy mortar, give way. Officials record the death of two workers, buried under the falling bricks.

Police bulletin, 20 July 1976:

> Over 1100 police personnel coming from all ranks have undergone voluntary sterilizations in the last fortnight. Among those who have undergone operations are senior officers including two district superintendents.
>
> On an average about 75 police personnel got themselves sterilized every day in different hospitals and camps. Senior Police Officers visit hospitals and other centres daily where police personnel undergo sterilization. The officers also pay frequent visits to the sterilized policemen in their homes to enquire about their wellbeing.

Earlier, a systematic drive was launched to motivate and educate all ranks of Delhi policemen about the benefits of the family planning programme.

The Delhi Police Welfare Society president, Sushila Mathur, wife of the Inspector-General of Police Bhawanimal, has done a yeoman job in propagating the family planning programme in Delhi Police.

Police bulletin, 2 August 1976:

Inspector General of Police Bhawanimal announced at a Vanomahotsav meeting at New Police Lines in Kingsway Camp that 2000 Delhi police personnel had undergone voluntary sterilizations in the past twenty-five days.

Inspector General of Police Bhawanimal was gheraoed by policemen at an Old Police Lines meeting. The IGP had just told the policemen to take part more wholeheartedly in family planning. 'If I have one more child, shoot me, sir,' says one constable, the father of two children.

An irate Bhawanimal shouts at him, 'Shut up! Who is talking of shooting? We are talking of a national programme.'

Another constable corners the IGP, saying, 'I am a Brahmin, sir, I have to take my holy bath every day. If I have my bath after getting operated, I'll catch an infection, sir.'

'Take the man away,' says the IGP. 'We will have everybody pleading that he is a Brahmin.'

Office of the DPR, Delhi Administration, 13 February 1976. The following press note is released for publication:

A motivational committee on family planning was set up last month by the Lt. Governor of Delhi under the chairmanship

of Mrs. Vidya Ben Shah, president of NDMC, Other members are:
1. Commissioner, Family Planning, Government of India.
2. Commissioner, Municipal Corporation of Delhi.
3. Secretary Medical, Delhi Administration.
4. Director Health Services and Family Planning, Delhi Administration.[3]

In addition, The Lt. Governor has now nominated Shri (sic) Ruksana Singh as the only non-official member of the Committee.

Jama Masjid Chowk, 18 April 1976, midday. A seventeen-year-old boy clings to one of the pillars below the Jama Masjid police chowki screaming at the top of his voice, *'Main nahin jaunga, main nahin jaunga* [I will not go].' He is being beaten by a group of police constables but the boy won't let go of the pillar. Finally, his fingers are pried open with a baton and the boy, still screaming, is dragged towards Dujana House Family Planning Camp. A few burqa-clad women watch the scene quietly from afar.

Somewhere in a house in Jama Masjid, 18 April 1976, late night. A women's get-together. 'We have got to do something about this nasbandi business,' says a matronly burqa-clad figure. 'Now they are dragging beggars to be sterilized, next they will drag our husbands.' She added, 'We must stop that lady somehow. First she comes and tells us to stop wearing the burqa and then she wants to castrate our husbands. We must stop her somehow.' Another woman says, 'If we start some sort of boycott, we have the Imam's and Mir Sa'ab's blessings.' There are hurried consultations for a while before the meeting breaks up.

Jama Masjid Chowk, 19 April 1976, midday. The Dujana House Family Planning Camp van screeches to an abrupt halt. A burqa-clad woman has lain down on the road right in front of the van. A couple of police constables rush out of the van. 'Hey you, get out of the way!' 'No, I won't. You are taking my Usman to the nasbandi camp. No, I won't, I'd rather die first,' cries the woman. 'What are you talking about? No.' But the woman is adamant. The police constables get angry. One of them catches the woman by her hair and drags her out of the way. A crowd has gathered already, and a deep growl emerges from it as they see the woman being dragged away. '*Arre,* what are you trying to do? Can't you see she is a woman?' says Mirza angrily. Mirza is promptly arrested. Meanwhile, the captives of the van have managed to open the door and, taking advantage of the preoccupation of the policemen with the crowd, have escaped.

Dujana House DDA Housing Complex, 19 April 1976. Fourteen-year-old Nazleen got the shock of her life when she opened the window of her second-floor flat. 'Hey, Amma, come quick! They are beating up the Begum Sahiba.' Buxom matron that she was, Jamila Begum ran as fast as she could from the kitchen. 'Mashallah, they have got the lady at last!' she cried.

Below, Ruksana Sultana, the family-planning chief, was trying to fend off the angry burqa-clad women who had surrounded her. Someone tried to grab her hair, but the begum managed to brush her off. 'Murderess, adulteress, how dare you come to Jama Masjid and castrate our men!' shouted one of the women. It was a moment of panic for the begum but fortunately for her, she was whisked away by her aides into a waiting car. She was shivering with fear and rage.

Upstairs, Nazleen lamented, '*Ish,* she managed to escape and I had been hoping that she'd get beaten up.' 'Arre, let that lady come back once again here,' said Jamila Begum, adjusting her spectacles, 'you will see what a beating she gets.'

Dujana House DDA Housing Complex, 1 April 1977. Janata Party flags fly arrogantly from the top of all buildings except a first-floor veranda where a large Congress flag flies defiantly. This is the house of Mohammed Zulfikar, Congress worker. He is no ordinary Congress worker. Mohammed Zulfikar was arrested under the Maintenance of Internal Security Act (MISA) in April 1976 for not saluting Begum Ruksana Sultana. A large, stolid man, Mohammed Zulfikar adjusts his fez as he says, 'I have been in the Congress for thirty-five years and will be on it for the rest of my life, but I don't salute just anybody.' Nobody in the area has once asked Mohammed Zulfikar to take down his flag.

Raj Niwas, 19 April 1976. Lieutenant Governor Krishan Chand issues a press statement.

> Certain reports are reaching the administration that some interested persons are bent on creating conditions in which the work of family planning cannot be carried on in an orderly manner.
>
> The facts are that as a result of the persistent efforts of the motivational committee on family planning headed by Smt. Vidya Ben Shah, President, NDMC and of Ruksana Sultana Sahiba, 15000 persons, male and female, have offered themselves voluntarily for measures which check the reproduction of unwanted children permanently. The people are motivated because large families, particularly in the city areas, live in very trying conditions.
>
> I want to make it clear beyond doubt that if any obstruction is caused to the doctors, the nurses or the personnel and workers engaged in promoting the family planning programme, very drastic action will be taken against the offending persons.
>
> Today itself in Dujana House, where a family planning camp was opened only four days ago, over 300 cases have

already been treated. We are at the beginning of the work
and by no means at the end of it.

Old Secretariat. Ageing Chief Executive Councillor Radha
Raman gives his sanction to the release of an article prepared for
publication under his name. The article says:

The Five Point Programme of the dynamic and youthful
leader Shri Sanjay Gandhi has had a tremendous impact
on the masses. It has electrified the entire national scene.
An atmosphere of constructive activity has been created.
Through this programme the citizens of India have been
presented with some well defined activities wherein they
could engage themselves and feel the pride of participation in
a new peaceful socio-economic revolution.

He has given to the people a simple and easily workable
programme of action through which any responsive
citizen can help strengthen the economic and social fabric
of the nation through voluntary individual action without
dependence on Government agencies. These programmes
which will have significant economic impact will at the same
time help bring about a healthy change in the physical and
mental environment of the country. As is well known by
now, the 5 pillars of this human programme are: the ideal of
small family; transformation of human environment through
tree plantation and cleanliness; mass enlightenment through
tree plantation; eradication of illiteracy; speeding up socio-
economic revolution by cutting at the roots of social evils
such as dowry and vulgar display of wealth and fighting the
canker of casteism which has been eating into the vitals of
Indian society.

Delhi has taken the lead in implementation of this vital
programme and its results are quite visible within a short time.
The entire social and physical environment of Delhi today

reflects the change brought about by the efforts to implement this vital programme effectively.

Summer 1976. In the crowded female ward of the Hindu Rao Hospital on top of the Ridge, the senior doctor grumbles as he steps over the sick women carpeting the floor of the ward.

He looks around for the other doctors who are supposed to be assisting him. They are not present. With a shrug, he tells the visitor, 'Why don't you write about this? Here we have so many patients. Many of them require surgery. But there are no surgeons. They are all at the family planning clinic, performing vasectomies and collecting Rs 2 for every gash they make.'

Summer 1976, Victoria Zanana Hospital, now called the Kasturba Gandhi Hospital. The smell of antiseptic lotion and blood, and the sweat of fear hover in a haze over the beds stuck close together in the wards.

In the maternity wards, the women are being put three to a bed. One has her head in one direction, the second in the opposite. The third is allowed to place her head wherever she wants.

In the septic ward, the nurses greet familiar faces who had come to the tubectomy camp a week or ten days ago. They had then been given their money and gifts and been sent away. They are now back with their stitches broken, with pus oozing out. 'There were deaths too,' a nurse says.

The Nagar Palika School of the NDMC, 21 August 1967. The NDMC vigilance officer calls a meeting of principals, teachers and officials. The vigilance officer reads out to the teachers the order issued by the NDMC member secretary, asking teachers to motivate as many people as they can for sterilization.

At the Nagar Palika School, three days later, the principal holds an hour-long meeting with the teachers to discuss the family-planning directive of the member secretary. He pleads for more cases from his schoolteachers. The teachers elect a treasurer for a special family-planning fund.

26 *August 1976*. The principal calls the teachers to a staff meeting and tells them of the exhortations of the deputy education officer to all principals. He says the teachers must give top priority to the family-planning campaign. The meeting goes on for more than an hour. Ultimately, the teachers give an undertaking to get 'cases' before 30 August.

The same school, 27 August 1976.

Principal sahib calls a special meeting of all teachers in connection with family planning which went on till 5.15 p.m. The principal asked each teacher personally what he or she was doing about it and how far they had been successful. The principal also reads out the NDMC asking for daily reports on the progress of the campaign.

The same school, 30 August.

The principal holds a special meeting of the teachers and asks each one of them whether they had called such parents who were eligible for sterilizations. And if they had not called the parent so far, they should do so immediately. The figures collected from the teachers show that 125 cases have been sterilized. The principal says that two cases have been collected today and two more will be collected by tomorrow.

(From the records of NP Boys Higher Secondary
School, New Delhi.)

Autumn 1976. Assistant teacher P.S. Yadav, on deputation to NP Middle School at Tilak Bridge, went to the school to collect his salary. He did not get it. Instead, he was given an order which read:

Pay of Sh. P.S. Yadav will be released on production of a motivation slip of a family planning case as a general policy in this respect. He may collect pay as soon as the case's motivation slip is deposited with the undersigned. Signed by Shri Niwas, Headmaster, Nagar Palika Middle School, Medical Institute.

DDA Vice Chairman Jagmohan's office, 18 April 1976. A delegation of the residents of the Turkman Gate make a desperate plea to Jagmohan to immediately stop the demolition of buildings or give suitable alternative sites. 'We want to live all together in Seelampur Welcome,' they tell him. Chowdhry Kaimuddin, a member of the delegation, is stunned to hear Jagmohan shriek 'Live all together! Do you think we are mad that we will destroy one Pakistan to create another Pakistan?'[4] One by one the members of the delegation leave in shocked silence.

Turkman Gate, 19 April 1976. A phone call from the deputy commissioner in the Turkman Gate police chowki. 'Hello, what is the situation?' asks the deputy commissioner. First silence, and then, from the other end, someone said, 'Murderer, bastard!' A hoarse voice filled with hate repeated the words. 'Who is that? Is that Turkman Gate police chowki?' the deputy commissioner panicked. 'This is your *baap* [father] speaking, you bastard,' the voice spits. The deputy commissioner puts the phone down and picks it up again. He orders the subordinate, 'Send reinforcements to Turkman Gate at once. They have taken over the police chowki.' This was during the brief moment of glory for the Turkman Gate people, their one-hour capture of the police station.

(An eyewitness)

Turkman Gate, 19 April 1976. Eighty-year-old Abdus Sattar had just finished his prayers when the police broke open the main gate of Dargah Faiz-e-Elahi masjid. Abdus had worked in the mosque for many long years and had been sweeping the floors of the masjid for longer than he could remember. Never had he witnessed such a scene of bedlam—screams, lathis, tear gas and blood. The terrified man crouched next to a wall. But soon the tear gas reached the corner where he was hiding. Coughing desperately, Abdus ran for the door. He was caught and dragged by his neck by a burly constable. 'I will come with you, but just let me go to the latrine once,' cried Abdus. The answer came in a huge blow to his head. Then everything blacked out for Abdus Sattar.

Pir Mohammed of Katra 3339. Fatak Teliyan will never forget that sub-inspector. 'Point him to me in a crowd but I will spot him. Yes, I remember his burly frame. He was very tall, over six feet, short, thick neck and beady eyes.' Pir Mohammed is sure. And of all the things he remembers about the sub-inspector, Pir Mohammed will never forget the strength of his arm. 'One hit from that hand, and you'll never get up again. He didn't have to use lathis, that one.'

Messrs Girdhar Lal Panna Lal. This lace and *gota* factory was one of the oldest industrial units in Turkman Gate. On the morning of 19 April 1976, the workers of the factory, numbering around sixty, reported for work as usual. When violence erupted all around the factory, the proprietor appears to have slipped away, leaving the supervisor and the workers to defend the factory. The workers did this, both against the demolition squad and the infuriated mob which was fighting the armed policemen. The workers, however, didn't fight the policemen as they only wanted to save the factory machines. The supervisor is reported to have rung up the police to come and evacuate the workers as they could not hold out any longer.

Soon the police came, but not to rescue the workers. Before the workers could open the bolted gates, the police broke them open and poured into the factory. Then the workers were mercilessly beaten up with lathis, bayonets and rifle butts and thrown into police vans. All of them were jailed. The only fault of the workers was that they had stayed on in the factory to defend the machines.

Katra 3393, Turkman Gate, 19 April 1976. Husnah Begum lay huddled, quivering with fear, as she heard the sound of gunfire and screams outside her room. Her little boy, Akbar, cringed next to her as there were loud knocks on the bolted door. 'Open up! This is the police,' shouted a voice. The woman and her child remained silent. 'We will break down the door if you don't open up,' the voice shouted louder. Akbar drew even closer to his mother. Then a loud crunch and the door gave way. Husnah Begum closed her eyes. She tried not to open them, throughout her ordeal with the foul-smelling constable. Her soft whimpering only once rose to a scream when she heard the cries of little Akbar as a rifle butt smashed him against the floor. A strange darkness now surrounded her.

~

Incomplete List of Persons who died in police firing or demolition operations on 19 April 1976. The list cannot be exhaustive till normal conditions are restored after termination of curfew:

1. Mohammed Arif son of Mohammed Bashir, factory worker (rolling-machineman) in the factory of Hamidduddin situated at 2811, Pahari Bhojila. Survivors: one wife, two children and mother. Age 24 years, resident of 2593 Kucha Meer Hasa, Jama Masjid.

2. Mohammed Rauf son of Mohammed Munir resident of House 2393 Kucha Meer Hashir (Chitli Kabar) Bhootnay Wali Gali.

3. Zahiruddin son of Nasiruddin, Kheer Wala Phatak, Kabristan, Age 23 years.

4. Jannat Begam sister of Mohd. Ibrahim, Age 30 years, resident of Phatak Taliyan.

5. Salauddin son of Mohammed Yamin, aged 19 years resident of 1942 Kucha Chelan.

6. Suleiman son of late Bashir, Phatak Meer Hashim, (Chitli Kabar.

7. Grandson of Hafiz Barkat (Name being found out), died in furniture shop opposite Gali Nanwa Teli, Turkman Gate.

8. Iqbal (other particular not known).

9. Son of Abdul Haq (name yet to be ascertained) resident of Mohalla Gadhaywala, Turkman Gate.

10. Abdul Malik, Age 22 (postmortem in police hospital).

11. Sagir Ahmed son of Majid Ahmad, Age 16 years, resident of 3889, Gali Khan Khana, Jama Masjid.

12. Mohammed Shabid, son of Mohammed Yasin, Age 18 years, resident of 1974, Suivalan, Jama Masjid.

Persons seriously wounded on the spot but whose survival or death is yet to be confirmed.

1. Bhola resident of Phatak Telian.

2. Shahabuddin Alias Babua, resident of Phatak Telian.

3. Bodam son of Matino, resident of 3030 Gali Ansari, Kalan Masjid, Turkman Gate.

First list of persons remaining untraced so far:

1. Wahid Ali son of Salimuddin resident of 2820, Pahari Bhojla.

2. Ghoti Begum wife of Baby Khan, Gali Saidan Kha, Pahari Bhojla.

3. Mohammed Rais son of late Mohammed Hashim, Gali Takhatwali Suivalan.

4. Afraz Begum wife of Azizudin, 1243, Rakabganj, Turkman Gate.

5. Mohammed Suleiman Takhatwali, Suivalan.
6. Razia Begum wife of Mohammed Akili, resident of
    1140 Turkman Gate, Takabganj.
7. Badruddin son of Islamuddin, 1212 Rakabganj,
    Turkman Gate.

Jama Masjid Chowk, 1 March 1977, midnight. The people
have been waiting for the leaders to come. Bahuguna is spied
perched precariously on the press-gallery table, nervous to
go farther through the 20-foot-deep crowd. But the crowd
beckons. 'Come Bahugunaji, it's only us, the people; we
will make way for you.' And Bahuguna takes up the offer.
He embraces a thousand cheering supporters as he is swept
towards the dais. But there was no sign of Babuji. 'Won't
Babuji come?' The anxious query is repeated. And finally
he comes. The familiar giant figure, escorted by a few Janata
Party workers, walks over to the dais. The slogans and cheers
and clapping threaten to tear down the very foundations of
the masjid.

Shahi Imam Syed Abdullah Bukhari is a splash of colour. His
robes are red and green; his dark glasses bring out his peaches and
cream complexion, and his sceptre rises and falls in flamboyant
gestures.

From the middle of the seething mass of humanity, a black
banner rises. Like a giant black bat, it hovers over the crowd
and a strange hush falls on the Jama Masjid square. The banner
says: 'We the people of Turkman Gate want to come back from
where we have been driven away.'

The shahi imam raises his hand. 'We the people of Turkman
Gate and Jama Masjid have paid in blood and dishonour of our
women. And we know who had ordered our suffering. It is not
the Hindus, not the Sikhs, not the Christians. It is not the RSS.
It is the government.[5] And now, my brethren, the hour has
come. We are to choose whether to keep this government or

not. So, my brethren, I give you a slogan; a slogan that I want you to repeat again and again till it brings down the edifice of this barbarous government. Brethren, repeat after me, 'Hindu, Muslim, Sikh, Isai, bhai bhai, bhai bhai!' The imam raises both his hands. And the slogan is taken up from one corner of the vast crowd to the other, till it rumbles and echoes down the lanes and by-lanes of Jama Masjid.

Polling day at Turkman Gate, 16 March 1977. An irate presiding officer at the Turkman Gate polling booth gets tired of explaining to the stream of voters pouring in how and where to put their ballot paper. 'Why don't you do one thing?' suggests one voter. 'We are all voting Janata, so what is all this secrecy about? Just do the job for us. But be sure that my vote goes to Janata.' By 3.30 p.m., out of 856 votes cast at the booth, only fifteen were believed to have gone to the Congress.

Town Hall, Delhi, 27 May 1976. At 3.30 p.m. a group of reporters enters the commissioner's room for the biweekly press conference. This would be one of the most important press conferences during the period of the Emergency.

In the cool, tastefully decorated room, a group of senior officers of the corporation surrounds Tamta. A photograph of Indira Gandhi adorns the wall. In front of the commissioner is a glass-topped model of Jama Masjid set in rolling acres of green. In symmetrical columns beside it rise four scale-models of multistorey buildings.

'Gentlemen, we plan to clear the entire Chawri Bazar and redevelop it on commercial lines. The municipal corporation will finance it out of the Rs 5 crore they have won from the NDMC in the power dispute. The scheme is being undertaken as a pilot project to initiate redevelopment of the old and decaying areas of the walled city,' Tamta says. The road to Daryaganj will be 150 feet wide. The buildings will have twelve floors.

Daryaganj, 15 July 1976. Soft-spoken Congress leader Shiv Charan Gupta, a former member of Parliament, said, 'The citizens have written to the corporation to extend the date of filling objections up to 15.8.1976 as 10 days' time is not sufficient to study the scheme and file the objection as it involves demolition of 1357 parties, resettlement of 2140 families, shifting of 134 factories and 228 godowns and 10 schools, alternative premises for 1126 shops and 5 hotels and disturbances to 33 temples and 3 mosques, but so far there is no indication of any extension.'

The scheme is not according to the provisions of the master plan. It does not conform even to the provisions of the draft zonal development plans of the area published for public objections in 1971 and not finalized as such. The first phase of the scheme from where the corporation wants to start 'operation demolition' is not shown as a clearance or redevelopment area in the draft zonal development plan of Dariba, Maliwara, in which this portion falls.

The government might be doing some fresh thinking about Old Delhi. If so, a master plan for old built-up areas should be prepared and the public taken into confidence as it would vitally affect the future of 13 lakh people living there.

Chawri Bazar paper market, July 1976. 'Come and collect Rs 350. Come and register yourself for family planning,' a corpulent young man exhorts passers-by.

Young men, sons of the big paper merchants of the bazaar, have formed themselves into an association dedicated to national goals. At the colourful shamiana, in front of the pyramids of tins of vegetable ghee, men queue up as loudspeakers blare the popular hits of Mohammad Rafi. Many of them work in the paper shops, and some are rickshaw-pullers and hawkers of fruit chaat.

Chawri Bazar. 'Sanjay Gandhi ki Jai!' The handsome, balding young man smiles as he slithers out of the car. A group of officials surrounds him in an inner circle. The young man stands up to speak. 'The Chawri Bazar scheme is not final. We will review it.'

1, Safdarjung Road, 9 November 1975. From early morning, they began collecting at the House. The senior officers had come in their cars. The junior ones on two-wheelers and the large body of the employees in municipal trucks and other chartered vehicles. This was going to be an unprecedented procession to the prime minister's residence. Over 10,000 officers and employees of the Municipal Corporation of Delhi (MCD), including its two undertakings, the Water Supply and Sewage Disposal Undertaking and DESU—would greet the prime minister and express their determination to improve civic services.

Leading the vast cheer group was the squat figure of Tamta. The heads of departments and zonal assistant commissioners solemnly led their batches, some of them carrying placards and banners probably for the first time in their lives. And if there was a smirk on the faces of many of the junior employees, it was because they knew that they wouldn't do much work for the better part of the day. No work either for the doctors, nurses, teachers, fire-service units and sweepers. They were all busy expressing their determination to work harder.

Instructions had already been given on what to do the moment the prime minister appeared, and when she made her appearance, the 10,000-strong rally shouted out slogans and clapped.

The prime minister thanked them 'for their continued support in all exigencies and Emergency' but also reminded them that 'we have an ancient Indian tradition to maintain balance in the moments of sorrow and happiness'. The most important thing, she said, was to maintain 'unity', solidarity and progress of the nation with full responsibility, dedication, discipline and hard work. Loud applause and repeated slogans of 'Indira Gandhi zindabad'.

'We have made much progress in the field of education, health, agriculture and industry,' she continued. Loud applause. 'But some vested interests from within and outside did not like our working and created obstacles in the progress of the country by disregarding the established norms of democracy.' Loud applause again.

The prime minister stopped abruptly. Someone had blundered. Officers looked around sternly to spot the culprit. Giggles were stifled hurriedly by the employees and the poor DESU clerk who had started the clapping almost by habit tried his best to retreat.

The crisis was soon over. The prime minister continued on a solemn note, 'If I wanted, I too could follow the life of ease and comfort, but I have chosen the hard way only in the larger interests of my countrymen.' Uneasy silence at this point. Nobody wanted to start clapping, after the blunder a few minutes back. But a senior officer came to the rescue. Rising up from where he was sitting, he raised a fervent cry: 'Indira Gandhi zindabad!', 'Desh ki neta Indira Gandhi!'

(A participant)

Delhi University. Statement by Abhimanyu Sharma, department of anthropology:

When the newspapers did not come out that day we knew something had happened. By midnight disturbing rumours had reached us and we tried not to listen to the loud knocks in the night. By morning news came that Dr Paliwal of the Botany Department had been arrested.

In our professors colony, the community was advised not to meet the arrested families. In the campus, in five days we counted at least 375 arrests. Some of them we heard were released later.

Jawaharlal Nehru University (JNU) campus, 25 September 1975.
Young Prabir Purkayastha lounges along with three girl students on the lawns in front of the School of Languages. Around 10.30 a.m., a black Ambassador drives through the main gate of the campus. Four burly men in civvies get out of the car, walk up to Prabir and ask him if he is Devi Prasad Tripathi, president of the students' union. Before he can answer, Prabir is collared by the men and dragged towards the car. The girls try to stop the men, but are shoved aside. Prabir is pushed into the car which has already started moving. The boy makes one last attempt, manages to free himself and falls out of the moving car. The car screeches to a halt as the two men run up to Prabir and pick him up. Again, the struggle to get free, but this time the men manage to get hold of Prabir. Now there is no escape. The car zooms off, but in the confusion leaves the two men behind.

Meanwhile, the girls scream and a crowd gathers. One of the men manages to escape but the other is captured by the students. Soon, a jeep full of armed policemen enters the campus. While they hold the students at gunpoint, their colleague clambers into the jeep. The jeep zooms out.

Delhi University, faculty of science. The new term, July 1975.

We were warned repeatedly to be careful. Particularly not to indicate any sort of politics in our class room lectures. Absolutely nothing. Then they sent us a code of conduct. They even set up a vigilance squad. There comes the dog squad, the teachers would say whenever one of the members would be seen in the department.

The dog squad would come and shout, 'Where is the Register?', 'Who has not come?', and 'Why?'

A departmental head would tell his visitors, 'That fellow is critical, what do you think, should we get him nabbed?'

(Report by Abhimanyu Sharma)

Indra Vikas Puri. Little children search for water amidst the rubble. The water supply department had cut off the connection early that morning. An elderly constable gives a child a drink out of his own glass.

The children's parents are busy putting the remains of their belongings on to trucks for the long trip to Trilokpuri. They are being allowed to take only essential belongings on the DDA trucks.

Policemen on horseback, their truncheons in hand, pick their way through the debris, exhorting the men and women to hurry up. 'We cannot wait here for you.'

The children are crying for lunch. There is no lunch because the DDA officials had come to the area early in the morning, warning that residents would get only four hours to demolish their houses with their own hands, after which the bulldozers would move in.

Trilokpuri. One hour later. The unending convoys of noisy trucks have been arriving since morning. In this truck from Indra Vikas Puri, four families have come with their belongings. Four women with sixteen children. The men have stayed behind to take care of the bricks and the asbestos sheets and the charpoys.

The women carry slips of paper listing the plot that will be their home. A foreman guides them to the place. The children help the mothers sort out their belongings. They place their belongings on their plot and wait for the fathers.

They also wait for water; the more hopeful ones for food as well. Their turn for water will come after two hours, because the leaking tanker always runs dry just before it reaches their plot.

Mangolpuri Resettlement Colony, 17 July 1976. The blocks of houses are only half built. A strong stench from the excrement of a thousand naked children stifles the air. It becomes worse towards 'T' block. Deep within this block lives the family of Dwarka Prasad in a hut and a situation which seems to be far worse than that of the Delhi Gate area which was cleared.

There is gloom in the family, for Dwarka's seven-year-old son, Prem, died of chickenpox a few weeks back, just twenty days after they had been resettled in Mangolpuri. 'He was a strong child. Prem was always playing and frisking about, says a haggard Bhagwano, wife of Dwarka.

'*Pata nahi,* what happened to him; he suddenly took ill. Two days of fever and then spots all over his body,' she says. 'We tried to get a doctor,' Dwarka interrupts, 'but where do we get a doctor in this wilderness? We finally got one at Sultanpuri 2 kilometres away and after we paid a large sum of money, he agreed to come. But no use, my Prem died within a day.' 'He died in great pain and the doctor took so much money,' wails Bhagwano. Now her youngest child has fever, recurrent attacks of vomiting and diarrhoea. Bhagwano is resigned to her fate.

Newspaper report, 18 July 1976.

The people sent to the Mangolpuri resettlement colony do not know the difference between symptoms of cholera, dysentery, amoebic dysentery, enteritis or diarrhoea.

Not one doctor, not even a compounder has come to this DDA-created instant colony. So the people do not know what exactly has affected every second child below five years of age, or is debilitating in an unending attack of fever, dysentery and vomiting.

The people also recognize malaria. Many of them are this day shivering with malarial chills. They can also tell when so-called drinking water is not drinkable because it may have

silt, be too briny or may have been contaminated when the
vast area covered by stinking human faeces soaks in the rain
which trickles down to the sub-soil reservoirs that feed the
handpumps and the occasional tube well.

But threats of epidemics—according to them, the
mahamari has already begun—touch only the surface of the
many ills that plague nearly 30,000 families which have
suddenly discovered that this spot in the vastness of an obscure
corner of the capital is to be their home from now on.

Khichripur, one monsoon evening. Union Minister of State for
Works and Housing H.K.L. Bhagat, who is the local MP,
has come to the camp here to supervise operations against the
flooding.

'Why don't you put a pump at this place to remove the
water?' the politician asks the civil servant pointing to the vast
expanse of water that surrounds the place.

'But, sir, it will do no good. We will pump out some water
but more will flow in from the surrounding area. We will never
be able to drain it dry.'

'Never mind all that. These people expect me to take some
action. They must see a pump working here.'

Khichripur, some weeks later. The people living in the hut in
the last row find they can no longer just walk on to the lane.
The lane is now at least 6 feet higher than the front of their
house.

The husband buys a truckload of earth and raises his floor
to the level of the lane to keep the water out. But there is an
unexpected problem. The roof of his hut is now only 4 feet
from the floor. The entire family has to sit it out until he gets
some labourers so help him raise the roof. And outside, the small
drain has become a miniature chasm, 6 feet deep, between the
new road and the floor level.

Mangolpuri, 17 July. Municipal worker Subhash Chand has three peculiar problems. And he does not know what to do. He has been married six months and his bride is away at her mother's. The DDA man has come and warned that if a single plot or hut is found deserted during a sudden check, it will be confiscated and allotted to someone else. Subhash has taken the remainder of his leave and plans to sit it out for that period. The alternative is to construct a pucca house. That will cost more than Rs 5000. But a house can be locked and can carry a nameplate to prove that it is occupied.

Subhash goes to his officer and seeks a loan. The officer asks him if he can get a sterilization case. Even if he could get one, he would get only Rs 2000 from the office; he would still need Rs 3000 more. The bank which has repeatedly advertised its fantastic philanthropic scheme asks him to produce the certificate of his own sterilization. 'But how can I get myself sterilized? I am only twenty-four. And besides, I have been married only six months,' says Subhash. 'That is none of our business,' says the bank official.

Outside Jahangirpuri DDA office, 15 March 1977, midnight. Large crowds mill about the office. 'They are handing out allotment slips for shops and plots if we give an assurance that we will vote for H.K.L. Bhagat,' says a bystander excitedly. 'But the bastard is taking some money for a slip, I heard,' says another. 'Oh, he is taking just Rs 30. Imagine a plot for a shop just for a vote,' answers the first one. But the DDA officer wants to go for his dinner. 'I'll just be back,' he assures the crowd.

Hours pass, but no sign of the officer. The crowd is getting fidgety. Meanwhile some newspaper reporters arrive on the scene in a car. Suddenly the crowd is galvanized into action. 'H.K.L. Bhagat zindabad!' they shout in unison. The reporters are hard put to explain that they are not Bhagat's men. The reporters explain that the DDA cannot give allotment slips as it is illegal to give them on the eve of the elections. 'But, I tell you they gave some of the people', 'Why, the officer took Rs 30 from me and gave me this slip', 'You mean they have tricked us?'—the crowd keeps grumbling and asking questions, hoping that the DDA officer will turn up.

Ultimately, the officer in charge of the local police post lands up with a contingent and shoos the crowds off. 'It's all a rumour,' he tells the crowd, 'now go back and sleep.' Grumbling angrily, the crowd moves off. He turns to the reporters and grins. 'That bastard DDA officer is a clever one, he even got some money out of the bargain.'

Rajpur Road Programme implementation committee office. Committee meeting in progress. The topic under discussion is the rising price of pulses. 'We should reduce the price by five paise.'

'No one will notice a five-paise reduction. It should be more.'

'*Theek hai.* We will reduce the price of the pulses by ten paise till the next meeting.'

Old Secretariat, 23 September 1976. The following note is dispatched.

    Y.P. Puri
    Dy. Registrar
    Delhi Administration
    Cooperatives Deptt.
    DO No. 7832-3

Please refer to my demi-official letter No. F7/1/76-Estt/ Coop 7667-71 of 18 September 1976 regarding the Family Planning Programme, achieving target of 2000 cases given in this behalf.

I send herewith a copy of the minutes of meeting held under chairmanship of E.C.(D) on 9 September, 1976. Since the Family Planning is a national programme, the target in this behalf has to be achieved at any cost. It will therefore be your personal responsibility to stress on the staff the dire need of achieving the target. You may also personally go to the field and contact the concerned office-bearers of societies for that purpose. A special drive needs to be carried out in right earnest for that purpose. I may however make it clear that adverse action is likely to be taken in case you and your staff do not come up to the expectation in achieving the target.

I had earlier asked for a daily report in the matter, which I regret has not been received from your end. The same may be sent to me immediately.

Sd/-
Y.P. Puri

Rajpur Road programme implementation committee office. Meeting not in session. An official says, 'Very soon the top officers like Tamta and others stopped coming to the Programme implementation committee meetings.' The issues were getting much too small for these bigwigs who were anyway taking orders from the very top. And so they would generally send subordinate officers to take their place at the meetings.

The petty politicians, the small officials and that peculiar category of non-official, non-politician hangers-on had the committee all to themselves over small matters. Of course if there were big issues, then the decisions were taken by the bigwigs. But not on Rajpur Road.

Town Hall, 15 March 1976. Commissioner's orders to the assessor and collector:

There will be no poster or slogan writing on the city walls after April 1, 1976. The municipal corporation has decided to ban the display of posters or slogans on the walls of houses, on buildings or offices within the jurisdiction in the Union Territory of Delhi. The Assessor and Collector has been issued instruction not to accord permission to display posters or slogans. Last year the department accorded permission to paste 1,70,000 posters.

The Hindu Rao Hospital, monsoon 1976, midnight. The taxi races to the Emergency casualty room. The relatives pick up the youth lying in the back seat and seat him before the young casualty medical officer. 'I can't breathe,' says the patient. 'Have you brought along your ration card?' asks the doctor. 'Or a sterilization certificate?' 'No,' says the patient's relative. 'Get it. And pay Rs 5 at the counter,' says the doctor.

'Can't we do all that later? Won't you give him some medicine?' asks the relative. 'These are orders,' says the doctor.

Town Hall, 4 December 1976. Press statement:

> Director of Health Services of Delhi Administration Dr O.P. Sharma and Municipal Health Officer Kewal Krishna reiterate in a joint statement that no inoculation was ever given in sole, palm, toe or thumb. They said any case which had been inoculated in sole, or palm may be brought to the notice of the authorities. They have deplored the fact that despite categorical statements from the authorities, some confusion still persists with regard to inoculations being administered to the children.
>
> They have clarified that only routine immunization is being carried out against communicable diseases. The vaccine injected has neither any harmful effect nor anything to do with the sterilization of the children.

Fire Brigade Lane, office of the DPCC, March 1977. 'It has got nothing to do with elections,' says Chief Executive Councillor Raman. 'The family planning disincentives have been withdrawn.'

'It has got nothing to do with the election,' says General Secretary Bansi Lal Mehta. 'The unauthorized colonies are being regularized.'

Office of the senior vice president, New Delhi Municipal Committee, March 1977. Vice President Charanjit Singh sits disconsolately at his massive desk. More perked up is Arjan Das, who sits next to him, his leg dangling from the armrest of the chair. 'We are increasing the wages of the NDMC staff,' says Arjan Das, an erstwhile motor mechanic. 'Mr Arjan Das is the patron of our employees. He has had talks with us,' says Charanjit Singh from behind his gold-framed spectacles. 'It has got nothing to do with the forthcoming elections,' they both add.

Old Secretariat, February 1976. The lawns of the local government's headquarters are agog with excitement. The pandal is brightly decorated. The policemen are standing in neat and sharply defined lines.

'Sanjay Gandhi zindabad!' Executive councillors lead in the echoing zindabads. *'Yuva neta, desh ka neta, Sanjay Gandhi zindabad!'* shouts the crowd of unemployed graduates who have gathered for the allotment function for minibus and other permits to them.

The excitement reaches a climax. It is announced that the garlands that have graced Mr Gandhi's neck will be auctioned to collect funds.

The bids come fast and high. Their first halt is at Rs 10,000. From among the audience, the voice calls higher and higher. A second voice paces him up to Rs 50,000.

Everyone present holds his breath. Only the hands move to clap with every fresh bid. The bids close at Rs 51,000. The first garland is Mr Sagar Suri's to keep for Rs 51,000. The second garland is taken by a transporter. His bid: Rs 51,000. The applause, which had halted for the climactic moments, bursts forth in an orgasmic spasm.

A government office, 1976. 'He is [a] born administrator, a fantastic mind. The other day he went to take his flying exams. The examiners told him it requires not only the flying lessons, but also a theory test. He said, "Give me the book, and take my test tomorrow." The next day the examiner is surprised. He not only gives all the correct answers, but even tells the examiner where the book makes a mistake. He is given his licence promptly. He is very fast. He is very quick to grasp the essentials. It is a pleasure to take orders from him. He expects you to do work. He punishes hard, but he also rewards well.'

(The chief officer of a big government department on Sanjay Gandhi.)

1, Safdarjung Road, late 1975. 'They come quite early, by about 7.45 a.m. Municipal Commissioner B.R. Tamta, DDA Vice Chairman Jagmohan, V.S. Ailawadi of the NDMC, Minister H.K.L. Bhagat, Lt Governor's Special Secretary Navin Chawla. Deputy Inspector General P.S. Bhinder is also occasionally here.

'They wait in the anterooms, sometimes with Dhavan [prime minister's secretary] and talk about Delhi affairs. They eye each other with rabid suspicion. He [Sanjay] calls them in one by one. He listens to their situation reports, and tells figures. Sometimes he taunts them that the other fellow is far more active. The person promises to be better by tomorrow.

'Sometimes he calls all of them together. This is when the big schemes are chalked out. This is when the officers bid for more portion of the work to be done. It is like a grand auction.'

(An eyewitness).

Vikas Minar, New Delhi, 28 February 1977. The DDA releases a press handout:

It is clarified for the information of the general public that the proposals to redevelop Turkman Gate area are only at the preliminary stage. Public objections/views have been invited and the scheme would be finalized in due course of time in the light of the objection/suggestions received.

Rashtrapati Bhavan, 23 April 1977. The distinguished gathering leafs through the brochure as the acting President confers the awards at the special investiture. Page 15 of the brochure reads:

PADMA BHUSHAN: SHRI JAGMOHAN

Shri Jagmohan, born on 25th September, 1927, has made significant contribution to the formulation and implementation of Delhi's Master Plan. He has specialized in formulation and implementation of Schemes of massive housing, creation of new woodlands and parks and rejuvenation of historical places. Under his able guidance as Chairman, Delhi Development Authority has successfully undertaken a massive clearance operation of about 7 lakh of squatters and slum-dwellers living in sub-human conditions in various parts of Delhi City and resettled them in 27 newly developed colonies with all public amenities within a short span of about 8 months. Shri Jagmohan has broken new ground in redeveloping in Jama Masjid-Red Fort complex, shifting the hazardous industries and trades to newly developed industrial Areas, redeveloping and beautifying areas around historical monuments.

Shri Jagmohan has travelled widely and represented India at a number of conferences. He has been given Cultural Award by Australian Government for his special work in the sphere of housing, redevelopment, slums and squatter's settlements, redevelopment of old and historic sites and for his book 'Rebuilding Shahjahanabad'. He has also contributed articles to various leading magazines and newspapers.

Shri Jagmohan is not present.

Vikas Minar, DDA headquarters, 30 April 1977.
The following letter is received:

Sir,

I want to bring your kind notice that I got myself sterilized on the assurance of Mr Tikku that my son who is working in the DDA will become regular. But I am sorry to say that nothing has been done so far besides my many requests.

It is therefore requested that you may kindly intervene in the matter and try to solve my problem at your earliest.

Thanking you and hoping for a favourable reply at your side.

Yours faithfully,
N.C.

chapter one

THE STORY OF TURKMAN GATE

~

Early on the morning of 13 April 1976, a rusty old bulldozer wheezed and creaked down Asaf Ali Road towards Turkman Gate. Behind it, at a leisurely pace, followed a truckload of labourers and a jeep. The strange caravan rolled on regardless of the curious stares of the passers-by and the barking of street dogs.

In the jeep sat DDA *tehsildar* Kashmiri Lal. The tehsildar was a worried man. His orders were clear, but he knew in his heart they weren't as easy as they sounded. 'Take it easy at first,' he had been told. 'Don't give any signs that might panic the people. Do it stage by stage.'

Stage by stage, he thought. These people are so touchy it would just need a small incident to create an explosion.

This was not the first time he had led a demolition squad to Turkman Gate. He had come twice before, and both times the demolition squad had been beaten back. He still remembered the huge lathi in the hands of the burly dairy owner. Single-handedly he had beaten off a whole police posse. But those were the days before the Emergency, he thought. For the first time, a tight smile played on his lips.

33

The demolition caravan screeched to a halt before the Turkman Gate transit camp. Word had already spread that the demolition men were coming. The tehsildar's jeep was immediately surrounded by a crowd of residents, their eyes glowing with resentment and suspicion.

'It's nothing, *mian*, we are just going to take away the residents of the transit camp to a better place in Ranjit Nagar. There won't be any problems, I assure you,' Kashmiri Lal told the crowd. There was grumbling among the residents of the transit camp but not really much surprise or resentment. The forty-odd families living in the camp were among the 120 families who had been shifted from Dujana House when the jhuggis there had been cleared. They had been promised accommodation in the housing complex to be built there. Over the years, eighty families had been shifted back to the new whitewashed concrete blocks at Dujana House. Now it was the turn of the remaining forty families to go, but since there was no more space at Dujana House, they would be accommodated at Ranjit Nagar. The people were unhappy. They did not get the Dujana House flats. But Ranjit Nagar was not too bad.

Kashmiri Lal thought that he had made a good start as he surveyed the labourers bringing down the walls and roofs of the houses with picks and rods. The camp residents had been given enough time to move their belongings, and their friends in neighbouring houses had helped to take their luggage out. It was slow work but there was no resistance at all. Maybe these people have learnt their lesson during the Emergency. Kashmiri Lal was beginning to feel much more confident.

The demolition continued through 13 and 14 April. For almost the entire transit, there were no incidents. Yet there was something disturbing about the rubble-littered land where the transit camp had stood just two days back.

'There is something I don't like, mian, about this breaking down of the transit camp. You don't think they might come for our houses next?' old Hafiz Mohammed asked his friend Mirza that evening.

'Arre, what are you talking about! *Yeh kabhi ho nahin sakta* [This can never be],' Mirza was sure. 'You and your suspicions. You are becoming a nervous wreck as the years go by.'

But late that night Kashmiri Lal was seen, along with two other DDA men, hovering around the Badi Masjid of Turkman Gate. They were talking and arguing. One of them was taking down notes.

'What are these DDA men doing here at this time of the night?' Mehboob Ali asked his friend Akbar when he spotted the three.

'You are a big Youth Congress leader here, why don't you ask them?' said Akbar who was jealous of Mehboob Ali's power as secretary of the local Youth Congress.

Mehboob Ali ran after the DDA men, but they had already disappeared into the darkness. Something fishy was going on, thought Mehboob, and decided to find out the next morning.

Nobody in Turkman Gate expected the bulldozers to come back on the morning of 15 April. The transit camp had been cleared. What else did the demolition men want? But in the morning two bulldozers came to Turkman Gate. Tehsildar Lal got down from the jeep and faced the angry crowd.

'It's nothing, friends,' he told them with sweetness in his voice. 'We want to break the footpath. I request all of you who have houses next to the footpath to remove your belongings so that they don't get damaged.'

'But you don't need bulldozers to break footpaths,' said the angry crowd.

'I assure you that no houses will be demolished. We will only break the footpath,' repeated Kashmiri Lal, disregarding the question.

The people's suspicion had been aroused. About 100 people, mostly Youth Congress workers, went to the Congress

Metropolitan Councillor Arjan Das. Arjan Das was a powerful man. A one-time motor mechanic, he had risen meteorically in the political hierarchy because of his close association with Sanjay Gandhi. Das was the main cheerleader for Sanjay Gandhi's five-point programme, and it was rumoured that there was little he could not get done if he wanted to.

Arjan Das was surprised when he heard of the bulldozers.

'It just cannot be. There isn't any plan at all for the demolition of houses in Turkman Gate. The transit camp was one thing, but the rest of the houses will stay intact, rest assured,' he told the crowd.

But the crowd would not listen. If there are no demolition plans, why were the bulldozers there?

'Okay,' said Das, 'a few of you come along with me in my car and I'll try to contact some minister.' Mehboob Ali was among the seven who accompanied Das in his car.

First they went to Information and Broadcasting Minister Vidya Charan Shukla's house.

'Wait outside, I will be back,' Das told the people. It was a long wait for them, however. At last he returned.

'The minister has rung up DDA Vice Chairman Jagmohan and told him to order the bulldozers back. So you can go back in peace. The demolition men won't touch your houses,' he told the waiting people.

The people thanked Das profusely and went back reassured. But when they reached Turkman Gate, they saw a scene of havoc and devastation. The bulldozers were no longer standing idle on one corner of the road. They were moving in to level the debris of nearly fifty houses that were standing on the same spot just a few hours back. More than thirty of the demolished houses were private property. Men, women and children squatted outside in stunned silence, their belongings piled up beside them.

As soon as Mehboob Ali and his friends reached the spot, the people surrounded them.

'What sort of people did we send to talk? See what they have done. Now who will save us?' shouted the people. 'A fine Youth Congress secretary we have here,' sneered Akbar. 'He goes to talk with the councillor and meanwhile the bulldozers smash through our houses.'

Mehboob Ali quietly said that he would try again. He ran back to Arjan Das. The councillor raised his eyebrows when told of the demolition.

'This is really incredible! *Chalo*, we will go to Ruksanaji, she will know what do,' Das said.

At the prefabricated asbestos-sheet family-planning centre of Dujana House, less than 2 kilometres from Turkman Gate, sat Begum Ruksana Sultana. The camp had been inaugurated by Krishan Chand that day. Glamorous socialite, boutique owner, and after she met Sanjay Gandhi, the leading social worker of New Delhi, Begum Sultana had become a veritable queen in recent months. She had come to the walled city just a few months back a total stranger but now hardly anyone was ignorant of her name. She had started out urging the women to cast aside their burqas.

'See me, I am a Muslim but a modern Muslim. Why should we be afraid to hide our features?' the lovely begum had said.

Though there was not much of a response, the begum had consistently kept coming to Jama Masjid. And if the people there resented her presence, they had also become aware of the power she wielded. She had got together some of the most notorious lumpen elements of the area like Razoo goonda, Zia and Keramatullah. They were her aides now and the terror of the area. There were standing orders at the Jama Masjid police chowki that no cases should be registered against the three. There was hardly a shopkeeper in the area who had not bribed them in order to be left alone. With the setting up of a family-planning camp at Dujana House, the begum had really consolidated her position. True, she had not been able to make many men of the area volunteer themselves for sterilization, and had to remain content with the police rounding up beggars and *tangawala*s for her camp. But, after all, it had been only a few days; soon the people of the area would have to recognize her power. Forcibly if need be. The begum had given her word to Sanjayji.

A few people were already aware of the begum's power. Veteran Congressman Mohammed Zulfikar lived right above the family-planning camp, but had not been smiling or saluting her though he passed her almost every day. Zulfikar thought he could get away with it as he was close to the Metropolitan Council Chairman Mir Mustaq Ahmed who, along with the shahi imam, were the two most respected leaders of the area. Mir Mustaq couldn't do much for Zulfikar. Just a few days ago, Zulfikar had been arrested while he was having dinner. It was a good example to others. Lately she had been noticing far more people bowing and smiling at her. As far as Mir Mustaq went, she would take care of him very soon. 'We'll see how long he can go on calling me a whore in private gatherings,' the begum darkly muttered.

Begum Sultana sat in the little boudoir she had made for herself next to the family-planning office. Her delicate nose wrinkled at the earthy smell all around, and her make-up was turning limp in the hot atmosphere as she impatiently brushed away the flies buzzing around her.

Mehboob Ali had met Ruksana Sultana when she had attended a *jalsa* next to Turkman Gate in February. She had even promised to build a community centre there within a few months. Mehboob Ali had pinned his hopes on the begum. He had in fact defended her hotly when his friends had called her a *randi*. 'She is a good Muslim. What if she does not wear a burqa? She understands our problem,' Mehboob Ali had argued.

'No,' said Ruksana Sultana to Arjan Das, 'I have not heard of demolition plans in Turkman Gate,' when they arrived at the camp. She agreed to come along with them to Turkman Gate and talk to the DDA officials.

It was late afternoon by then. Twenty more houses had turned to rubble by the time they reached Turkman Gate. The begum and Arjan Das called the DDA officials aside and had a long talk with them. Mehboob Ali who also wanted to hear what they were talking about was told sternly to stay away. 'Are you a fool? I am trying to help you people, and you try to make a mess of it,' the begum told him. After the huddled conference, the begum came and told Mehboob Ali that she had given instructions for the bulldozers to be called off. True enough, the bulldozers went back and demolition operations were stopped. Hope rose in Mehboob Ali's heart again.

'But,' said the begum, 'this is a very complicated situation. I want a small delegation of you to come to my house this evening to discuss matters. By then I will know the exact position.'

In the evening, a delegation of seven went to the begum's residence on Jantar Mantar Road. The begum was not available. The delegation was told to wait outside by Razoo goonda and his gang. 'The begum is very busy but she left a message with me for you,' said Razoo. 'She told me to tell you that the begum is ready to take up your case only if you immediately set up a family planning camp at Turkman Gate and supply at least 300 cases within this week.'

Mehboob Ali could not believe his ears.

'But how can we set up a family planning camp when our houses are being demolished? Our women and children are sitting out on the road. What sort of bargain does the begum want to drive? How can we possibly give her 300 cases in a week? Tell her we will set up a family planning camp but just give me some time. Already the people are burning with anger. Who would want to get sterilized at this time?' Mehboob Ali pleaded.

'Okay, I will give her your reply,' Razoo said and went inside.

He was back in a minute.

'The begum says that if you don't want to cooperate with her you can go to hell. *Jehannum mein jao.*'

'But the begum had promised . . .' Mehboob Ali still tried.

'*Abbe chal*, get out before the begum gets really angry,' said Razoo. Mehboob knew better than to argue with Razoo goonda. The delegation left quietly.

The same night they decided that the only person who might listen to their problems was Subhadra Joshi, the local MP. Joshi had won hands down both times she had stood for elections to the Lok Sabha from the area. Not only was she popular, she was also known to be close to the prime minister. Lately, however, she had been rendered almost a nonentity as she had antagonized the authorities with her resistance to the Jama Masjid demolition drive which had started last November. She had also not been kowtowing to Sanjay Gandhi. She had been under a cloud and it was for this reason the people of Turkman Gate had not approached her. But now there was no way out. She at least would give them a patient hearing.

Early next morning, a group of people went to Joshi's house.

'You should have come to me earlier,' she chided them, 'but I'll see what I can do.'

But first they had to get a signed memorandum, stating the number of people staying in Turkman Gate, how long they had been staying there, the number of voters and other miscellaneous information.

'Prepare a memorandum and I will see if I can give it to the prime minister.'

Meanwhile, the bulldozers at Turkman Gate inched their ugly snouts farther and deeper. There were three of them now, working at full speed. The DDA officials had started giving allotment slips for plots in the Trilokpuri and Nand Nagri resettlement colonies to people whose houses still stood. A clear indication that more and more houses would be demolished. There was also a noticeable change in the attitude of the DDA officials. No more sweet words. Now they gave orders. They were brusque with the people who went up to them and asked them on what basis their houses were being demolished so arbitrarily.

'We have our orders,' was all the DDA officials said.

'But we have been staying here for generations. We are no jhuggi dwellers. We have been paying the house tax even,' pleaded the residents. 'Still if you think that we have to be removed, give us some suitable alternative accommodation. Send us to transit camps on Mata Sundari Road or Minto Road, not to open fields in Nand Nagri and Trilokpuri. How will our women keep purdah? Where will our children study? Tell us how we will earn our bread miles away from our locality? We are not dogs that you can drive us away from our own homes.'

The people went to Chowdhry Mohammeddin Elaichiwallah, a grand old patriarch of the area. Photographs of him with the prime minister and President lined the walls of his sitting room. But they turned out to be more useless than the junk which Chowdhry Elaichiwallah sold in his factory.

'Chowdhry Sa'ab, we have beaten back demolition squads many times before and they had not intended to do even one-tenth of the damage these people have done. Tell us, Chowdhry Sa'ab, shall we sit quietly and watch our homes being destroyed one by one, our women and children pushed out on the streets?' the people demanded

'These are strange times, my brothers, we can't act like we did before. Any sort of resistance, and destruction for all of us is certain,' the shrewd old patriarch said and scratched his flowing white beard.

Not that he had not already tried to stop the demolition. He had been told to shut up. 'Don't complain too much. You are already in disfavour as all old Congress hands are. If you interfere too much now, none of your old associations will save you,' he had been told. The old man could not possibly show his hand.

Yet he was the leader of his people. After the people had gone away disappointed, Elaichiwallah stared for a long time at the photograph which showed him hugging President Fakhruddin Ali Ahmed.

'Only you would be ready to help but, *Khuda jane,* you too have become powerless,' Elaichiwallah said with a deep sigh.

The people now feared for the Badi Masjid of Turkman Gate itself. They repeatedly asked the DDA officials whether the masjid property too would be demolished. To this, the officials assured them that it would not be touched.

'Nothing is written in our orders that we clear the masjid too,' they told the people. The DDA officials were obeying orders by the letter. Don't rush things, slowly increase the tempo.

Do it stage by stage, they had been ordered.

Early on the morning of 17 April, a small band of Youth Congress workers led by Mehboob Ali met the prince himself. Sanjay Gandhi greeted them coldly when he heard what they had to say. They presented him with a memorandum signed by more than 1000 people of Turkman Gate demanding the end of the demolition drive.

The prince was a man of few words. He nodded once and the meeting was over. After they left, the prince tore up the memorandum into neat little shreds. He had little time for the rabble. He had to catch a plane for Simla.

Meanwhile the bulldozers continued their devastation at Turkman Gate. The DDA had already gone back on its promise that the masjid property would not be touched. They were giving out allotment slips to people who had houses on the masjid property. Any sort of protest was answered with a shout, 'Do you want an allotment slip or not, or do you want to lose your allotment plot as well as your house?' Tension was building up fast at Turkman Gate. The rows of women and children on the road grew longer and longer, and the piles of belongings lying out in the open grew higher. Most of them refused transportation to their new plots—they had heard what sort of places Trilokpuri and Nand Nagri were.

Some of the residents who had been sent there had come back and told terrible tales.

'Just a swathe of barren land, Chacha,' Arif had come back and told his uncle, 'and the flying dust. See my red eyes. One couldn't survive a day there, I tell you.'

The residents squatted grimly in the open at Turkman Gate, preferring it to the alien land they had been banished to.

In the evening, some of the squatters were approached by the DDA officials.

'Look, if you want a place other than Trilokpuri or Nand Nagri, we can suggest a way out. Just sign a statement that your houses have been demolished according to your own wishes. We will give you a better alternative place to stay,' one of the DDA officials told them.

'We sign this statement and then you forget about your promise. What sort of fools do you think us to be? Once we sign this statement, our hands are tied. We can't even complain.' The residents had decided not to believe a single word of what the officials told them.

'And how about the rest of the residents? What will happen to them?' they asked.

'Well,' said one of the DDA officials, 'if you think that you will be able to save your friends, you are mistaken. We have orders to clear this place right up to Hauz Qazi.'

Then the officials walked off.

Soon after, the residents were surprised to see Jagmohan himself get out of his car. The DDA vice chairman's visit raised hopes again. First, the officials offer bribes to sign a statement, and then the vice chairman arrives at the spot. There must be some pressure on them to stop the demolition, the residents thought. Jagmohan, however, stayed for only a few minutes.

'I believe you have some objections. Send a small delegation of your leaders to me tomorrow and I will talk to them. I can't discuss in the crowd,' Jagmohan told the anxious crowd surrounding him.

'But all the while the discussion goes on, your bulldozers keep on razing our houses,' someone from the crowd complained.

Jagmohan allowed himself to smile.

'The DDA does not work on Sundays. Tomorrow there won't be any bulldozer,' he said.

For the first time in five days, the bulldozers did not come to Turkman Gate. Jagmohan had been right. The DDA did not work on Sunday. The residents had got a day's respite.

Around 11 a.m. on Sunday, a delegation led by Elaichiwallah went to meet Jagmohan. They waited for a while and were then ushered into the room of the vice chairman.

'Tell me briefly, what exactly do you people want? I am terribly busy and can spare you only a few minutes.' Jagmohan did not look very amicable.

'We will be brief,' said the leader of the delegation and put forward a list of demands: (a) the immediate ceasing of demolition, if possible, (b) the allotment of alternative 45-yard plots in Seelampur Welcome or other suitable transit camps if the Turkman Gate area had to be demolished, and (c) an assurance that the masjid will not be touched.

'If you have to remove us, remove us all to some large area where we can carry on our respective jobs and trades. Don't scatter us all over the outskirts of Delhi,' the men pleaded. It was at this point that Jagmohan flared up.

Recollecting the meeting later, Chowdhry Kaimuddin, who was in the delegation, said, 'I do not know what exactly aggravated him. But I think it was because we said that we wanted to be all together. He burst out suddenly, "Do you think we are mad to destroy one Pakistan to create another Pakistan?"'[1]

There was a stunned silence as the import of Jagmohan's words sank in. 'We will give you plots in Trilokpuri and Khichripur, and you will have to go like the five lakh other people we plan to resettle. This is one time you people will not get any special privileges,' Jagmohan continued.

'And remember,' Jagmohan warned, 'if you don't go, and make the foolish mistake of resisting the demolition operations, the consequences will be serious.'

Jagmohan stared fixedly at Elaichiwallah. The old man lowered his eyes and led the delegation out. War had been declared.

There were still some attempts by the leaders to contact ministers and councillors. Works and Housing Minister Bhagat flatly disclaimed all responsibility for the demolition. 'I am ignorant of any demolition plans,' said the minister, disregarding all attempts to draw his attention to the fact that not only were there plans, but that they were also being carried out.

Chief Executive Councillor Raman too pleaded ignorance and, in his usual ambling, incoherent style, told the Turkman Gate delegation: 'Surely they must be mistaken.' This time the delegation did not even try to convince him.

Later that evening, Mehboob Ali and a few other residents went to Joshi and presented her with the memorandum she had told them to prepare. She promised that she would come to Turkman Gate the next morning and talk to the DDA officials. She is also reported to have told the delegation to collect as many women and children of the area as possible, and stage a dharna at the demolition site. But she later denied this, attributing this to a misunderstanding.

Early on the morning of 19 April 1976, there was a lot of commotion in Turkman Gate. The women and children were collecting near the yawning, vacant rubble land that had been steadily growing larger and larger over the past few days. By

8 a.m., nearly 500 women and 200 children were squatting on the demolition site. All of them wore black armbands.

Mehboob Ali was among the people who were organizing arrangements for the women and children. Two large drums of drinking water had been arranged for them. Soon it would become hot and their thirst would have to be quenched.

The people were expecting Joshi to arrive by 9 a.m., as she had promised. But the hours rolled by and there was no sign of her. By 11 a.m., Mehboob Ali knew that something was wrong. Subhadra Joshi was not the sort of person who would not keep her word. He decided to telephone her and find out. She seemed cold and distant on the phone.

She said she had not been able to come but had been trying to contact various important people on the phone and had not been able to do so yet. She would come as soon as she was able to talk to one of them.

But could she not come over right now, asked Mehboob Ali. Soon the demolition men would come and there must be someone here to stop them.

'I will try my best,' she said as she hung up.

Subhadra Joshi knew differently. She was lying. She would not go to Turkman Gate. Not because she lacked the guts. With her long experience with bureaucracy, she had realized that the fate of the people of Turkman Gate was beyond her control now. Since early morning she had been dialling various numbers—numbers of people who had just a few months ago bent over backwards to please her. But now not a single one of them was available. Bhagat's personal secretary said he was not available. Jagmohan has gone out, said the DDA office. After she tried five different numbers in vain, she knew she was defeated. The prime minister was not in town, ruling out the possibility of a last-minute appeal to her. Even more than Elaichiwallah, Subhadra Joshi felt that she was somehow letting the people down. But she could think of no conceivable way to help them.

The sun rose higher over Turkman Gate. The women and children squirmed uneasily as sweat trickled down their bodies. How long would they wait for Subhadra Joshi? 'Not to worry, not to worry, she has promised that she will come. Just sit quietly,' Mehboob Ali advised them. Around 11:30 a.m. the bulldozers came. They were a little late today. They would make up the time soon.

'What is this gathering about?' shouted a DDA official. 'Get out of the way at once.'

Nobody answered. The women and children continued to squat grimly, pretending not to hear the DDA official's threats.

'Are you deaf? Move or I will order the bulldozers to go over you,' shouted the DDA official.

He was met with a fixed glare of 500 women and 200 children. The DDA official shrank back, overwhelmed at the intensity of hatred he saw in those eyes.

At noon, when the sun had reached its peak, the first contingent of police arrived. Seven trucks of armed Central Reserve Police Force (CRPF) men moved into Turkman Gate. They were in uniform, complete with riot shields, tear-gas guns and rifles. Some of them even carried tommy guns. They seemed prepared for a riot.

A near-riot had already taken place less than 2 kilometres away at the Dujana House Family Planning Camp.

For days, resistance to the Begum Ruksana Sultana Family Planning programme had been growing in Jama Masjid. The women of the area had been growing ever more apprehensive at the happenings at the Dujana House camp. Till now no local men had been touched but from early morning the women saw hordes of beggars, rehriwalas and labourers being dragged by the scruff of their neck towards the Dujana House Family Planning Camp. The operations had started a few days back. The family-planning van and two private cars would go out early in the morning. Inside the van would be Razoo and his gang as well as a few police constables. The vehicles would return after some time packed with ragged men, many of them mere adolescents. They would first be taken to the Jama Masjid police chowki and then dragged to the Dujana House Family Planning Camp just a few paces away. Then down into the basement to the sterilization operation theatre where a group of doctors and nurses would conduct rapid-fire surgeries on their screaming victims.

Just the morning before the women had seen a seventeen-year-old boy clinging to a pillar of the Jama Masjid police chowki screaming, *'Main nahin jaunga, main nahin jaunga.'* He was being beaten mercilessly with lathis by some constables but the boy just would not let go of the pillar. They finally pried his fingers open with a baton and dragged him down the road towards the camp. The boy was a *pardesi*—a total stranger to the women but his desperate screams had not only touched their hearts but also brought on fears about their own boys and husbands.

Later that night the women held a meeting in a house at Jama Masjid. Something had to be done to stop this carnage, they decided. One of them brought a message that if they were to organize a resistance campaign, it would have Mir Mustaq's blessings. Begum Ruksana had to be taught a lesson.

Around 10.30 a.m. on Monday, the family-planning van returning with a fresh load of victims for sterilization screeched to an abrupt halt in front of the Jama Masjid chowki. A burqa-clad woman was lying on the road right in front of the van. A couple of police constables rushed out.

'Hey you, get out of the way!'

'No, I won't. You are taking my Usman to the nasbandi camp. No, I won't, I'd rather die first,' cried the woman.

The police constables were puzzled. There was no Usman they had caught that day.

'What are you talking about? There is no Usman in the van, just some beggars we picked up from the station,' said the policemen.

But the woman was adamant, she would not move. The constables became angry. One of them caught the woman by her hair and dragged her out of the way. There was an angry murmur in the big crowd which had by then surrounded the policemen. 'Arre, what are you trying to do?' said Mirza, a venerable resident of the area. 'Can't you see that she is a woman? How dare you touch our women!'

But while the policemen were busy with the crowd, the inmates of the van, who were being taken to be sterilized, had managed to open the door and were running away as fast as their legs could carry them. There was much jeering and laughter by the crowd. Infuriated, the police arrested Mirza.

News of the arrest spread like wildfire in the Jama Masjid area. The shopkeepers called for a hartal and, by 11.30 a.m., shops began to shut in the area, right up to Turkman Gate, including the whole market adjoining Daryaganj, in Suiwalan, Dehra Behram Khan and Syed Ahmed Road. Small groups of people stood on the road and complained that police high-handedness was going too far.

All this was being watched by the two most prominent leaders of the area.

Jama Masjid Shahi Imam Bukhari fumed and ranted as he watched from the masjid the manhandling of the woman and the arrest of Mirza. His worst suspicious had proved correct. The imam traced this latest incident to the series of outrages by the police on the people of Jama Masjid ever since the riots there on 2 February 1974 when he himself had been put behind bars and ten people had been cut down by police bullets and innumerable others injured. The police had to release him after a series of riots by the people of Jama Masjid but the imam had never forgiven the Congress government. The Emergency had put the imam in a vulnerable position but scarcely did a Friday go by when he, in his sermon, did not criticize the powers that be. 'This government is worse than the RSS,' the imam used to shriek in his sermons.

Mir Mustaq was also watching from his office on Jama Masjid. The veteran Congressman's power as Metropolitan Council chairman had been slowly whittled away after the Emergency. Now he had no say at all in what happened in the capital. He had watched helplessly the advent of Ruksana Sultana in Jama Masjid and her growing power. He had only been able to retaliate by abusing her in private, but he knew that if it came to a showdown now, he might lose. He had not been able to do anything to help Mohammed Zulfikar—a favourite of his—when he was arrested a few days earlier. Just a week ago, he had publicly come out against the authorities at a meeting in Jama Masjid on Jallianwala Bagh day. He had warned that if the high-handedness of the police and local authorities continued, there would be terrible consequences. As if in answer, Krishan Chand had announced the next day that any interference in the family-planning programme would not be tolerated. Outwardly, Mir Mustaq swallowed all the humiliation and still maintained good relations with the authorities. But his heart burned with resentment.

A group of women had come to Mir Mustaq in the morning, demanding that he intervene and close down the Dujana House camp. He had rung up the lieutenant governor but was told that the camp had been opened on 15 April and would continue till enough sterilizations had been done. Krishan Chand hung up and Mir Mustaq had told the women that he was helpless.

The group of women had also approached the imam and he too had tried to stop the camp for the day. He had repeatedly warned that there would be trouble unless the camp was closed. But the authorities had paid scant attention to his warnings. The imam had told the women to act as their conscience told them to do.

Young Nazleen lived in the second-floor flat right above the Dujana House Family Planning Camp. Her mother had told her to stay indoors for there had been an uneasy tension in the locality since morning. But through the window she had been taking a good look at the tamasha going on outside the family-planning camp. She had gone inside for an hour to study for her upcoming examination. When she came back to the window, she got the shock of her life.

'Hey, Amma, come quick! They are beating up the Begum Sahiba,' she called. Buxom matron that she was, Jamila Begum ran as fast as she could from the kitchen.

'Mashallah, they have got the lady at last,' she cried, surveying the scene below.

An angry group of women had surrounded the family-planning camp.

'Close the camp immediately,' they demanded of Ruksana Sultana who looked shaken.

She had not bargained for such violent resistance from this rabble.

'The camp will go on till we get enough sterilization cases,' she screamed back at the women. 'Don't you dare tell me how and when to close the family planning camp. Instead of creating a scene here, why don't you motivate some men in your homes to come and sterilize themselves?' the begum told them.

This was too much for the women. They surrounded the begum. Someone tried to grab her hair, but the begum managed to brush her off.

'Murderess, adulteress, how dare you come to Jama Masjid and castrate our men! We will lynch you, you bastard,' the crowd shouted. It was a moment of panic for the begum but fortunately for her, she was whisked away by her aides into a waiting car. A few stones were pelted at the car, but the begum managed to escape.

The women then turned their attention to the row of victims sitting in the tents outside the camp awaiting their turn to go to the operation theatre.

'Come away with us, we will hide you. There is nothing
to worry, the begum has fled.' The women beckoned to them.

It was a strange sight. Big, burly men being rescued by the
veiled heroines of Jama Masjid.

Meanwhile at the Jama Masjid chowki, two family-planning
camp cars had been stopped by another band of women. The
cars were bringing a fresh batch of victims for the camp. To
open the doors of the cars was the work of a moment for the
women and the men were set free in a trice. The family-planning
camp aides had never before seen the women so angry, and even
Razoo goonda thought it better not to intervene.

It was too good to last. Truck after truck of police
reinforcements arrived. The women retreated hurriedly after
one of them was caught, beaten up and then pushed into the
police van. The women climbed up to the terraces while the
police challenged them to come down. From the terraces the
women screamed abuses at the police. Their blood was up.
They wouldn't give up so easily.

It was around this time that the message from Turkman
Gate was flashed to Jama Masjid. 'They are massacring us here at
Turkman Gate. Come and help us if you can.'

The message took the family-planning camp out of the
minds of the people of Jama Masjid. Men, women and children
ran through the lanes and by-lanes towards Turkman Gate.
The people of Turkman Gate were their relatives and friends.
If they were being attacked, that was where they would fight
the police.

The two parallel dramas of Turkman Gate and Dujana
House had at last converged.

The sun blazed on in all its fury at Turkman Gate. The blue-
domed Dargah Syed Faiz-e-Elahi mosque on Asaf Ali Road had
by now been totally encircled by policemen whose numbers
had been increasing every fifteen minutes. Asaf Ali Road was
lined with police trucks. The CRPF, DAP, Border Security

Force (BSF), the local police—all armed personnel available to the State were now in Turkman Gate. In their hands bristled bayonets, lathis and guns. Facing them still sat the 500 women and 200 children. A strange madness had descended on the people of Turkman Gate. Undeterred by the hot sun, unintimidated by the guns and bayonets, they refused to let the bulldozers advance over their homes.

Mehboob Ali's heart was in his mouth. With every police truck that came into Turkman Gate, his heart sank further. He had kept off the demolition men for a while saying that Subhadra Joshi would be coming any moment. But there was still no sign of her. If she did not turn up soon, anything could happen. Yes, Mehboob Ali brooded, anything could happen.

The DDA officials again approached Mehboob Ali.

'We tell you once again, remove these women and children. Stop holding up our work.'

'If you just wait a few minutes for Mrs Joshi,' Mehboob Ali pleaded.

'I tell you, your Mrs Joshi won't show up,' said an official. 'She is hiding in her house. Nobody is coming to help you.'

Mehboob Ali kept quiet. The officials were right. The people of Turkman Gate had been left alone to face the bulldozers. Nobody was there to mediate for them.

The police now approached Mehboob Ali. 'Remove those drums,' they said, pointing to the drums of drinking water.

'But there is only drinking water in them,' Mehboob Ali explained. 'Remove them. That's an order.'

The drums were removed. There would be no drinking water for the women and children now.

A sea of khaki was engulfing Turkman Gate. In this vast army of policemen, the generals stood out. Deputy Inspector General Bhinder was there. So were Superintendents Ohri and Nikhil Kumar. And pacing up and down was the subdivisional

Magistrate R.K. Patiande—the same magistrate who had ordered the firing at Jama Masjid in February last year.

Conferring with the police officers was the chief of the Nehru Brigade. Some men of the Nehru Brigade also stood by the policemen. They seemed to be working out a plan.

Mehboob Ali watched the chief of the Nehru Brigade uneasily. That man is bad and he is up to some mischief, he thought.

It was time for namaz at the Faiz-e-Elahi mosque. The menfolk had already reached the masjid when a few of the women and children squatting in front of it also got up to say their prayers.

No sooner had this happened, than the chief of the Nehru Brigade and a few of his men shouted, 'They are going to throw stones. Stop them!'

Mehboob Ali rushed to stop the women and children from getting up. But it was too late. Someone had picked up a stone and chucked it at the women. Turkman Gate was already at a flashpoint. Pandemonium broke out.

The women and children had been waiting for nearly seven hours in the hot sun. Seven hours they had sweated it out patiently. They had been constantly shouted at by the officials and the police. Their drinking water had been taken away. Their blood was already boiling when the Nehru Brigade man threw the stone at them. It was like tinder to fire.

Picking up stones from the rubble of their houses, the women and children threw them back at the Nehru Brigade chief and his group. They were beyond reason now.

Within a minute, the first group of policemen moved in on the women, wielding lathis. But the police retreated immediately as they were driven back by a veritable stone storm. The mob was growing in size and venom. Lathis would be useless against it.

The tear gas, then. The first tear-gas shell landed right amongst the women and children. An eerie scream went up among them.

It was not a cry of fear.

It was a battle cry.

Tear-gas shells were lobbed one after another and though the women had retreated from the demolition site, they continued the stoning from the rooftops and lanes of Turkman Gate. Some ran to the blue-domed masjid for shelter. But the majority stayed on to fight.

Hurried consultations took place among the senior police officers and the subdivisional magistrate. Tear-gas shells too seemed ineffective against the mob. Should firing be ordered?

The question was answered even as they were discussing it. A big stone knocked down a police officer. He lay groaning, blood streaming down his face.

'Fire!' The order came.

Fourteen-year-old Khurshid was running to help his mother out when a bullet smashed through the side of his face. He spun around and fell to the ground. He was pulled into a lane by some residents and given first aid. Later he was sent to hospital where the police got to him and put chains on his legs while he lay with his shattered face on the bed.

Abdul Mallu looked straight ahead as he ran. He had to reach the Faiz-e-Elahi masjid. In his left hand he carried a few rotis and some curry for his mother waiting at the masjid. He had just about reached the steps of the mosque when the first bullet caught him in the leg and he crashed down on the road. He was up like a flash. His muscular eighteen-year-old body could take a leg wound in its stride. He had to reach his mother.

The second bullet caught him high up in the chest, knocking the wind out of him. He sat down suddenly. As if in a haze, he could see three policemen running towards him. Run, his instincts screamed at him, but he felt too weak. His legs refused to take his weight and he slumped down just as the policemen reached him. 'Finish the bastard,' he heard one of them say. And then, as his lips formed 'Amma Jan,' a rifle butt crashed down on his head.

Imam Hafiz Mohammed of Dargah Faiz-e-Elahi masjid had nearly finished the Monday prayers when the police came to the mosque. For the last fifteen minutes he had been fervently praying to Allah to stop the massacre outside and protect his congregation. But Allah seemed to have deserted the mosque and its imam on this day.

The masjid's imposing main door had already been bolted to prevent the police from coming in but it was just a precautionary measure. Imam Mohammed had not really imagined the police would enter the holy place.

When there were loud knocks, Imam Mohammed had thought that the police were trying to scare them into opening the door. But a loud crunch on the door dispelled his illusions. The police were using a battering ram. He had fixed the gate just a month ago and the bill had come to over Rs 7000. The imam's heart sank as he realized that the door would be the least of the things damaged that day.

The congregation was getting restless. The battering outside had risen to a crescendo. Finally, with a crash, the door broke open and the policemen poured in.

'Stop, this is the house of Allah!' the imam screamed, his face a mask of fear and anger. But his voice was drowned in the screams of the 300-odd men, women and children as the police fell on them.

There was no escape from the police lathis in the confined space of the mosque. One by one, the people were being dragged out.

But it was by no means an easy task for the police. The people clung desperately to the walls and windows of the masjid. They clung on despite the rain of lathis and blows by the police. The masjid to them was still safer than the rampage going on outside.

'Okay, gas the bastards out of the masjid,' ordered a police officer. Two tear-gas shells landed right inside the masjid. In the closed space, the gas was murder. This brought the people running out like ants from an anthill. Just a few minutes of the gas and a person could choke to death. Little Usman had lost track of his mother in the bedlam. Because he was small, he had been able to dodge the lathis and blows till now. But gas was another thing. His eyes blinded by tears, Usman ran hither and thither inside the mosque, but in the mad stampede he could not locate where the door was. His breath came in heavy pants.

'Amma Jan,' he screamed, 'where are you? Save me.' But Amma Jan was enveloped in the blanket of gas which was slowly choking the life out of Usman. Someone stepped on him heavily but Usman was beyond feeling. The gas had taken his life.

Eighty-year-old Abdus Sattar crouched terrified next to the wall. He had been the sweeper of the masjid for longer than he could remember. Never had he witnessed such a scene of bedlam. Screams, lathis, tear gas and blood—Abdus closed his eyes and prayed to Allah. But soon the gas got to him. Coughing desperately, Abdus ran for the door.

He was caught just as he had managed to grope his way to the door. Dragging him by the neck was a burly constable. 'I will come with you, but just let me go to the latrine once,' cried Abdus. The answer came in a huge blow to his head. Then everything blacked out for Abdus Sattar.

Imam Hafiz Mohammed had managed to retreat into one of the inner rooms of the masjid.

'Hai, Allah,' he prayed, 'help your children! How long will this massacre go on?'

'Where are you, Allah?' came a voice behind him. In the doorway stood two police constables and a Nehru Brigade man. It was the Nehru Brigade man who spoke.

'Bring your Khuda, imam, and see what we do to him. Come on, let's see, bring out your Allah, I want to see him,' he jeered.

'I am the imam of the masjid. Do not touch a holy man. My blood will be on your head,' the imam shrank back. His heart gave a sudden leap as he remembered that his little son was sleeping in the next room.

'Where have you hidden the rest of them, imam? We know that some of them are hiding in the next room,' he said as he smashed open the door of the next room. The imam ran to stop him but he was grabbed by the neck by one of the constables.

'Ah, what have we here! Your son, imam,' the Nehru Brigade man's voice a sibilant whisper.

'Don't hurt him, he is only a little boy,' the imam cried.

'Arrest both of them,' the Nehru Brigade man ordered.

'Okay, I will come along with you, but don't hurt my son.' The imam had surrendered. But his little boy tried to run. A lathi landed on his thigh and he fell on the floor. The imam jumped to guard the boy. The blow of a lathi crashed on his left arm, breaking it instantly.

'Soften up this dog of an imam a bit. It will take some of the love of Allah out of him,' the Nehru Brigade man barked.

Imam Hafiz Mohammed prayed on while the blows rained down on him.

'Allah, all these insults, all this humiliation to you, and your imam. Punish them, Allah. Let them remember what they did to your masjid forever,' the imam prayed as he was dragged outside.

In just half an hour, the masjid had become an abattoir. Blood pooled on the ground and the air was noxious with fumes of tear gas and the groans of the injured congregation. Doors, windows and furniture had been smashed and the cash box of the masjid containing a few thousand rupees had been looted by the marauding policemen. It had been a wholesale affair.

Outside, on the road the battle was not so unequal. There was space to fight back and men had joined the women to keep up the stone storm which still kept the police at a distance from the houses of Turkman Gate. Fresh reinforcements had come from Jama Masjid to help the people and the mob had swelled to over 3000-strong.

DIG Bhinder himself was in charge of the operations but never had he seen such unbending resistance from a mob. Normally, the first few rounds of gunfire are enough to dispel any mob. But these people were madmen. They still would not allow the bulldozers to come in.

Right in front of him was a man jumping up and down. A giant of a man. In one hand he held a lathi, and with the other he lifted his lungi and showed his genitals to the DIG. His abuses reached Bhinder even over the sound of gunfire and screams.

'What are you staring for?' Bhinder shouted at a subordinate. 'Get the son of a bitch.'

It was easier said than done. The first policeman to reach him was smashed down like a matchbox by the man. So were the second and the third. The man stood like a colossus daring to mock the whole of Delhi Police.

They got him finally. About a dozen policemen brought him down with a crash. For minutes all that could be seen were the flailing lathis falling on the supine body of the giant. But not a scream escaped from his lips. Not even a single groan. His body twitched spasmodically even after the policemen had left him and then finally lay still.

Another man was spotted on a terrace, lifting his lungi and showing his genitals to the police below. Orders were given to shoot him down. For some time it seemed that he bore a charmed life against bullets. He remained a grotesque, obscene figure silhouetted against the sky, screaming imprecations against the battery of guns firing at him from below, till he gave a sudden jerk, lifted his hands and fell like a stone off the terrace on to the road. A bullet had found him at last.

But for all their heroism, the people of Turkman Gate were slowly being pushed back by the police, when suddenly help came from unexpected quarters.

A mob of more than 500 men came from the direction of Delite Cinema on Asaf Ali Road and attacked the police force from behind. They had been enraged because one of their womenfolk had been shot down as she was passing Turkman Gate just a few minutes back. The men, like all residents of poor colonies, had no love lost for the police and the death of one of their women had put all considerations out of their mind.

Barely had the police recovered from this surprise attack, when another mob attacked them on the left flank. This mob came from the Hamdard Dawakhana side. Some of their relatives too had been injured in the firing and lathi charge.

Taking advantage of this, the fighters at Turkman Gate again pushed forward, pelting stones, soda-water bottles and acid bulbs at the retreating lines of policemen. They were more organized now.

A crowd surrounded the police chowki and the two or three constables inside barely managed to escape with their lives. The people had taken over the police chowki.

There was jubilation among the people. This was the police chowki where many of them had been brought before. They had been arrested, harassed or beaten up here. Now, they controlled the chowki.

The phone rang inside the chowki. Someone from the crowd picked it up. 'This is the deputy commissioner speaking. What is the situation?' the voice on the other side said.

'Murderer, bastard!' a stream of abuses poured into the receiver.

Sitting in his office, the deputy commissioner panicked. 'Who is that? Is that Turkman Gate police chowki?'

'This is your baap speaking, you bastard,' replied a hoarse voice filled with hatred.

This was too much for the commissioner. He slammed the phone down and then picked it up again. 'Send reinforcements to Turkman Gate at once,' he spoke into the phone. 'They have taken over the police chowki.' The commissioner then called for his driver. 'Turkman Gate,' he ordered as he settled down in the back seat of his car. So far, the police had fired sporadic volleys. After the capture of the police chowki by the crowd, they fired in a steady stream. They were shooting to kill now.

The western horizon was red. It was four in the afternoon and blood flowed down Turkman Gate. Their short-lived jubilation had turned sour as the bullets cut them down one by one. Nobody, not even the people of Turkman Gate, could take so much punishment.

The mob was being pushed back again.

'Run, run for your life, *bhaiya*. Run back into the lanes,' even as Rais Ahmed told his brother this, he saw him slump down with a bullet in his chest. He ran backwards, dragging his brother's limp body. Must get to a doctor, he thought to himself.

But where could he find a doctor at Turkman Gate at that time? The injured who could be retrieved from the battle lines by their friends and relatives had been brought to a lodge deep inside Turkman Gate, where a makeshift hospital had been set up by the people. Torn clothes substituted for bandages and the women cleaned up the wounds as best they could. For the seriously injured, there was little hope of survival.

The sea of khaki now threatened to swallow Turkman Gate. The crowd had fled the police chowki and there sat the deputy commissioner making hurried phone calls. 'The situation is coming under control, sir,' he spoke into the phone.

'Good,' the voice on the other side said, 'but be sure to smash all resistance completely before you stop.'

The police had come right up to the inner ring of houses of Turkman Gate and scores of them began to enter them. A new wave of carnage had started.

Katra 3393, Turkman Gate. Husnah Begum lay huddled, quivering with fear, as she heard the sound of gunfire and screams outside her room. Her little boy, Akbar, cringed next to her as there were loud knocks on the bolted door.

'Open up! This is the police,' shouted a voice.

The woman and child remained silent.

'We will break down the door if you don't open up,' the voice shouted louder.

Akbar drew even closer to his mother. Then a loud crunch and the door gave way.

Husnah Begum closed her eyes. She tried not to open them throughout her ordeal with the foul-smelling constable. Her soft whimpering only once rose to a scream when she heard the cries of little Akbar as a rifle butt smashed him against the floor. A strange darkness now surrounded her.

Just a few yards away, pretty, bright-eyed Salena Begum was fighting like a wild cat with the burly constable who had broken into her room. The constable had already felt her nails and teeth.

'This is a tough bitch. I can't manage her alone. Come and help me,' the constable called to one of his friends outside.

Two constables against one woman. Yet Salena fought. Biting, kicking and screaming, she dragged both of them from one corner of the room to the other as they tried to tear off her burqa. Salena Begum would go down the hard way.

The scene had shifted from the demolition spot to inside the houses that remained standing in Turkman Gate. The firing had subsided as the police steadily poured into the lanes and by-lanes hunting for their kill.

Inside the Girdhar Lal Panna Lal lace and gota factory, one of the oldest industrial units of Turkman Gate, were trapped sixty workers. They had reported for duty as usual in the morning. When violence had erupted all around the factory, the proprietor had quietly slipped away, leaving the workers and the supervisor to deal with the situation.

The workers were defending the factory like their own homes. The machines were their bread. Nobody, neither the demolition squads nor the mob outside, would be allowed to touch the machines, the workers had vowed.

But the situation had rapidly worsened. The main gate was bolted, the fleeing mob might enter the factory and set it on fire. The supervisor panicked. He phoned up the police chowki and asked for help to evacuate himself and the workers.

The police came soon after. But before the workers could open the gates for them, the police broke through the gates themselves. Hundreds of them poured in through the gates and fell like wolves upon the unsuspecting workers.

They were beaten up mercilessly and then packed like dogs into police vans. The only fault of the workers was that they had stayed on to defend the factory.

Curfew was declared at 5.30 p.m. And then followed a systematic wave of looting and raping. Most of the men had either been arrested or fled from the area. Only the women and children remained unguarded in their houses.

Razia Begum had been waiting for her husband for over an hour in her house but there was still no sign of him. There was a knock at the door and she eagerly went to open it. She found a police constable instead of her husband.

'Take off your earrings,' he ordered. Razia gave him her earrings.

'Where do you hide your other jewellery?' Helpless, Razia directed him to the little box where she kept her jewellery, their accumulated savings.

'And now your clothes.' Razia pointed to the suitcases beside the bed.

'Not the clothes in your suitcase. The clothes on your body.' The constable bared his betel-stained teeth.

Razia's eyes widened in terror. With a wild lunge, she managed to dodge the constable's grasping arm and ran out into the veranda. Beyond it was a 40-foot drop to the pavement below.

'Come back, woman! What are you trying to do?' the constable shouted from behind her.

Razia Begum closed her eyes and jumped. The pavement rose to meet her with a sickening thud.

It was getting dark in Turkman Gate. Red flecks still coloured the dark sky as the sun sank farther. A hush had fallen, though occasionally the silence would be broken by screams or hysterical sobbing.

Not a light came on in any of the houses. The electricity had been cut off. So had the water and telephone connections. It was as if Turkman Gate had been disowned by the rest of the city.

The silence was broken suddenly by the weird cranking and croaking of machines. It seemed as if some primordial monster was laughing in the face of Turkman Gate. The bulldozers had started moving again.

Arrayed like a tank squadron, sixteen bulky shadows came to life as the light of day went out completely. Their ugly snouts shook as they moved forward. They seemed to be chortling with glee. There were no obstacles in front of them now.

Nineteen-year-old Suleiman heard the sound of the bulldozers as he crouched inside a half-demolished house. He had managed to escape and hide here. Nobody would think of looking in here. He was a bit worried about his brother. They had arrested him. Tomorrow he must try and bail him out, Suleiman thought.

The sound of bulldozers did not mean anything to Suleiman at first. It must be the police trucks leaving, he thought. The sound came closer.

Suddenly, it flashed through Suleiman's brain: This was no truck. Trucks don't make this sort of noise. What could it be? Suleiman wondered as the noise grew louder and louder. He dared not look out lest he be discovered by a passing constable. The noise seemed to be heading towards the house in which Suleiman crouched. And as it was almost upon him, Suleiman realized it was a bulldozer that was advancing upon him.

He opened his mouth to scream but his scream was drowned in the growl of the bulldozer as its 12-foot blade smashed its way into the house, mixing Suleiman's body in the rubble. Then the monsters moved on to destroy it further.

The darkness was suddenly lit up by high-powered searchlights, and the waste that was Turkman Gate lay stark and bare under their piercing rays.

The sixteen bulldozers kept on moving.

They did not stop that night, nor the next day or night. In fact, the bulldozers worked round the clock till 22 April, till they had obliterated all signs of life as well as death in Turkman Gate.

The rubble of Turkman Gate was scooped up into trucks and thrown behind the Ring Road every day, where buzzards and jackals were seen rummaging through it. Only the stench of rotting flesh which hung for days together over the rubble remained to tell the story of the life-and-death struggle of the people of Turkman Gate.

chapter two

THE BULLDOZERS

~

19 July 1975, Kalan Mahal, Jama Masjid

The Emergency was twenty-four days old. The employees of the DDA and the MCD had for more than a month busied themselves at the house of Prime Minister Indira Gandhi. From the morning of 12 June, they had demonstrated their support for the prime minister, pledging their loyalty to her. As the officials supervised the arrangements for water and barricades, for transport and urinals, the men and women of the capital's civic organization braved the searing June winds and sat for hours to listen to the woman they had come to see.

On 19 July 1975, the officers decided that the time had come for action. In their last confabulation together, the senior staff of the DDA and the MCD, led by their redoubtable chiefs, had decided that the first operation would be carried out in the Jama Masjid area. They discussed the date for the operations. There were too many factors to be taken into account, all too many things to be remembered, noticed and included in the deliberation.

It could not be a day earlier, because 17 July was a Thursday and any deed done on a Thursday would be hotly discussed and debated at the Friday congregations in the mosque. It could not be Friday at all. And the next week would upset the programme that was even now being chalked out for a really good drive in the city. Saturday, 19 July 1975, was the unanimous choice. Almost never again would the officials waste days of action on such deliberations.

They struck at dawn. Even as the sun rose, contingents of police from the Central District moved in, blocking roads, keeping the curious away. Cleaning their teeth, gargling and still rubbing the sleep out of their eyes, the people of the surrounding areas gathered to watch. For the people inside Kalan Mahal, there was little time for munching the *datun* or rubbing the briny charcoal powder on their pan-stained teeth. Mothers preparing paratha and chai for the early child left the *angithi* and gathered close behind the *tat* curtains as the strange officials announced that they should leave their homes because the land was to be cleared. With a small posse of police following them, the officials repeated their warning to all the men.

The signal went out to the truck drivers to rev up their engines. The first truck drove up, its backboard down, its driver waiting. The officials barked commands. The constables moved in too, their lathis waving in tune with the shouts. Everyone was moved in time with the shouts. Everyone was moving, but not the people of Kalan Mahal. They stood in sullen groups, the women screaming imprecations, the men debating, discussing, questioning. But not budging. The sun was meanwhile rising higher and the day had started getting hot. The crowd had also started swelling. The officials could wait no longer. The warning was announced. Load your *boria bistar*, your pots and pans on the truck before the men with the *sambal*, the pick and the hammer move in.

The sambal had embedded itself into a wall when the father and his children put their baggage on the truck. The mother collected her aluminium utensils, put out the fire and came and stood next to the truck. The family waited and watched as they pried loose the bricks, as the sambals tore huge gashes in the walls.

The tempo was building up. Within minutes, the structures had been ravished irretrievably. The families boarded the trucks. They had been told they were being taken to Seelampur across the Yamuna. 'Khuda hafiz,' the women shouted to friends who followed the truck on to the main road. Men followed on cycles and rickshaws. It was not a short way to Seelampur as the trucks crossed the heavy traffic on the main road. Then over the old railway bridge, and jolting over every undulation in the road, to the piece of land where they would have to start life again.

As fast as the families left, the clearance staff set to work with the enthusiasm born of the knowledge that the head of the department was watching. Men and machines soon had Kalan Mahal bereft of any sign that people had ever lived here. Bereft of any sign of life.

With the last family on the truck, the tension eased. The senior police officer issued some more instructions to his divisional officers, slumped into his car and drove off to the headquarters in Daryaganj. The police force he had ordered to remain on perpetual guard in the area was considered strong enough to maintain the peace, if the residents presented any threat to it.

By noon, the demolition squad of the municipal corporation and their fellow workers in the DDA contingent reported to the superior officer that their work there was finished. The labourers gathered their sambals, picks, shovels and the rusty tasla and climbed on to the trucks neatly labelled 'ON GOVERNMENT DUTY'. The convoy drove off in a cloud of dust and noise. On to the main road. Their destination was the Ambedkar Stadium outside Delhi Gate 2 kilometres away. The trucks ground to a halt in the parking lot that generally plays host to the cars, scooters and cycles of the capital's most rabid sports fans.

With the elan of a well-practised team, the supervisors relayed orders as the men removed shamianas and brickwork from in front of the long row of shops, dhabas and restaurants that do business in the lee of the main stadium wall. The shopkeepers made as if to resist but had second thoughts. The Emergency was still all too recent, still all too unfamiliar. They did not know what would happen. The job was an easy one and the khalasis were soon back in their trucks. They had a short break for lunch.

After lunch, the squad was at it again, half a kilometre away. Near Delite Cinema. All too close to Turkman Gate. But at present, it was only the shopkeepers they were after. The encroachments had spilled on to the road, and the demolition squad dispersed. The shopkeepers picked up their chairs and stools, stray bits of wood and the odd glass tumbler that had escaped injury. In Kalan Mahal, neighbours who had left for work in the morning, with the demolition squad very busy, returned to find an expanse of open land, strewn with a few pebbles and the odd toy. In Seelampur, the housewives sorted out the belongings they had packed in such great hurry.

The sambal and pick would come to Jama Masjid again on 22 November. And again on 25 November and again later. Because in Town Hall, the British-made headquarters of the MCD, and in the prefabricated Vikas Minar structures of the DDA, the instructions had been received loud and clear. The city was to be cleared of all unseemly slums, all crowded and narrow gutters where men lived and bred and created problems of law and order, all places which reminded one of the rank hunger and poverty, places which had caused problems for the police. The orders had come from the very top. From 1, Akbar Road? Or from 1, Safdarjung Road? Employees in the DDA office were now considering very seriously how they should describe the address of the 'actual headquarters' of the gigantic organization that employed them all. The employees in Delhi finally settled on 1, Akbar Road. It made for a nice distinction. 1, Safdarjung Road was the official residence of the prime minister. The employees were firmly of the opinion that the rooms occupied by Sanjay Gandhi fell in the Akbar Road area. 'That's where the orders came from,' said the personal assistant of a senior officer. 'And the orders were simple. Do it, and do it fast. Do it now. We do not know how long the Emergency will have to be continued. The work must be over before that.'

For the 200 families living in Moti Bagh, Sarai Rohilla, in the seedier part of the capital, the morning of 30 July 1975 is important. They had been living there for years. In houses of earth and thatch, brick and asbestos, the 1500 men, women and children had so far rebuffed all demolition squads sent there. They would gather in stormy numbers. They would yell for their leaders. They would also dare the authorities to touch their homes. The authorities had so far not dared to.

Now they did. With the same precision as in Kalan Mahal, the formations closed in on the kill. The subdivisional police officer, Darshan Kumar, a big, bulky man in his loose khaki uniform, with the three stars of a deputy superintendent of police (DSP) adorning his shoulder straps, instructed his officers and men to take position. Meanwhile, he went into a discussion with the area subdivisional magistrate and the assistant housing commissioner who was in charge of the overall supervision of the morning's campaign. The official orders from higher-ups were that it was an implementation programme. The land belonged to the municipal corporation and it had already paid the compensation of the land to the Delhi Administration which had acquired the land for the construction of an overbridge to connect the Shakti Nagar area with the main bulk of West Delhi colonies. The Rs 1.2-crore overbridge was meant to have been finished by 1971. But the houses built in the area were posing a problem for the municipal corporation. It could not begin work till the residents were shifted. For years, it had tried to make them leave but had failed. Even the police had failed and, after many an encounter, the authorities had decided to wait for a more opportune time.

The opportune time had come, and this time they were prepared to carry out the orders. Under the watchful, enthusiastic eyes of the officials present, the demolition men raised their sambals and picks. Raised them over and over again, till the huts and houses were no more. The residents, totally cowed by the heavy police presence, made an attempt or two to resist. The leaders got into arguments with the officials, but the weight of khaki proved too much. Sullenly, the people picked up their belongings and boarded the trucks. With a sigh of relief the officials prepared their reports. A group of workmen set up a barbed-wire fence around the cleared sites. Then, as the whistle of goods trains and massive diesel engines echoed from the nearby tracks, the demolition squad picked up its rods and hammers, spades and taslas, and left. The operation had passed off with a rare smoothness that surprised the officials who were still thinking in terms of the pre-Emergency days when a demolition of the kind they had just done would have been an impossible thing. The people just would not have allowed it.

The planning was by now done in Sanjay Gandhi's room. Not the detailed planning, but the broad guidelines. It was not as if Sanjay was not bothered about details. He was. He cared exceedingly for details. He had personally inspected each minor detail on the rostrum that had been erected for his mother's rally at the Boat Club lawns at India Gate. Mrs Gandhi was scheduled to explain at a mass rally her stand on her defeat in the Allahabad High Court earlier on 12 June. The Allahabad High Court had, on a petition by Raj Narain, declared her election from Rae Bareli null and had debarred her for six years from seeking election.

It was 20 June 1975. Mrs Gandhi had not yet come to the Boat Club lawns. The rostrum was empty save for the lone policeman in civvies desperately trying to look like a politician and failing.

Suddenly, on the stage appeared Sanjay Gandhi, a balding figure in a white kurta-pyjama. He was followed by DIG Bhinder in uniform. The people gathered at the rally wondered who he was. Some who were from parts of New Delhi knew him to be the younger son of the prime minister, the fellow who had said he would make a car for the common man. But to the many from outside town, his presence made no sense. There was a scattered burst of applause, almost as if the people felt they might as well clap just in case he turns out to be somebody important.

But most people kept quiet and watched the two fellows on the empty rostrum—the fellow in white and the sardar policeman whose uniform seemed too loose to be neat. Sanjay Gandhi's first appearance on the stage from where his mother would speak was not very impressive. And therefore, the people wondered all the more how he was giving orders to the policeman and why the policeman was looking a shade too obedient.

The officers ruling Delhi were fiercely jealous of each other. And not without reason. Favours were given in the most unreasonable manner, and most disproportionately. Jagmohan had been bestowed with the Padma Shri while others who thought they were equally, if not more, worthy had been ignored. The officers realized that the only way to maintain the pre-eminence of one's position was to try and cosy up to the son of the big boss. Over the past two or three years, the officers had been busy consolidating their power. In the absence of a determined political leadership in the capital, officials had succeeded beyond even their own expectations. They had consolidated their power and established their authority, so much so that even the political hierarchy had found itself increasingly dependent on the bureaucratic bosses of the DDA, the municipal corporation and the Delhi state Small

Scale Industries Development Corporation for their political sustenance. Those in the know therefore were not surprised if they saw the de facto police chief or the head of a civic body paying courteous and humble respects to Sanjay Gandhi that afternoon at the grand rally at the Boat Club lawns. That was the way to become more powerful.

Atop the rostrum, Sanjay looked into all corners of the gaily decorated stage. Bhinder gave them a second look. They tested the height of the microphone bank and looked over to the lattice work that had been erected to accommodate the press reporters and photographers of a dozen nations. Sanjay expressed his satisfaction with a smile. Bhinder beamed his thanks. Mrs Gandhi drove up as the security superintendent of police had his men moved with the nervous excitement of laying hens. Mrs Gandhi mounted the podium. And spoke: 'The rally has not been called to pressurize anyone.' Thousands of employees of the MCD, the Delhi Administration and the NDMC applauded. They were clapping. But they were also discussing the strange thing they had seen just before the prime minister had arrived. As they dispersed from the Boat Club lawns, they talked of what they had seen. And going home in Delhi Transport Corporation (DTC) buses later that evening, they were still discussing if Sanjay Gandhi's presence on the rostrum had any significance.

No one knows the precise date or day that the first meeting was called at 1, Akbar Road. No one remembers a date, nor does anyone remember which officer was present and which officer was not. One of those who were present has even forgotten if he had been summoned, or had decided on his own to go because he felt his rival was bound to be present there. He certainly knew that summoned, invited or coming of his own accord, he did not want the other fellow gaining an advantage over him. How they had come to 1, Akbar Road no longer mattered.

The fact was that they were here at 1, Akbar Road. 'They would come and wait in the anteroom,' says one who was in a position to watch the activities on those hallowed grounds. Sometimes they sat with Dhavan (the prime minister's private secretary) and discussed other officers in the IAS or the police. They would sit till Sanjay could free himself from the Youth Congress and the other leaders who came to see him even before 8 a.m. The officers usually came at about 8.a.m. He would call them in. At first he called all of them together—Tamta, Jagmohan, Bhinder, Ailawadi who had just been appointed member secretary of the NDMC, Navin Chawla, the lieutenant governor's secretary, and municipal leaders or councillors; often the executive councillors would be present. Sanjay would listen to them narrate how their work was being hampered. He would listen as they spoke of their problems. Then he would issue his directions. The officers acted promptly.

On 23 June 1975, in the biggest operation they had ever carried out, the clearance staff of the west zone office of the municipal corporation began a day-long drive to beautify the Tilak Nagar chowk where a teeming bazaar thrived. Police Subdivisional Officer Daulat Ram, the police station incharge, Duli Chand Galia, and Subdivisional Officer Y.D. Vankata, responsible for maintaining the peace in the area, marshalled their forces. The forces included a 200-strong battalion of khalasis and other workers armed with pickaxes and spades, a dozen trucks and the police force of the sub-district. The men with crowbars and the policemen with tear gas and lathis moved in. Within the span of a working day, they cleared over 700 structures of wood and brick that had been built on government land. Once again, the massive police bandobast had successfully withstood sporadic resistance.

The spirit of competition was catching on. Like the various unidentified fevers that swept through Delhi occasionally, the mood spread amongst the officials. The words of praise at the morning conferences were heady indeed. And the lashes discouragingly strong. The competitive spirit appealed to Sanjay too. The youth in him apparently revelled in seeing people fight for his favour. He now called them in one by one. Only on rare occasions, or when something very big was to be planned, would all of them—each of them separately—ask him about the progress, tell him that the other parties had complained of tardiness, and then take instructions from him. The targets were chosen in a pattern. In addition to the official surveys that had been done, the local Youth Congress organizations too had their lists of jobs to be done.

The beautification drive was the easiest of things to participate in. All one had to do was to prepare a list of the dirty areas. The rest was done by Sanjay Gandhi. He had taken over the men who ruled the various civic organizations. They in turn governed their subordinates in the same manner that he governed them. Quick results were the criteria. 'The essence of the Emergency is that work gets done on time, in time,' the civic bosses had announced to their staff. The organizations were honed to a perfect pitch to obey this dictum. No dissent, no resistance from worker or officer. That had become the order of the day.

It had all begun with the lieutenant governor himself. When he first came to Delhi, the political leadership welcomed him with open arms. The chief executive councillor found in the undistinguished retired Indian Civil Service officer just the sort of person he wanted after his stormy relationship with Baleshwar Prasad. That had ended when the Centre moved Prasad out in the wake of the scandal that came to be known as the 'VIP land grab' in which many of Delhi's senior citizens had allegedly been given out-of-turn allotments in a cooperative housing society in one of the capital's posh residential neighbourhoods. After the political fireworks seen in the Baleshwar Prasad era, the Congress bosses of the Delhi Administration thought they had found the ideal non-person in Krishan Chand. They were not mistaken.

Within days of the Emergency, Krishan Chand had become a nonentity and the fact was made apparent to him every second by the continuous presence of Navin Chawla. A Delhi boy, Chawla had been in the Indian Administrative Service for only a few years. He was well connected, well bred and was generally liked by his friends and colleagues who found in the bright young fellow a sense of humour and a tenacity for hard work. He was an additional district magistrate (ADM), one among many. But he was the most prominent of the lot. Although he was not by a long margin the most senior of the dozen or so ADMs who helped District Magistrate Sushil Kumar manage the revenue and law and other situations in the capital, he was lucky to be the chief of the area called New Delhi. As ADM, New Delhi, part of his duties was to ensure that peace was maintained in and around the Safdarjung–Akbar Road block of bungalows, where Indira Gandhi lived with her two sons and their wives and her grandchildren.

Chawla was also the district marriage officer and many a VIP had he bound to a wife with one sweep of his pen. Among them was Sanjay Gandhi. Chawla presided over the function in the house of family friend Mohammed Yunus where Maneka Anand, the amateur journalist daughter of an army colonel, became the legally wedded wife of Sanjay Gandhi.

'Navin rules us all,' a senior administrator grumbled. 'You antagonize him at your own risk, because the lieutenant governor is absolutely under his thumb. In fact, we call Navin the actual governor. Krishan Chand is just his lieutenant.'[1] The joke was a serious one. There was another confusion. Both Chawla and Krishan Chand claimed to receive their orders directly. Sometimes the orders were even a trifle contradictory. In such cases, it was for Chawla to see that Krishan Chand issued the necessary orders to make requests and demands; orders given face-to-face, as well as those conveyed through third persons or over the phone were given the cloak of officialese that would guarantee their legality. Krishan Chand was needed to sign the official orders.

One of his first orders after the declaration of Emergency was to appoint a committee to expedite the development and beautification of the Trans Yamuna area. On the committee were the municipal commissioner, the DDA vice chairman, Congress leader Bhagat and four others. Within days of the constitution of the panel, beautification work started in the densely populated area near the Yamuna River.

By early October, the demolition drives had become coordinated. In mid-October, the squad struck at Krishna Nagar, Green Park and the unauthorized colony of Arjun Nagar where the most peculiar thing happened. A bulldozer pulled down a portion of the house where Arjan Das lived. Das was no longer the small-time mechanic working at a garage on Roshanara Road. He no longer had his pyjamas stained with motor oil, his hands soiled with grease. After working with Sanjay Gandhi at the garage, Das had sought to shift to more respectable pastures. He too chose politics. From the garage, Das moved on to the Metropolitan Council of Delhi through the midterm general elections called in 1971. When the Emergency was clamped, Das was still said to be close to Sanjay Gandhi.

The demolition of the house of Arjan Das set off a wave of speculation in the city. 'Arjan Das is no longer in favour. Sanjay does not like him any more. Arjan Das is finished. He is out.' Das too was stunned by what was happening. A house more or a house less would not matter to him much, but it was not just a matter of a house. And so Das registered a loud protest. It would be the loudest protest heard during the entire demolition programme. The only other one would be the explosion at the Turkman Gate. Arjan Das's protest was heard. An official said the government had listened to the many complaints that had been received of illegal demolition. The government, he said, was aware of complaints that good houses were being demolished in a most unauthorized manner. The government would organize an inquiry. How could somebody just come and demolish a house that was in perfect order? Something must have happened to the DDA. But to people other than Arjan Das, another thing was becoming apparent. The DDA, which had begun late, was now edging out the municipal corporation.

The bulldozer that demolished the mechanic's house also pulled down the adjoining ones. The neighbours said Arjan Das himself had asked the demolition squad to clear the entire row when they demolished his house.

The bulldozer kept moving till it hit a three-storey house. Its blade struck the masonry; the house trembled and, from the first floor, a huge piece of concrete fell on the bulldozer. The operator barely escaped with his life. The machine remained trapped for seven days. The owner of this house sued the DDA for contempt of court, claiming he had the high court stay in demolition of his property. The DDA was claiming the demolition as its historical privilege. 'There can be no development without demolition,' Raman would say later.

The DDA firmly believed in it. So did Jagmohan. And because the DDA was the authority bound by an Act of Parliament to look after the development of Delhi, it followed as a natural corollary that demolition was its birthright too.

There was a voice of dissent. The municipal corporation did not think so. Although the Slum and Jhuggi Jhompri Department, complete with the commissioner in charge, had been transferred to the DDA some time ago, the municipal by-laws still left room for the corporation to show how active it could be. Its offices could show how much they believed in the 'work more talk less programme' of implementation. The earlier experiments with smaller demolition programmes had shown that a big show of force could, if used succinctly and with daring, cow the most vigorous of protesters. A bulldozer working with a phalanx of mounted and armed constabulary was a yellow prehistoric monster that could strike terror in the bravest of hearts, in the most organized of resistance efforts. Tamta planned another campaign for 23 November 1975. The target was the area around Jama Masjid. The directive was clear. To make Jama Masjid an exemplar of cleanliness. The medieval bazaar which had adorned the giant steps of Jama Masjid for hundreds of years would have to be purged. The directive was clear. The method had been perfected in field trials. But the problem still daunted the heart. It was not any ordinary area. Jama Masjid posed its peculiar difficulties. The police had of late been complaining that the Kabari Bazaar was encouraging petty thefts, especially of car parts. They also complained about what a headache the entire system was. One had to always keep a wary eye on matters here. The officers posted to the local chowki could not afford to relax. Often, in the past, the people had resisted any attempt by the authorities to meddle with their lives and lifestyle and, many a time, the reaction had been violent.

The decision was therefore to stick as close as possible to the directives. There was to be surprise, speed and police presence strong enough to quell any sound even before it vibrated through the air. The meeting ended. Orders were circulated through the police network that 22 November was action day. It was Wednesday and reasonably safe, the police moved in strength. First the traffic police in their white sleeves set about making the approach roads to Jama Masjid. out of bounds for all vehicles save debris-clearing trucks, bulldozers and police cars.

The magistrates and the subdivisional police officers supervised, as the DAP constables checked the chains tethering their rifles to their belts. Behind them, in distinct but small clusters, the gas squads readied their equipment: wide-barrelled guns and squat but neat canisters holding the tear-gas shells. As some distance, Tamta took care of last-minute details. Deputy Commissioner K.N. Sharma and assistant commissioners Sardar Beant Singh, R.K. Singh, Bansi Lal and G.L. Sharma, who had

not gone to their headquarters in such diverse places as Sadar
Paharganj and the New Delhi south zone, waited for the green
signal from Tamta. At a distance sat a DDA official, aloof from
these MCD men, but feeling pleased with himself. He was sure
he would enjoy himself thoroughly. With him lay the important
task of issuing the slips that would get these people another place
to set up shop. He had been told by his boss in Vikas Minar that
this bunch of shopkeepers would be sent to Mayapuri.

Tamta's signal came at 10 a.m. sharp. And then, from behind
the wall of the tall and burly jawans of the DAP, an army of 1000
labourers trooped out. They struck at three sides of Jama Masjid
simultaneously. The noise of heavy concrete blocks falling on
sonorous steel slabs rose to a crescendo. Clouds of dust rose in
the air. The picturesque surroundings echoed to the sounds of
turmoil. And over it all began the mechanical whine of heavy
vehicles moving in for clearance.

The 1000 labourers worked without rest, for the authorities
did not want the pace of the demolition to let up. A breathing
space could have disastrous results, could give sufficient time to
the shopkeepers to decide to do something to stop the operations.
The dust rose higher, and through its haze came the blare of
loudspeakers. Amplifying a tinny diction, the megaphone intoned
endlessly. Sometimes the voice would be cajoling. It would
request the shopkeepers to save their belongings voluntarily. At
other times, the voice would have an edge of menace about it.
It would utter sharp commands. In heavily accented Urdu and
Hindi, the voice would tell the people to take heed. 'Take heed,
for you will not be warned again. Take heed and remove yourself
peacefully,' the voice said.

The demolition was going on at a furious pace along the
three sides of the mammoth structure which had served for
centuries as the classic focus of city life, mosque and marketplace
with memories of *shahi* (royal) processions and the buying sprees
of Mughal princesses. The men with iron rods came to the

Shahi Gate, from the direction of the police station near the lane leading to Chawri Bazar and from Dariba Kalan. But there was a hitch. Some of the shops built in the alcoves of the masjid wall were displaying unforeseen strength, the careful craftsmanship of builders of a past generation had made the mortar harder than the hardest modern concrete. The lime slurry that withstood the test of long decades was successfully challenging the hired government brawn. Also, many shopkeepers carrying on the business of their fathers had reinvested their incomes in improving their shops, and the heavily reinforced structures could just not be demolished.

'We heard the roar of bulldozers. A number of bulldozers were active, because it takes a really heavy bulldozer to smash an RCC (reinforced concrete) pillar or an RCC slab. The ordinary D-4 Caterpillar bulldozer with its wire-operated blade will not do. It requires a D-8 or D-9 Caterpillar to really clean up the place,' said a bulldozer operator. The deadly Caterpillars lowered their heavy, hydraulic blades, and cleaved into the debris. Rock and brick crunched under their thick chain tracks; the bulldozers, heavy as they were, lurched. One Caterpillar stopped in its tracks and the operator came down to remove the stone that had lodged itself in the chain links. The bulldozers advanced again and again, levelling the ground, pushing the debris in front of the gigantic sweep of their blades.

The men at the front were still busy with the heavy steel levers. The lever would thud into the wall. The labourer would bend over it, twist it and pry a stone loose from the shop wall.

The lever thudded into the wall again. The worker suddenly jumped back in fear. Before he could exert any force on the steel rod, a massive stone had tumbled off the wall. With a crash, a chunk of masonry fell to the ground. Suddenly there was silence, louder for the noise that had preceded it. In the silence, the worker explained the situation to his officers. The officers went to the supervisors. By now all activity had nearly ceased at the

site. In the unexpected hush could be heard the loud screams of
a venerable elder, cursing the men, bringing Allah's wrath down
on their heads for their sacrilege. The engineers, however, were
concerned with the problem on the ground: that of meeting this
new threat which could well escalate into the ugliest incident
they could dream of. The superior officers were immediately
contacted. The chief had left the site for a while when work was
on in full swing. The officials now consulted the top engineers
they could find. A solution emerged.

The solution was to construct an 18-inch-thick brick wall
to buttress the main masjid wall whose mortar could then be
saved from further damage. A cynic also pointed out that the
wall would help to hide the ugly gashes made in the wall by the
sharp steel sambals that had been used to pry loose the moorings
of the shops. With the frenetic activity that had earlier in the day
marked the demolition, the corporation men began to construct
the new wall that would save the edifice from collapsing. They
worked fast and long. Slowly the wall rose, brick by cross-laid
brick. The time it took was not very long, but to the anxious
junior officers, it seemed like hours before the wall was at last
high enough to cover their earlier depredations.

Even more relieved than the engineers were the police
officers. The noises started again. It took the sixty trucks
umpteen trips to cart away the debris. It took the shopkeepers
even more trips to salvage whatever remained of their business.
Then they too trooped to the DDA desk.

The corporation boss had reason to be pleased with himself.
The Jama Masjid demolition drive, which had been attempted
without success over the years, had been carried out in one day.
So what if the day was a trifle eventful. Tamta relaxed. Already,
planning was under way for another demolition in the area, this
time on Esplanade Road where some shops had been thwarting
the anxiously desired beautification. Everyone warned that it
should be done as fast as possible, before any resistance could be

organized. Things could well get out of hand if the people were given too much time to dwell on the first day's demolition. And this time it could be even more vicious, because the cotton market and the row of commercial shops between Dariba Kalan and Esplanade Road had some wealthy shopkeepers. The shopkeepers, however, should not cause much trouble, it was said. They had money, but they could do precious little to approach anyone to stop the municipal corporation.

The demolition squads moved out of the area later that evening. But a strong police force kept vigil. Roadblocks were retained and vehicles coming to the masjid area stopped. Their occupants were questioned, and most were asked to take some other road. The hush of an unofficial curfew descended over the area. It would, like the police force, remain for some time.

The corporation could not wait long. The next demolition would have to be done before Friday, 28 November 1975. And so much of the work had to be completed before that date that there would be no possibility of it lingering on till Thursday evening. At the congregation on Friday, they knew that the topic would be discussed in hushed voices. They did not want to provide too many reminders to provoke an incident. And therefore, they chose Tuesday, 25 November, for the next drive.

Tamta wanted the drive to be conducted with the smoothness of a well-oiled clock. Already the endeavour was to show the progress of the work to Sanjay Gandhi as early as possible. That would be in keeping with the image of efficiency. That would certainly be the best way to prove the 'talk less, work more' idea that had gripped Sanjay Gandhi. Work more.

Ohri marshalled his forces. His deputies conveyed his commands to the inspectors. The platoons of constables were briefed by the havildars. Within minutes, the police fanned out to their practised positions. Wireless sets on motorcycles hummed with static. The jeeps of the gazetted officers hummed with a dozen voices coming over the radio waves. The civic contingent was also gathering its ranks. There were 1000 labourers and thirty-five trucks. The target was a row of twenty-eight shops trading in cotton, and a block of 200 shops that constituted a mixed commercial centre.

The generals were Tamta and K.N. Sharma, a pleasant-faced officer. The chain of command represented senior officials from all eight zones of the corporation. For most of the officers, it was in the nature of an on-the-job refresher course. They were in New Delhi's south zone, and the strategy of Esplanade Road could come in handy. They were from the rural zone, but could still gain something from witnessing at close quarters one of the biggest demolition drives ever undertaken in India.

The corporation demolition squad had by now achieved the finesse that comes with long practice. The shouts of the shopkeepers, the protesting youth and the businessman who felt he just had to hit the policemen to formally register his protest, were handled competently, with minimum waste of time. The trucks made well over 1000 trips to clear the area. If one now stood at Esplanade Road, he could look clear across to Jama Masjid. With grass growing all around, it would be quite beautiful, the officials could almost feel the greenery. Jama Masjid was now clean. The corporation's coup had been successful. Sanjay could now be shown tangible proof of the success of his clarion call. The Town Hall congratulated itself and smirked. It would smirk some more on 10 December, when Sanjay Gandhi would formally congratulate the civic officials for their good work.

The officials scrubbed themselves extra clean for the day they had anxiously been waiting for. Some had waited with trepidation. They had heard that this young man brooked no nonsense, that he was headstrong as a mule, and that if he was displeased, he would not hide it. Sanjay Gandhi drove up and was received by a crowd of officials who clapped a thunderous welcome. *'Shri Sanjay Gandhi ki jai!'* they shouted. They looked around for the others to join the chorus. The older officers smiled. A few younger ones responded. Officials and youth mixed with each other and soon the crowd was a homogenous one.

The people of GB Road, the area where the less pricey prostitutes of the capital do business in the name of dancing girls, watched the curious procession. Prostitutes and pimps, policemen and grain dealers watched and wondered as the fair young man was shown the area by an energetic Tamta, who had just started to display the strain of all that energy. The boys accompanying Sanjay and Tamta looked around and shouted, 'Sanjay Gandhi zindabad!' From the occasional door, someone joined in. The youth shouted, 'Tamta sahib zindabad!' The officials beamed.

The new mohalla bigwigs also beamed as Sanjay passed through Farash Khana and Ajmeri Gate. Turkman Gate was nearby, but Sanjay was not to visit the area today. Tamta took him to the interior lanes of Phatak Namak. The women and men peeped from behind the doors at the strange procession. Sanjay was walking fast, accompanied by Tamta and a gaggle of officials, all gesticulating wildly, bringing to the young man's attention the whitewashed wall, the yellow dustbins and the fly-killing Gammexane powder in the drains. The odour of urine was successfully camouflaged in the pungent smell of the powder.

'That is Sanjay Gandhi. *Indiraji ka launda hai* [Indiraji's son],' the women pointed out to their children. 'He looks just like on television,' a child observed. 'And that is the commissioner sahib,' one man told another. 'So this is why all those sweepers were here yesterday, spreading this white powder.' The jigsaw pieces fell into place for the householders. And so it went on in Mohalla Rodgaran and in Sirki Walan.

'First class,' Sanjay told Tamta. 'Thank you, sa'ab.' His cup was running over. 'Good work,' said Sanjay, and all the officials beamed. A formal vote of thanks was passed with a round of applause. The point was not lost on the officials of the municipal corporation. Tamta saw off Sanjay Gandhi. It was all too easy, this coup.

For Tamta, the applause was just a tribute to the position he had achieved in the municipal corporation over the years. Once a deputy commissioner here, Tamta had returned as commissioner, and was soon involved in a violent war of nerves with Mayor Kedarnath Sahani and his Bharatiya Jana Sangh party which had the majority in the municipal house. Kishore Lal was leading the minority Congress party. The ruling Jana Sangh was itself ridden with dissension, and too many of its members were willing to take issue with the leadership. One of them was Jagdish Anand who left the Jana Sangh, charging it with corruption and bossism. The suicide of leader Balraj Khanna, an Urdu newspaper reporter who took his politics seriously, also had shattered the morale of the Jana Sangh. Khanna's suicide, it was being widely alleged, was a result of psychological pressure. He was being investigated by the Central Bureau of Investigation, said Town Hall gossip.

Tamta's fight with the Jana Sangh had the blessings of the Congress party ruling in the Delhi Administration and at the Centre. Tamta revelled in that fight. He toyed with the Jana Sangh politicians, he played with them, and finally he got the Centre to throw them out of the Town Hall altogether. The government obliged him. Orders were passed superseding the municipal corporation. From being a tame second fiddle to a plethora of political bosses, Tamta found himself to be the top boss, totally and absolutely in command. An army of officers was ready to do his bidding as never before. Over more than 20,000 people he held the power of final arbitration. The supersession was in March 1972. By the time June 1975 came around, Tamta was in total command of the situation. As the sole power in Town Hall, he was also enjoying his own emergence as a prominent social, even political, figure, avidly courted by the lesser politicians. Even the bigger politicians had to come to him if they wanted any work done. Tamta was in close contact with the higher powers. The transition to 1, Akbar Road was smooth.

From 1, Akbar Road and the early morning conferences, the commissioner came to know one basic fact about Sanjay Gandhi. Nothing pleased him as much as the knowledge that instant action had been taken on his words, instant action which could be proved by statistics. Planning figures and demolition figures, and even the capture of stray dogs were all good. The feel of 1, Akbar Road was conveyed to the second and third rung of officials and, within a month, the lowest peon sitting on his door-side stool was aware of the desire to keep the numbers high. As they had found out in the July demolition drives of 1975, there was no need to be wary. The police would help, and the atmosphere of the Emergency was deterrent enough for anyone who sought to make trouble. From dusty files were hunted out all tasks that had remained incomplete. Local leaders, by now all of them belonging to the Youth Congress, helped chalk out the actions that were needed in their respective areas.

The orders went out to the dog squads. More than 20,000 dogs were hunted, caught and then killed in the district zones. The hawkers came next, and were hunted and prosecuted. The Emergency was only a month old when the zonal officer of Sadar Paharganj zone was asked by the commissioner to report to him the progress done in demolition drives in the previous fortnight. With a penchant for the smallest details, the zonal assistant commissioner, R.G. Singh, listed his achievements. There is a smirking sense of pride in the note Singh sent to the commissioner:

During the last fortnight, the staff of the licencing and enforcement branch of this zone, in cooperation with the staff of other zonal departments organized special drives to clear unauthorized encroachments.

On July, 24 as many as 100 pucca [made of brick and mortar] masonry constructions in front of the railway station were removed. At this very place about 150 encroachments on public land which included fruit and vegetable sellers, pavement tea-shops and cigarette stalls were removed. On the same day 12 licenced rehris dealing in fruit and drinks were seized.

The assistant commissioner also informed his boss how he had done the job:

This major clearance operation could not have been so much successful but for the active involvement of the sub-divisional magistrate, the sub-divisional police officer and the police station head officer who rendered all possible help and in abundance.

Singh went on to give all the details to Tamta. His staff had helped evict the people living on the land marked for the Sarai Rohalla bridge. They had removed all the shop projections and encroachments from the Azad Market crossing to the Kishanganj railway bridge and had beautified the area. They had also removed some shops. Licensed and unlicensed mobile stalls on rehris were also removed throughout the area. Squatters were evicted from the Subzi Mandi vegetable market area. The clearance drive in Paharganj had been carried out promptly, as had the commissioner's directives in other areas. The statistics were impressive.

Also impressive was the drive to remove the thousands of cows and buffaloes kept within city limits by milkmen. The beautification order requiring all shopkeepers to have a standardized elongated billboard on their shops also enforced. Within days, 1,00,000 boards were shortened, much to the delight of carpenters who suddenly demanded and got up to Rs 50 for a day's work. 'Voluntarily' the shopkeepers paid the carpenter. They had seen what happened if the boards were not shortened and the sunshades reduced to the new standards. If you did not break your own shop projections, the corporation would do it for you and send you the bill, the commissioner had told the shopkeepers. Within days, they found he was not lying. A strong posse of labourers struck at the Ajmal Khan market one morning. And when they left that evening, mounds of rubble and heaps of shattered wood planks remained to speak of the corporation's earnestness.

Demolition was tagged on to whatever drive was in force. A sample from a diary of the Karol Bagh zone read:

Whitewashing of curb stones . . . 35,000 feet
Grill repaired . . .1,000 feet
Whitewashing of trees . . . 20
Houses whitewashed . . . 2,013
Prosecutions launched . . . 298
Dogs killed . . . 165
Rats killed . . . 295
Unauthorized constructions demolished . . . 71
Trees planted . . . 50
Bougainvillea shrubs trimmed . . . 7 parks
Jhuggies removed . . . 58.

The statistics fever was at its height. It was a new year, 1976. Tamta passed an office order giving seven days' time to the residents of the capital to modernize their plumbing. Dry latrines would have to be converted into flush-type ones.

Soon thereafter, the bomb burst. The commissioner announced the Chawri Bazar redevelopment scheme. The demolition around Jama Masjid had proved (had it not?) that these areas could be cleaned and beautified. It was a plan conceived at the 1, Akbar Road meetings and had received enthusiastic support from everyone. The DDA was all for it, the commissioner agreed and the police concurred. Such a plan would solve many problems that had been a headache especially for the police and the civic departments. The decision was taken to announce the plan.

It was announced on 27 May 1976—exactly eleven months after the declaration of Emergency—at a press conference convened that hot summer day in the cool room of the commissioner in the Chandni Chowk Town Hall.

Tamta sat at his table. With him were his chief engineer, the chief architect and town planner and sundry other officers. In front sat the reporters from New Delhi's newspapers. The boards in the room displayed maps and artists' impressions of what the plan would do to the Jama Masjid area. On the table was a glass-topped model. It showed a tiny Jama Masjid dwarfed by four gigantic blocks of buildings. It showed a rolling green park and wide black ribbons for roads.

Tamta spoke. 'After achieving considerable success in clearing up some areas, the municipal corporation is now contemplating a comprehensive scheme for environmental improvement and redevelopment on modern lines of the commercial area of Chawri Bazar. The scheme will initially cover about 18 acres which has been divided into two major chunks located on either side of Chawri Bazar, stretching from the back of the Jama Masjid up to Chowk Badshah Bulla.'

'The scheme,' Tamta continued, 'is being undertaken as a pilot project to initiate redevelopment of old and decaying areas of the walled city, one of the most densely populated in the capital. The proposed buildings would each be twelve storeys high.'

For once, and for the only time, the Akbar Road gambit failed. It was only a month after Turkman Gate. Nearby Dujana House, where Ruksana Sultana Singh worked, was a perpetual source of tension. The police became worried as the newspapers announced the Chawri Bazar scheme: 'This is it. This is why they butchered Turkman Gate. They want to remove all human beings from the area and build a super modern market here.' The men, women and children nodded in understanding and in fear. Turkman Gate was not a mere memory. Even now armed police marched in heavy-booted vigil through its by-lanes. The old men in their ancient houses and the old Congress leaders thought it was time to register a protest. The first protest was not strong. But it was apparent that for once, the rich paper traders of Chawri Bazar, the poor artisans of Badshah Bulla and the aristocrats of Gali Khankhana had united. This was no warning of a mere demolition. This was something more serious. So serious, in fact, that they needed some more time before they could breathe easy enough to study the plan and object to it. The shock had been too great.

In sharp, staccato happenings, the Chawri Bazar resistance was born. The rich paper merchants did it their own way. Their sons had helped collect funds for Sanjay Gandhi's five-point programme. They thought it would help. The old-timers and the cultural elite were banking on something more sophisticated, also more ephemeral, but still strong enough to make them shed their fear. In a letter sent to both Sanjay Gandhi and Indira Gandhi, Mohammed Mustesan Faruqi, who organized a movement under the name of the Shahjahanabad Development Society, said: 'The picturesque buildings around Jama Masjid that are sought to be demolished under this scheme cannot be rated as slums. They in fact form a historic complex symbolizing a typical Indian culture pattern and adding to the area. To raze them to dust and to erect multistoreyed structures for commercial purposes instead, to be auctioned to the highest bidder, will mean an untold loss to the thousands of families living there in peace for centuries. Bulldozing them in the name of redevelopment will be against the declared policy of our beloved Prime Minister Mrs Indira Gandhi.'

The stately Faruqi continued, 'The new structures proposed will mar the beauty of the historic Jama Masjid itself. It will be a terrific blow to the historical significance of Shahjahanabad as it is one of these areas of the walled city where one can read its history in every brick and stone. In fact the area is unique in this respect. And of course, the corporation's scheme does not conform to the Master Plan for Delhi, nor to the Development Act, 1958 and the Municipal Corporation Act, 1957.' He added, 'If the scheme is ever implemented, it will be a terrible blow to the people of this area and will lead to their decay and ruin.'

The Shahjahanabad Development Society published a pamphlet, 'Shahjahanabad Speaks', and printed a folio of photographs of the area. The photographs showed beautiful and stately buildings, but no slums.

The tempo was now building up. The Shahjahanabad Development Society dared the authorities again. Even as policemen desperately trying to look like civilians collected copies of their letters, the society published details of what the scheme would do to them. The list was titled 'How many to be ruined' and went on:

Properties 1327, families 240, shops 1126, offices 126, godowns 228, temples 13, mosques 3, schools 10, and hotels 5.

Congress leader Shiv Charan Gupta appealed to a wide band of intellectuals. 'The government might be doing some fresh thinking about old Delhi. If so, they should take the public into confidence.' And somebody pointed out, filing a long objection to the scheme, 'How is the Corporation handling it? Is it not supposed to be the DDA's baby?' The central government had not bargained for this hornet's nest. Union Housing Minister K. Raghuramaiah said, 'The redevelopment project is with the DDA and it is reconsidering it.' The DDA was amused at the corporation's plight.

A few days later, Sanjay Gandhi visited the Chawri Bazar area. He saw a family-planning camp. And then he announced that the Chawri Bazar scheme was being shelved. The people cheered. The paper merchants jumped with joy and their sons congratulated themselves. Said a press note on 28 February 1977:

It is clarified for the information of the general public that in the light of the objection received, the preliminary scheme drawn up by the Municipal Corporation has been dropped. The entire project was transferred to the DDA which has drawn up a revised scheme.

From the DDA's point of view, it was a fair lesson that the upstart municipal corporation had been taught. Such grand projects were their speciality. The DDA vice chairman had built up the organization to handle schemes of just about this magnitude. It had the resources and it had the money. Over the years, the revolving fund meant to finance the construction activity of the DDA had been multiplying with every new commercial scheme. It was a heady time for the DDA. And a heady time for Jagmohan, the man with the boyish fluff of hair on his forehead, who took one look at table models and told you how much money the DDA would make. Already its revolving fund meant to finance low-cost housing for the city's residents had reached dizzy figures through investment in real estate meant for some of Asia's biggest commercial ventures.

With his long experience, first as the housing commissioner and then as the implementation commissioner, Jagmohan had learnt the most effective manner of driving a point home. As soon as he became the vice chairman, he set about implementing the lessons he had learnt under different commissioners. It had taken him guts and years of work to rise so high. From a relatively junior posting in the Punjab Provincial Civil Service, Jagmohan had come to DDA at the instance of the lieutenant governor.

With his youthful appearance and jaunty airs, Jagmohan soon established himself as a person who would always meet the strictest demands made of him. His seniors had found him possessed of superhuman ambition, but knew him to be useful. To further his own career, Jagmohan could easily dazzle his superiors with evidence of phenomenal work. He rose fast. By the time he developed insights into the workings of the DDA, he was ready to take over. He succeeded S.G. Bose Mullick as vice chairman in early 1971 and immediately embarked on honing the DDA into a sharp tool that would get him the results he wanted to show to the higher-ups. The results that he knew would have to be shown if the DDA had to get sole power over the fate of Delhi. In the DDA's power lay his own.

The DDA is supposed to have a thirteen-member governing board. Under the lieutenant governor who is the chairman, it has a vice chairman, a member for finance, an engineering member and representatives from the elected municipal corporation and the metropolitan council and from the central government. But even before the Emergency, Jagmohan had succeeded in dominating the board so completely that no one else could be heard. After the municipal corporation was superseded, the municipal commissioner became the sole civic representative, and even the nominal opposition that the Jana Sangh had been providing was removed. 'Jagmohan was enjoying it thoroughly,' says someone who worked with him for many years. He had also devised a scheme to contact the middle rung of executives and engineers to give them orders directly or to convey his displeasure. Jagmohan ruled the DDA so absolutely that when the organization shifted to its twenty-one-storey headquarters at Indraprastha on the banks of the Yamuna, a carte blanche was given to the decorator charged with making the vice chairman's lounge and office presentable.

Somewhere along the line the vice chairman also shifted his focus. The DDA had been charged by its creators to build houses and develop the city as a whole. Jagmohan had shifted his focus to major commercial activity. Now he also decided to go back on a belief he had himself held when by comparison to his present status *he was* the lowly implementation commissioner. 'If we do not copy the affluent countries, and if we abandon costly schemes of housing and slum clearance and encourage our architects to plan and build simple yet beautiful colonies, the twin challenges of massive urbanization and abysmal poverty could be met.' The thesis was slowly revised. There followed an interim period when money was spent on improving the lanes and lights in slums. The politicians liked it; it helped them tap the solid slum vote bank. But now there were no elections, and not many politicians. It was the right time.

It was the right time, agreed everyone who was sounded out at the Akbar Road meetings. Already Tamta and his municipal corporation had started work in this direction. The DDA had got increasingly involved and in massive publicity campaigns indicated that it was ready to do all the work itself. The challenge had to be met.

It had been decided that the time had come to remove every jhuggi jhompri from the last remaining slum, and as fast as possible. The order went out to prepare the contingency plans. The massive D-8 and D-9 bulldozers were conditioned for prime service. The new orders were framed. The element of surprise was of the essence, and the target would be disclosed at the last possible minute. The demolition squad and its police escort would prove sufficient. A direct liaison was arranged with the Delhi Police. The grand strategy was prepared.

'Only one or two men knew of Jagmohan's targets for the day. These men would assemble their squads and take them to the chosen spot. Simultaneously, the police would be brought to the area. The lighter bulldozers were brought on trucks. The authorities looked away when the heavy bulldozers broke the metal on the roads on their way to the demolition sites. We had all been told of the importance of surprise and the importance of the job. This was to be the work's biggest drive—like Janakpuri was Asia's biggest residential colony,' said a DDA official.

When the newly expanded DDA demolition squads hit a place, the place stayed hit. The people were told to voluntarily pull down their houses if they wanted to save the bricks and the asbestos. They were told that if the DDA tore down the houses, they would not be able to salvage anything. They were told that they had time till noon. And that the DDA would itself remove any structure that remained after noon.

At Indra Vikas Puri, the men, women and children took the officials literally. With their own hands they sought to remove the stone slabs and wooden beams, but it was not always possible to do it by lunchtime. Not that there was any lunch that day. But it was more difficult in Serai Beri near the Qutub, and in the ironically named Sanjay Nagar near Kotla Feroz Shah at the border between Old and New Delhi.

'If the slum had huts, the DDA would use its bulldozers. Even the heavy bulldozers do not have the strength to barge into a well-structured house. One tried to. It got stuck,' the bulldozer man said. 'Also, the delicate fuel injection system of the bulldozer is at the top, barely protected by a metal sheet. If a brick falls on it, it is finished. Bulldozer operators do not dare go to a wall that is over six feet high because they get injured. In such houses, the labourers have to use their sambals to reduce the structure to manageable rubble. The bulldozers then push it into a pile for the trucks to cart away.

'But the bulldozers really enjoy biting into the mud of earthen huts. A D-9 bulldozer can start at one end of a row of small huts and just push them out of the area. The blades are up to 12 feet across and hydraulically operated. They level everything.

'The lighter D-4 bulldozer cannot do much of this type of hard work. But they can help with the levelling, especially where the huts are made only of mud and thatch. The D-4 bulldozer's blade is a dangerous thing. It is operated by a cable and jumps over anything that comes in its way. Unlike the heavier types, this blade will not push a man away if he decides to lie in its path. The blade will just pump over the man, and the Caterpillar tracks will crush him. That is a bulldozer operator's nightmare.'

The DDA was marshalling all the bulldozers it could find in the capital. The heavier ones were only with government agencies; they were all deployed. They also came from the Central Public Works Department and from the local works department of Delhi Administration. The smaller bulldozers were hired from private operators. 'We charge Rs 60–70 per hour for the bulldozer. We have bought them from disposal auctions for Rs 25,000 and let them out to government agencies for road building and dam work. The DDA routinely hires our bulldozers for road purposes,' said Gupta, owner of a bulldozer.

'They, the DDA, seized the bulldozers of another person,' says Gupta's son. 'But the bulldozers could not be used for heavy demolition.'

'I saw the heavy bulldozers in action in the Jama Masjid demolition drive.'

The bulldozers did not take much time to level the two slums that flanked the All India Radio transmitting station, off the DU campus. Within a few hours, the bulldozers had left the area a ploughed field, with a small mandir sitting conspicuously in the middle. The slum had been set up at the time of the general elections five years ago by a Congress leader of the area to offset the Jana Sangh vote that was sure to come from the second slum set up by his Jana Sangh adversary. The Jana Sangh politician was absent. The Congressman was present during the demolition, but it had been months since he found that the DDA area officer was not going to listen to him.

As the hungry machines chewed up homes, Jagmohan's representative sat at a table and chair nearby, guarded by a police posse. He was distributing the slips of paper that would get them a place in the area they were being sent to. 'Come up. Bring out your ration cards. You want the slip or not? Don't want it? Then go to hell, you bastard. Who do you think you are? Come on, next one.'

As the people waited by the piles of their belongings, the first trucks lumbered laboriously on the road now hidden under broken plaster and bricks. There were not enough trucks. 'Just take your essentials. And don't everyone get on. What do you think, is it a bus or something? Just the essentials, if you do not want your stuff to be thrown out.'

'Where are the other trucks you said would come?'

'How do I know? Do not bother me.'

In another colony in Sadar. 'Listen friend,' said the DDA worker, 'I sympathize with you. My own house has been demolished.'

Demolition is unavoidable in the planned development of Delhi, said Raman while inaugurating a project. Like the other established politicians in the capital, the chief executive councillor of Delhi had just pledged solidarity and support for Sanjay Gandhi's programmes. He was as impotent to do anything as Bhagat, the Union minister of state for housing and therefore the top man for the jobs in the capital. The best Bhagat could do was to slow the pace in his constituency across the Yamuna. No other politician could do even this.

The bulldozers moved on, slowly and with finality. Their tracks made patterns on the freshly turned earth. Over the tracks were imprinted the marks of the threads of the truck tyres. Superintendent of Police Rajinder Sahay, harassed by a long stretch of duty at the Sadar demolition, complained, 'These people have not sent as many trucks as they had promised.' Someone had decided to make some money in the confusion by charging for 100 trucks but sending only eighty.

The people chartered their own trucks. The rates shot up and for night-time jobs the rates were higher still. And the trucks would not take too many things—not big beams or stones or people, or pigs. For slum dwellers in north Delhi, transporting their pigs was a big problem. Pork prices slumped as the pigs were butchered under the double ultimatums of the municipal corporation and the DDA bulldozers.

On the way up were the demolition figures. Within months of the first meeting at Akbar Road, Jagmohan was in a position to report that more than 50,000 huts and houses had been demolished. The police too corroborated the positive effects of the extensive demolition. Bhawanimal and Bhinder smiled as they spoke of the declining trend in the capital's crime pattern.

Like a well-drilled army, the DDA machine was proving to its sole commander its worthiness. The machines did not stop in the heaviest of rains or on the hottest of days. No soldier on the war front could have given a better display. With the Turkman Gate episode safely in its past, and the municipal corporation stumbling pitifully on the Chawri Bazar issue, the DDA was emerging on the top. Tributes were paid to its performance and that of its boss in the capital's equivalent of a state assembly. Even as sporadic complaints appeared in the newspapers of the crumbling plaster of DDA-built houses or of the exorbitant amount of money it was demanding for its houses, the DDA kept its focus on the jhuggi and the jhompri.

With half its engineers supervising the demolition drives, the other half was placed on the vast stretches of fields in the corners of the capital. For what was once its chartered activity, the building of houses, the DDA now found few men to spare. Houses, however, continued to be built, and promptly a regulation was made that they would be allotted to those making the payment in full. The full payment now went up to Rs 75,000. Prices for plots touched the half-million-rupee mark. Two plots meant for nursing homes went to a South African Indian millionaire for Rs 7 lakh.

But the other commercial ventures of the DDA were not faring as well. 'Nehru Place is desperately in need of clients,' a senior civic official said. Jagmohan had raised the problem at the meetings at 1, Akbar Road. 'The corporation has been ordered to cut off the water and power connections of all commercial establishments in south Delhi and to tell the people to move to Nehru Place,' he said. Many did, reluctantly, and after cursing those controlling their destinies.

The man in control of the DDA settled in for a long and fruitful reign. He had made the supreme sacrifice. He had given up his coveted membership of the Indian Administrative Service. He had shifted to the deluxe office in the swanky high-rise, just like the executives do in Hollywood films. And he had been told he would get the Padma Bhushan in the next honours list. A UN agency had commissioned him to write an expert article. 'He will make 50,000 bucks on it, the bum,' said a junior official. After greeting the youthful man at Akbar Road, Jagmohan reported, 'We have removed all jhuggies from the city. We have demolished 1.2 lakh housing units in the slums. That's 7 lakh people.' Chief Executive Councillor Raman summed it up. 'We have made striking achievements that were considered impossible, thanks to the new climate.'

chapter three

OUT IN THE WILDERNESS

~

Dwarka Prasad stared moodily at the road receding behind him. It was a longer distance than he had imagined. The truck seemed to go on and on. Beside him on the truck huddled his family and belongings—his wife, Bhagwano, aged thirty-five, and his three children, Prem, Annu and Babua, the baby in his arms. He eyed his belongings. He had not been able to salvage much. Just one rusty trunk, a couple of faded mattresses and the battered pots and pans. Not much to start a home anew with, he thought bitterly. As Dwarka looked at the road, it seemed as if his whole past was running away from him.

Dwarka's past was the Delhi Gate bustee where he had grown up. It was here that his father had come after the partition of India in 1947 and opened a tea shop. He was a hard-working man, his father. Over the years, he had built up the shop, bench by bench, teacup by teacup till it had become one of the most popular tea stalls of the area. It was here that he had got married. Dwarka looked at Bhagwano. Poor woman, she seemed to have aged in the last few days. Yes, life had been hard work, but it was looking up slowly, Dwarka had got a job in DESU and Bhagwano looked after the tea shop after his father died. Thank

God his father had not been there to see the bulldozers raze the tea shop, Dwarka thought. The old man would have jumped in front of the bulldozers to save his shop.

The DDA had given him just fifteen days' notice. 'You live in an unauthorized colony. The colony will be demolished. You shall be resettled in Mangolpuri. So, prepare to move out,' the notice had informed him. Dwarka had immediately run to all his friends with the notice. Can this be true? he had asked them. Even earlier, there had been rumours of the demolition of their colony. But nobody had believed them. How could anybody demolish a colony which had been thriving there for decades?

Realization had come only when the demolition squad was at his door. The last-minute packing had left Dwarka a mental wreck. What to take? What to leave behind to be crushed under the bulldozers? It was difficult to find takers for the furniture of the tea shop. Nobody was willing to buy any stuff in the colony. Everyone was too busy selling off their own furniture. Finally Dwarka gave away the furniture to his relatives. It had been a dead loss. Bhagwano was half asleep as the baby suckled at her breast. She had not slept for the last few days. Now the rolling of the truck brought delightful slumber. But her thoughts would not let her sleep. 'What will we find when we get to this Mangolpuri?' The question kept recurring in her mind. With a woman's instinct, Bhagwano sensed the ordeal before her. She did not want to reach Mangolpuri. Let the truck go on and on, Bhagwano thought.

The only person in the family happy about the shifting was seven-year-old Prem. The other children, three-year-old Annu and the baby, were too young to understand what it was all about and had been alternately crying and laughing. But Prem was absolutely exhilarated. Shifting meant that he would not have to take his exams in school. Prem hated examinations. What he liked to do was play all day. Mangolpuri sounded interesting. He could not understand what his parents were worried about.

It was a change at least, Prem thought to himself, as he frisked about from one corner of the truck to other.

Dwarka and his family were among the 1.5 lakh families being shifted from all corners of the city to be resettled on its outskirts. It was an integral part of the five-point programme of Sanjay Gandhi and the fulfilment of Jagmohan's vision. No more ugly sores on the capital's face. The slums were being cleared by massive demolition operations. No more rabble choking up traffic and encroaching on the government's property and sensibility. Seven lakh people were being banished to the periphery of the city. Delhi would be the most beautiful city in the world, Jagmohan had dreamed. The only city, in fact, which did not have any poor living in it.

Jagmohan's DDA had been quite specific about its reasons for the resettlement. Just after the Emergency, it had announced its resettlement project. A pamphlet read:

> The urban poor live in dilapidated settlements that cling precariously to hillsides, line smelly canals, block roadsides, or crowd inner-city alleys. In their tattered misery, they mock the aspiration of all those who yearn to make their cities sophisticated and modern. Furthermore, these human beings are unwelcome because they build shacks on urban land to which they have no legal right and for which there is little or no infrastructure of public services. It is only in the context of this magnitude and complexity of the problem that the 'Delhi Squatters Resettlement Project' can be understood.

Yes, the complexity and magnitude of Dwarka's life had suddenly increased. From being just one person with a family he had become a part, admittedly a small part but still a part, of the giant exodus from the city. Dwarka was no longer an individual. He was now an integer in one of the biggest experiments of the Emergency in Delhi.

All this could not have made much sense to Dwarka as he stared at the road receding behind him. To himself, he was still very much an individual. Ecology, congestion, architectural symmetry—these terms of reference were meaningless to him. His problems lay in Prem's education, his wife's health and his own job. His squalid surroundings in the Delhi Gate slum might have been an eyesore to the DDA. But to him it was home. The barren fields that flashed past the truck might grow into future urban townships for the DDA. To Dwarka it meant coming out in the wilderness.

The landscape was getting more and more deserted. How many miles had they covered by now? Ten, maybe fifteen, miles. Dwarka had never come this way before, but it seemed that he was not in Delhi any more. Could the truck have taken a wrong turn, Dwarka wondered. But no, big bright-yellow boards pointed with a red arrow: 'This way to Mangolpuri.'

There were other boards too. A large field where a flock of sheep and goats lazily grazed sported a huge noticeboard. 'College', the noticeboard proclaimed.

Prem found this terribly amusing. 'Look, Pitaji, college,' he pointed out gleefully to his father. The sheep and goats seemed a vindication for his general contempt for education. 'I'll go to this college,' he announced, ignoring the black look his father gave him.

A few fields later was a board announcing 'Cinema'. The only inhabitant on this field was a large mournful-looking cow. 'Cinema, cinema,' giggled Prem till his father gave him a hard smack. 'One more word from you and I'll throw you out of the truck,' Dwarka shouted. He was losing his temper.

The DDA publication had waxed eloquent on the 'infrastructural and environmental facilities' provided at the resettlement colonies. These facilities include construction of pucca roads, brick-paved lanes and by-lanes, water supply through tube wells, handpumps and municipal sources, community latrines, dispensaries, super-bazaars, local community shopping centres, schools, playgrounds, cinemas, woodlands and parks. The truck had reached the outer limit of rural Delhi by now, and there rose on the distant horizon a faint red smudge. The smudge grew bigger as the truck drew closer. Now a row of tiny brick hutments could be seen. It was hidden for a short distance by a bend in the road and then, as the truck rounded the bend, the Mangolpuri resettlement colony was upon them. Almost treeless, the brick hutments that criss-crossed one another in geometrical patterns were mostly half built. Some did not have roofs, others had only two walls. The structures seemed so peculiar and misshapen that were it not for the naked children running in and out of them, they wouldn't have seemed like houses at all.

A terrible stench arose as the truck drew closer and closer to the colony and all of them covered their noses. The truck was passing a row of latrines. There were eighteen of them, Dwarka counted. All without roofs or doors—they were full up even at noon with men, women and children defaecating. Then right into the heart of the colony, the truck came in and screeched to a halt. Dwarka stood erect on the truck to survey his new home.

Mangolpuri lay grinning shamelessly under the hot, bright June sun. There was a starkness about its squalid surroundings that stunned at first sight.

Dwarka was not expecting a plush house. For most of his life he had lived in slums. Filth, congestion, narrow roads and open drains—he had grown up with them. Dwarka was desensitized enough to live in the most squalid of slums.

But there was something inhuman about this colony. Everything was in symmetry. There were straight roads and neat little plots facing each other in long rows that stretched way beyond where the eye could see. There was nothing unplanned about the colony. It was a child's planning. Convenience had been sacrificed for symmetry and the order had a lifeless quality about it.

The women sitting at the doorways of the hutments had a strange, ferocious look in their eyes and the children looked wild and emaciated. Even the dogs here seemed mangier, baring their yellow fangs at the truck.

'Chalo, bhai, get down from the truck with your belongings,' the truck driver shouted, breaking Dwarka's reverie. 'I have to make another trip,' he added.

Dwarka felt like telling the driver that he wanted to go back with him. But there was no place to go back to. He had to stay here. This was his new home.

With Dwarka and Prem carrying the luggage, and Bhagwano, the baby and Annu trotting behind, the family walked down the row of hutments and plots to their plot in T-block.

A 25-square-yard plot of land. That is all Dwarka had as a home now. He had been prepared for this. He had brought some poles and a piece of canvas with him. This was the makeshift home that Dwarka made for his family.

Later, he would get bricks and build his house according to DDA specifications. As he lay in his tent that night, Dwarka felt like a defeated man. His past seemed too distant to be real. His present was too transitory to think about. And his future? Dwarka closed his eyes to his future and fell asleep.

The next day Dwarka went to meet the DDA engineer to find out about building his house. He was already in a foul mood. In the morning when he went to ease himself, he had found a queue, almost a kilometre long, in front of the latrines. He had waited in the queue for one hour and then come away disgusted.

Now he had to wait in another queue in front of the DDA engineer's tent. Finally, after waiting for more than three hours, his turn came.

'Yes, what is your problem now?' asked the florid DDA engineer in an irritated voice. He had been dealing with residents of the colony one after the other from morning till evening for many months, and he was sick and tired of their ignorance and problems. He had at first tried to be gentle and helpful. But it is not easy to be gentle and helpful when you know that half of the problems you have been called upon to solve cannot be solved in any case. These people were doomed for the first few months. It was better they realized that as soon as possible. 'I came yesterday. My name is Dwarka Prasad. I have been allotted a plot in T-block,' Dwarka tried to smile ingratiatingly. 'I just wanted to know, what are the DDA specifications to build my house and how do I go about it?' Dwarka asked diffidently. 'Haven't you read the handbill we distributed, idiot?' the engineer shouted. Dwarka claimed ignorance of any such handbill. 'Okay, listen, these are the specifications. One room, covered by a roof, one window and a space for a bathroom inside. If you like you can build a small patio outside. No *kuchcha* structure allowed. And remember, careful about sanitation. Don't let your kids shit outside on the road. Disobey these rules, and we demolish your house,' the engineer fired rapid instructions at Dwarka.

'About shitting, I just wanted to say that I waited for more than an hour in front of the latrines but I could not get in,' Dwarka began.

'Where do you think you have come, idiot, Defence Colony?' shouted the DDA man. 'Why don't you build an attached bathroom in your plot itself? Then you don't have to wait. You fancy yourself to be different from the others, do you?'

Dwarka quailed under the storm of jeers and abuse from the engineer. 'And another thing . . .' The DDA man stopped Dwarka as he was stepping out of the tent. 'Don't try to complain about the lack of facilities here to any councillors or ministers who might come visiting. You try any funny business and we show you who's boss. Understand?'

His face burning with humiliation, Dwarka went back to his tent. 'What happened?' asked Bhagwano. 'Oh, nothing, just don't let the children shit outside the house. I don't know where they will shit but if they shit outside the house, the engineer said that he will demolish our house,' he snapped back.

'And have you asked about the milk?' Bhagwano asked again. Little Annu was a sickly child. She needed milk to recuperate.

'Damn, I forgot. This engineer was such an unhelpful chap. All he did was jeer and abuse.' Dwarka cursed aloud. 'I'll see if some of the other residents know where to get milk,' he told Bhagwano and stepped out into the blazing sun again. 'You want milk, friend!' jeered one of the neighbours. 'Have you tasted the water here yet? Just taste it and you will forget about milk. It is such a heavenly taste, you won't want to drink milk after that,' the jeers continued.

An elderly man was more helpful. 'Sometimes a milk van comes but you have to be really fast to get some milk out of it. Usually the milk bottles are taken away in less than five minutes. Some vendors also come to sell milk, but it is more water than milk. And they charge fantastic rates,' he said.

The jeers on water continued to ring in Dwarka's mind. 'Is there any more water in the *matka*?' he asked Bhagwano when he got back to the tent. They had brought a big matka full of water with them and that had lasted them till the morning. 'I have brought some water from the handpump but it looks a little peculiar,' Bhagwano grimaced.

'Give me a glass.' God, he felt thirsty. The water did look funny. Yellowish in colour. It smelt a bit funny too. Dwarka took one sip and immediately spat it out. 'This water tastes absolutely bitter,' Dwarka said, his face contorted. 'This couldn't be drinking water, you foolish woman. You must have brought some shit water or something,' he shouted at his wife. Bhagwano started crying. Irritated, Dwarka again stepped out into the sun.

He tried the handpump at the end of the block. Again that bitter taste. There must be somewhere one can get drinking water.

He met the elderly man again. 'Sorry to disturb you again. But can you tell me where I can get drinking water?' The man directed Dwarka to the handpump a few blocks away. There, he said, the water is better.

Got to drink water. Dwarka remembered that he hadn't had a drink of water since morning. The distance to the block seemed miles. There must be a big crowd there if that was the only handpump for drinking water in the colony, Dwarka wondered as he walked.

But there was no crowd. The handpump at the block was in fact deserted. Thank God! But no water seemed to come from the pump though he worked the lever again and again. 'The pump has broken down,' came a harsh voice from a nearby hutment. A lean-faced man stood at its doorway. 'And pray why won't it break down? Ten thousand people using it every day. What pump can stand it? You bastards from other blocks came and spoiled it, understand? And now we have no pump.' A stream of abuse followed Dwarka as he walked away.

'I have boiled the water,' said Bhagwano when he reached the tent. Her eyes were still swollen from crying.

'Give me a glass,' Dwarka said. He swallowed the hot, bitter liquid in one gulp.

'Give me another,' he said. He felt thirsty.

Yes, Dwarka had slowly learnt to swallow the bitter life at Mangolpuri colony. His new house had come up in fits and starts. It had cost him a pile of money. He had not realized that building material would turn out to be so costly. Sand had cost him Rs 1.50 a bag and cement Rs 22. But when he came home and opened the bags, he found that only half the sand bags were full.

Dwarka had given up the idea of a pucca roof. Ceiling stone was selling at Rs 70 a gross. He had run out of money by that time. The canvas sheet which had served as a tent for the first few days was now his roof.

The house that Dwarka built was a regular little black hole, ill-ventilated and with hardly any space to move about. It became a furnace in the day and was too stifling to sleep in at night. The only opening in the house was the door and that too was facing another row of similar hutments on the opposite side.

The family slept outside on two charpoys. Dwarka and Annu on one and Bhagwano, the baby and Prem on the other. Thank God it was still summer, Dwarka thought. If it were raining, where would the family go?

The first rains came when the family had completed exactly a month in the colony. The day had been cloudy and Bhagwano would have enjoyed the cool air had it not been for Prem. The boy had been growing wilder by the day. There was no school to go to and he had the whole day to roam about in the colony.

Early in the morning, Prem would go out and return home only for his food. He was the only one in the family who had thrived in Mangolpuri. Dwarka himself had grown thin and emaciated, his eyed were sunken with worry and work. Bhagwano looked over fifty now. It was back-breaking work, managing the family while Dwarka was away. Little Annu grew more sickly every day and would cry for the smallest of reasons, which often led to cruel beatings from her mother. The baby had a virulent attack of diarrhoea, probably because Bhagwano's milk had dried up and it had to take the strange concoction which passed off as milk that Dwarka bought from a local vendor.

Prem had almost become an adult at seven. His compulsive frisky nature now manifested itself as a constant rebellious manner and he did not care for even Dwarka's anger these days. He hardly listened to his mother. Today, Prem had fought with a boy of S-block and had badly bruised him. His mother had collected a big crowd and come to Bhagwano and abused and threatened her. Normally shy and timid, Bhagwano had been scared to death.

They could not afford to antagonize the older residents of Mangolpuri. They were a wild bunch. God knows what could happen. Dwarka stayed away the whole day and she was all alone in the house. She would complain to Dwarka today about Prem. The boy was becoming impossible. Dwarka had come home in a dark mood. He had been abused by his foreman today. Dwarka had again reached the office late. It was more than 25 kilometres from Mangolpuri to the DESU office in Indraprastha Estate and he had to change buses thrice. He would start early in the morning at six, but it still took him more than two hours to reach his place of work. Apart from that he was paying a heavy bus fare every day. And on the top of this, his foreman had been telling him that he was late every day. Today he had been given an ultimatum. If he came late again, three days' wages would be cut.

Dwarka had come home with a foul temper and a bad headache. He had slumped down on the charpoy, and the breeze was just beginning to cool him down when Bhagwano told him of Prem's fight with the boy in S-block. That was the last straw. Dwarka was furious. Prem had come prancing in as usual at dinner time to walk right into his father's wrath. Dwarka beat him mercilessly, banging his head against the wall.

'Get out of my house, you swine!' Dwarka shouted. 'You are no longer my son. Next time you come for food, I'll thrash the life out of you.' Prem had slunk away, whimpering loudly.

The family had gone to bed early that night. Dwarka stretched out on the charpoy alone. The boy had still not come back. Well, if he nurses so much anger at the age of seven, it's time he learnt a lesson, Dwarka thought darkly.

Dwarka had just dozed off to sleep when he felt the first heavy drops of rain. He opened his eyes and saw that the sky had clouded over. The downpour began even as the family gathered the mattresses and rushed into the house with the charpoys.

Dwarka watched the downpour get heavier and heavier. The wind had become a gale. And soon they had to shut the door to stop the rain from coming in.

Bhagwano was worried about Prem. Had he been able to take shelter in the rain, she wondered. She should have stopped Dwarka from beating him up so badly, she brooded. Who would give the boy shelter in the rain in this godforsaken colony? Bhagwano listened to the wailing of the wind outside.

Bhagwano's reverie was shattered as a big drop of rain splashed on her hand. She looked up with a start, and her heart sank.

The roof was leaking.

The canvas which had served them well for a month was at last cracking under the onslaught of the wind and the rain. 'Water is coming in through the roof,' she screamed to her husband.

Dwarka jumped up from the charpoy. Yes, the rain was slowly punching holes in the canvas and the wind had unravelled one of its bindings on the wall. The canvas might get blown off any moment.

'Hold on to the canvas,' Dwarka screamed to his wife as he desperately clung to the loose end of the canvas. Bhagwano gave the baby to little Annu who had also woken up, and tried to straighten out the canvas roof, but lost her balance and ended up pulling out another corner of it.

At once there was pandemonium in the pitch-dark room. Part of the canvas gave way, and now the rain came in devastating torrents, drenching nearly every corner of the room. Startled, Dwarka let go of his end and the whole canvas collapsed, leaving the family in the house with no roof.

The rain lashed the family for three hours. Bhagwano wrapped the baby in her arms and bent double protecting it from the rain, while Dwarka strove to cover Annu as best he could. For three hours, the family was exposed to the worst vagaries of nature, their belongings slowly becoming limp and useless.

And during those three hours, Dwarka wondered what sins he had committed in his past life to be subjected to this torture. Even a dog found shelter on a night like this but his family had no place to go.

In the morning, when the rain had stopped, Dwarka fixed the roof with a new canvas, reinforced with some timber he had stolen from another hutment nearby. He had reached a stage where he would do anything for his family's survival. In just one month, Dwarka had learnt the laws of the wilderness.

Prem came back two days later with a swollen face and high fever. He was so ill that he could not even tell them where he had been for the last two days. The fever rose the next day and Prem became delirious. The boy seemed to be in great pain and in just a few days, had lost energy and weight.

When spots began to appear on Prem's face, Dwarka panicked. He knew the symptoms of chickenpox. He had to call a doctor. But where would he get a doctor in this wilderness? There was not even a compounder available to give medicine. Dwarka rushed around like a madman to get some sort of medical man to treat his son.

At last he got through to a doctor with an MBBS certificate and a dilapidated clinic nearly 2 kilometres away in Sultanpuri. The doctor was ready to come but only on payment of Rs 50 in cash. No, he could not take the money later.

'Where is the guarantee that you will give the money later?' he asked Dwarka. 'Besides, on principle, I don't visit patients. I lose too much time for practice. For you, I am doing this extra favour because your son seems to be very ill.'

From where would Dwarka get the money? He had put every paisa of the family's accumulated savings into the house. His wife's jewellery had also gone into it. In his Delhi Gate slum, he could have easily got the money from the local moneylender.

But in Mangolpuri who would give him money? Nobody knew each other in this wilderness.

The only possession which Dwarka still had was a family heirloom that his father had given him. Dwarka was very proud of this watch. Besides, it was vital to him as it helped him keep time when he went to the office in the morning.

But he had to get a doctor. Dwarka sold his father's watch for Rs 60, the best price he could get in such a short time. He would pay Rs 50 to the doctor and the rest for medicines. If Prem would just last out till the beginning of the next month when Dwarka got his pay, he could take him to a better doctor.

The doctor came and prescribed a few medicines for Prem. A very bad case of chickenpox, he declared, but the medicines that he prescribed would keep the boy alive, the doctor had promised. But nothing could save Prem. Two days later the boy died. Life in Mangolpuri had claimed one member of the family in no more than a month.

Prem's death had been the final break with the past for Dwarka and Bhagwano. The tragedy had broken them completely. Both of them had given up hoping for a better life. They were too busy with day-to-day survival to think about the future.

Little Annu had a recurrent fever and a series of raging attacks of diarrhoea. The bitter, silty water which the family was forced to drink was probably the reason for the diarrhoea. The child had shrunk unbelievably in a month's time. She showed signs of acute malnutrition.

But Dwarka was no longer running around for a doctor. He was resigned to his fate.

The brutalization of Dwarka Prasad and his family was not an isolated quirk of misfortune. It was part of the grand resettlement plan dreamed up by Jagmohan to resettle 1.5 lakh families, involving a total population of nearly 7 lakh men, women and children.

The pompous pronouncements from the DDA office
scarcely acknowledged the actual horror of life in colonies like
Mangolpuri. It was too busy conjuring up grand visions of
fairylands to sell to the public. Whether on paper or in speeches,
the DDA described as the ideal urban township what was
actually a wilderness.

To see the resettlement colonies through the DDA's eyes
was indeed a surreal experience. A DDA publication on the
resettlement project claimed:

How far has Delhi Development Authority come and how
fast. Housing half a million people in its resettlement colonies
and planting half a million trees in a brief span of eight months
is itself indication of hard work, disciplined effort and zeal and
initiative on the part of the DDA. Only a few months ago the
trans-Jamna area where about 2.5 lakh squatters have been
shifted under the resettlement scheme wore a deserted look
in the absence of single human soul. Today one is dazzled by
seeing new township humming with full activity.

The new townships, Khichripur, Kalyanpuri, Trilokpuri,
Himmetpuri and New Seemapuri in the trans-Jamna area
have all facilities. Wide roads, tube street lights, community
centres, TV auditoriums, dispensaries, schools, shopping
centres, DTC arrangements, children welfare centres, parks,
woodlands, lakes, social welfare centres, cinemas, all these
have been provided to the residents who have been given
developed plots of 25 square yards each. Similarly in other
areas, resettlement colonies like Dakshinpuri extension,
Kanpur, Tigri, Madangir, Madanpur Khadar, Garhi, Sun Light,
Gazipur, Seelampuri, Gokalpuri, Nand Nagri, Seemapuri,
Shakarpur, Mangolepuri, Nangloi 1,11,111, Jhangripuri,
Sultanpuri, Chowkhandi, Hastal, Khyala, Ragbir Nagar,
Pandav Nagar, Narian have been developed by the DDA
which are a scene of intense human activity and self-help.

Isn't it surprising that in as short as a period of eight months 27 resettlement colonies have been developed for as large a population as seven lakhs. Most of the residents have already built houses on the plots provided to them while others are still building according to an economical sample design provided in each colony.

It is by no means that simple to realize the mobility that has been shown in bringing the new township in such a small period which otherwise could have taken years. So many hands worked in so short a time to offer a better environment to a large segment of population. It was this segment of population which led life in shanties and slush under sub-human conditions.

The DDA very well realized that life for half a million will not be that cheerful in new locations unless something better was offered to them. In slums the resettled people had suffered in sun and rain; in new homes they have to fear none—neither the sun nor the rain. But the DDA realized their need for shade. Hence the programme to plant half a million trees best suited for the new environs.

The resettlement colonies where green buffers will emerge after half a million trees sprout up will not only give better look but will have many features like parks, playgrounds community tot-lots, lakes and gardens. It is good that DDA has chosen to plant trees like eucalyptus trees which will be helpful in reducing the sub-soil water of the trans-Yamuna area.

The resettlement of squatters in the new townships is not confined to merely giving them a plot of developed land with roads, street lights, community centres, dispensaries, shopping centres, parks, playgrounds etc. It is something much more. Delhi Development Authority has taken adequate care of the social and economic needs of the shifted population. One thing which baffled everybody in the course of shifting the squatters to the new areas was their employment. DDA very ingeniously sited the townships in areas which had ample employment potential. The townships are more or less surrounded by large industrial commercial institutional and horticultural areas which have a large scope of providing employment of the casual labour and skilled persons. The squatting population of Delhi comprises these three categories. In a comparison worked out by the DDA, it was brought to light that the shifted population had limited employment opportunities in their old surroundings. The main outlet of their earning was domestic service, as their old locations were neither nearer to the industries nor were influenced by the major construction and horticultural works in their vicinity.

The other thing which baffled during the course of shifting was the transport facilities. In the townships and their new link with the city. In this direction the transport authorities and the local administration have rather done a yeomen service by flooding the new townships with new routes. The man in the new townships is now better placed in the matter of community and civic facilities, transport and employment than he was at earlier an unauthorized, unplanned unhygienic shack.

The gigantic work which DDA took up to resettle lakhs of squatters in new environs is coupled with a great foresight in bringing about complete transformation of Delhi and New Delhi areas. The areas which looked slushy pockets of slum are either neatfully landscaped or provided with shopping housing and institutional facilities. The areas under the unauthorized occupation of the squatters were otherwise needed for the planned development of Delhi in accordance with the Delhi Master Plan.

With the resettlement of squatting population, DDA has, therefore, achieved four objectives; (1) to provide house sites to those who live unauthorisedly on public land in sub-human conditions, (2) to reclaim the areas which were earmarked for a specific use under the Master Plan, (3) to clear slums from the congested parts of the city and to provide better accommodation to those who lived in hovel like structures amidst suffocation and congestion, and finally (4) to undertake programmes for the facelift for Delhi.

The above was the story which the DDA told the people of Delhi about the resettlement colonies. The mixture of half-truth and blatant lies passed off as the truth, with almost no contradiction apart from reports in just one newspaper which had the courage to publish at least a part of what was actually the condition in the resettlement colonies.

If the story of Dwarka Prasad's life in Mangolpuri sounds horrible, much worse was the condition of the residents of the cluster of resettlement colonies across the Yamuna bridge—Khichripur, Kalyanpuri and Trilokpuri.

Almost at the other end of the city from Mangolpuri, Khichripur held out the same symmetrical misery to its residents. The telltale row of brick blackholes, the straight but already buckled roads and a nauseating stench—all of these monstrosities Khichripur shared with Mangolpuri. Where it scored higher as a living hell was in the condition of its drains. The rains had played havoc with the drain alignment which was crooked to begin with. The bigger drains were now higher than the smaller drains in the lanes. As a result of this, water stagnated in the lanes, filling up vacant low-lying plots. They were too low for the water to flow back into the main drains. These pools of stagnant water were the breeding ground for a million mosquito larvae and the source of a wave of epidemics of diarrhoea and malaria.

Deep in the heart of Trilokpuri lived twenty-year-old Sundari, with her husband and a one-and-a-half-year-old daughter. The husband, a daily-wage worker in a government office, earned about Rs 150 a month. About Rs 40 was spent on the bus fare alone to take the man to his place of work. Some money had to be spared every month to raise their hut since they came to the new colony, Trilokpuri, seven months ago. The result was a thatched hut that would start leaking even in the slightest drizzle.

A few days after the first showers, Sundari's daughter had high fever. She would shiver continuously even under the two blankets the family possessed. It was only a week later that a visiting group of Red Cross doctors happened to examine the child. They immediately diagnosed the fever as malaria.

The family's luck was in. Red Cross doctors carried the rare chloroquine, the main drug against the disease, on them. The daughter recovered slightly after a dose of the drug. But medicines were useless if the patient spent the night under a leaking roof. A few days later, the fever returned. This time, the family took the child to Safdarjung Hospital, a 40-kilometre trip which itself must have put severe strain on the girl. She was admitted to the hospital and her condition was diagnosed as a case of diphtheria.

The girl died within a few days.

The Red Cross had set up a camp in each of the three colonies of Khichripur, Trilokpuri and Kalyanpuri. But the doctors there were overwhelmed by the large number of patients they had to treat every day. The main problem was that the drinking water itself was poison. The Yamuna which quenched the thirst of the whole of Delhi brought no solace to the three colonies though it flowed so close to the area that it posed a constant threat of flooding. The only source of drinking water was the unfiltered subsoil water drawn through handpumps—when the handpumps worked.

Then there were the latrines. The authorities had provided approximately one latrine for every 200 residents of the colonies, and the rush in the morning was something that had to be seen to be believed. This pile of excrement accumulated sometimes for three days together before it was cleaned out by sweepers.

Just about 50 yards from the colonies lay one of the biggest dumping grounds where night soil was emptied out every day. The stink apart—the piles of shit had not particularly contributed to the sanitary conditions of the area.

To deal with the explosive situation, the authorities had provided almost no medical facilities. True, there was a bright DDA board proclaiming 'Medical Clinic' in a large, vacant piece of land but, like all other DDA boards, it meant nothing. It had been left to the Red Cross team of doctors to control the situation and, while they were trying to do their best, it was quite obviously too gigantic a task for a voluntary organization.

The organization was footing a monthly bill of over Rs 3 lakh, but at least four times this sum was necessary to check the wave of epidemics. Nearly 200 patients queued up every morning at each of the three Red Cross camps. About 70 per cent of them were suffering from gastroenteritis. What was baffling the doctors were the repeat cases of gastroenteritis. The patient would be treated and get well but within a few days would come back with the same ailment. The repeat cases were as high as 40 per cent. Already two cases of gastroenteritis deaths had occurred in the nearby resettlement colony of Himmatpuri.

Stomach diseases were of course rampant in every family. Hookworm, threadworm, tapeworm and a variety of other worms which debilitate the victim and make him susceptible to other diseases were very common.

A variety of skin diseases, particularly in the children, was another problem the doctors faced. While there was an acute shortage of latrines, there were no bathroom facilities at all in the colonies. The residents were expected to make their own bathrooms on their 25-square-yard plot. This of course was impossible, when the residents did not have the means to build even a proper room. So they had been heavily dependent on the rare handpump which worked. But when the rains and the stagnant pools of water accumulated on low-lying vacant plots, the children could not be controlled. There among the faeces, muck and fifth floating in the pools of water, the children splashed about having their long overdue baths. The results were soon evident in the rashes, sores and patches on their bodies and faces. The doctors had repeatedly warned the parents not to allow their children to bathe in the pools of rainwater. But who had the time in the mad race for survival in the wilderness to look after their children!

Acute malnutrition was also evident in the emaciated and haggard faces and bodies of the young and old. The doctors had found it impossible to cure a patient if he was unable to take a proper diet. So the Red Cross had started a milk-feeding project where nearly 17,000 old and infirm residents, expecting and nursing mothers and children were given 250 ml of milk per head and multi-vitamin tablets.

But the Red Cross found charity just too expensive to sustain the thousands of jobless people in the colonies. These were the unfortunates who had lost their jobs because their earlier places of work were now too far to commute to. There was no rich residential colony or industrial complex nearby where these mostly domestic or casual labourers could find work.

Mangal Das, a greying peon, lived in Khichripur, a good 24 kilometres from the south Delhi office where he used to work. Initially he had tried to commute by cycle, but almost 50 kilometres of pedalling every day brought racking pains to his legs at night and almost every second day he had to take leave to rest his legs. Peons, however, are not allowed to take leave every second day and Mangal had been sacked. Now he and his family faced starvation.

The Red Cross had been able to give jobs to 150 people as part of a voluntary auxiliary paramedical force on a daily wage of Rs 6, working day and night to fight the epidemics. For this twenty-four-hour job, the Red Cross camp had been besieged by thousands of jobless. A hundred and fifty jobs were just a drop in the ocean.

Drawing on all its funds, the Red Cross had then started a wheat dole for 1000 needy families in Khichripur, Trilokpuri, Kalyanpuri and Himmatpuri. Under the scheme, 1 kg of wheat per day for 1000 families was given free. But this too was a drop in the ocean. The Red Cross would move out of the colonies by September. They had neither the resources nor the goodwill of the State to carry on. A Red Cross lady doctor made the mistake of complaining to a visiting reporter about the bad sanitary conditions and high incidence of disease in the colonies. The newspaper then made the mistake of publishing the doctor's name. The Red Cross had been pulled up sharply for this and the doctor severely reprimanded and threatened with dire consequences. The State was jealous of the monster it had created. It would not let charity spoil its plans.

The 7-lakh-odd people who lived in the twenty-seven resettlement colonies scattered on the outskirts of the capital shared one common characteristic apart from their general misery. They were all totally dependent on the organizations of the State for even the pettiest detail of their everyday life. Eating, drinking, defaecating, copulating and even dying—they were at the total mercy of the State.

Dying, for instance, was no way out in a colony like Trilokpuri. There was no cremation ghat at Trilokpuri and the price of firewood was four times the rate in the city. It took nearly Rs 200 to burn a body there. Which family banished there could afford a sum like that! Unable to bear the expense of firewood, the poor, regardless of whether they were Hindus or not, buried their dead near the nullah a few hundred yards from the colony. But even after this, they might not have got rid of their dead. Marauding dogs and jackals often dug the body up and brought the half-eaten corpses back into the colony. The wilderness seemed to haunt even the dead.

The routine harassment by officials was of course an everyday experience. For those who did not prostrate themselves with absolute humiliation at the feet of officials, life could be made more miserable.

Man Phool, a disabled ex-serviceman, for instance, was foolish enough to try and argue with a DDA official about the paucity of drinking water. The next day, he was told that his plot had to be allotted to somebody else and he'd better move to another one. This was just next to the latrines. Man Phool had to dismantle his house and build it all over again on another plot. Two weeks later, the officials appeared at Man Phool's house again. He was told a road was being laid through the plot given to him. Now Man Phool salaams the official whenever he passes by.

The essential vulnerability of the people lay in the lack of a community, the absence of organized leadership to mediate with the officials. Though they were 7-lakh-strong and shared the same misery day and night, the people had no bonds with each other. The wilderness was so totally oppressive that there was hardly any respite from it for a community to grow.

Whether they came from Turkman Gate, Netaji Nagar or Shahdara, the people had belonged to well-defined communities. They had their own leaders back in their old slums. Not that the leaders did not exploit or manipulate them. But still, in moments of danger and trouble the people could turn to them.

Here in the resettlement colonies there was nobody to bargain for them. The colonies did not have the homogeneity of a slum. Even in the poorest slum, the people could band together and fight off alien instructions by officialdom. Here the colony itself was alien. It was of little use fighting the ground they were standing on.

Some of them were leaders in their own right at the places from where they had come. Here they were nobodies. Like all the others, they cowered in their half-built hutments under the wind and rain and humiliation. For these erstwhile leaders, life in the resettlement colonies was particularly traumatic.

Choudhary Shri Parkash had been the undisputed leader of the slum at INA Market near Safdarjung. He owned the only general merchandise store in the colony, and everyone in INA came to him. Night or day, any time the people ran out of flour or rice, kerosene or dal, they came to him.

He would sell them the provisions on credit, and would wait till the seventh of the next month for them to pay him back after they received their salaries from their offices and factories. And for all that waiting, he charged only a small amount as interest. The people of INA paid him willingly.

They liked him too. Choudhary Shri Parkash was a good man. His relatives were big men back home in their Pauri Garhwal home. His elder brother was the biggest shopkeeper in the entire village.

Whenever someone came to Delhi from the village, he would come straight to Shri Parkash. He would find them a place to stay in the slum till they found a job and could build their own shack. Till then he would sell them provisions without asking to be paid in cash. The people of INA did not know what they would do without Shri Parkash.

He had been of help to the entire slum at INA. He had talked to the committee men when they wanted to challan every house for not keeping their area clean. And he was the one who had taken aside the DDA inspector when the latter had come to the slum before the Emergency and had said all the new huts would have to be demolished. Shri Parkash had paid the inspector out of his own money. He had told the people that they could pay him back the next month.

But in Dakshinpuri, Shri Parkash was a poor man, one of the worst off. When the DDA had demolished his shop in INA, he had lost all his goods. Others from outside the colony who owed him money had been removed to far-off places he did not even know of.

Shri Parkash did not have the money to start a shop in Dakshinpuri. The local wholesalers did not know him, would not advance him credit. He did not have the money to buy the provisions in cash. And he did not have the courage to sell provisions on credit to all these new people who were his neighbours in this sprawling place.

Shri Parkash found himself a nobody in Dakshinpuri. His own house had just three walls, with a thin thatch protecting his wife and children from the sun. Only two or three of his neighbours knew that he was once the Choudhary of the INA slum. And they looked the other way when going past his house, the broken-down hutment that was now the house of Choudhary Shri Parkash of INA.

The only ones who held some power in the resettlement colonies were the youth gangs—steadily growing in number—that roamed about terrorizing residents. Robbery and snatching incidents had increased as the colonies grew, and residents who returned from their offices at night often fell prey to these gangs. They were quite vicious and did not have an iota of mercy.

The police in resettlement colonies refused to register cases. They were getting a share of the loot from the gangs, which in fact had State protection and most of their members had joined the Youth Congress. The only people to whom the officials spoke politely were these gang members.

Ganesh lived in Kalyanpuri where, amidst all the kuchcha houses, was the solitary exception of the double-storey, cemented police station. When Ganesh's eighteen-year-old daughter was abducted, he went running to the police station. There, however, he was in for a shock. The police officer would not register a case. Ganesh knew that the police officers had some idea of who could have abducted his daughter. But he was helpless.

And along with all the pressures of life in the colonies was the constant knife of sterilization hanging over the heads of young and old. Municipal worker Subhash Chand was sandwiched by three different problems. He had been married for six months but his wife refused to join him at the colony. He was somehow managing alone when the DDA men came and warned him that if any plot was found deserted during a sudden check, it would be confiscated and allotted to somebody else. For Subhash, it meant either leaving his job or trying to construct a pucca house which could be locked and which could bear a nameplate. But a pucca house meant an expenditure of Rs 5000. So Subhash approached the local bank official who was supposed to grant housing loans.

Subhash asked for the loan; he was asked for his sterilization certificate.

'But how can I get myself sterilized? I am only twenty-four. And besides, I have been married only six months,' Subhash pleaded.

'That is none of our business,' the bank official replied. The resettlement colonies were steadily becoming concentration camps that broke down the personalities and individuality of people and communities.

The wilderness had been deliberately created to complete this task.

chapter four

THE DAYS OF THE LONG KNIVES

~

August 1976. The old man stood in front of the table and wept. The table was set in the car park, and the people getting out of their cars stopped to see what was happening. Why was the old, emaciated man in the white 'Khes' weeping. He was frail and weak and it was obvious that he had a fever. A crowd was collecting around the table. The man sitting on the chair opposite him was getting angry. 'Go home if you don't have the paper. Or sign this form. We will give you money, and many more things. You will not have to pay anything. Just press your thumb here.'

The senior doctor drove into the car park as the 9 o'clock siren sounded its first wail. As soon as he got out of the car, he stopped in his tracks. He thought there was something familiar about the old man. He had seen him around in the hospital somewhere in recent days. He called the man over. 'What is the matter, friend? What's up?'

The old man broke down completely. 'Doctor Sa'ab, help me. These people will not let me stand in the queue, they say I cannot get medicine for my fever. They want me to sign the paper for nasbandi [sterilization]. I don't need nasbandi. I need medicine for my fever. But they say I need the nasbandi first.' The old man sobbed out the story. He had come early to the Hindu Rao Hospital to be first in the queue. The hospital was a busy one, and patients had to come on time, or else it would be a long wait before one's turn came to see the doctor. He was standing in the queue waiting for the registration window to open when this man came to him.

'He was young and talked loudly. He stopped in front of me and asked me if I had undergone the family-planning operation. He said I will have to come with him before I can get my *parchi* for the hospital. I am telling him that I am over fifty-five, that my wife is dead, but he does not believe me. You tell him, doctor. You tell him that my wife died in this hospital only five days ago. In that ward over there, the zanana ward next to this car park. See, this is the parchi, the slip of paper that the sisters had tied to the body of my wife when she died in the ward. This they had tied to her white sheet, her shroud, when they wheeled her away to the *murda-khana* [mortuary]. I am keeping this slip, doctor. This slip was tied to my wife's body when it was in the murda-khana of this hospital. I am telling this young man my wife is dead. That I do not need nasbandi. I am a widower and I am too old. I have fever. I need medicines.'

'Stop bothering this man, you rascals,' the doctor shouted. 'Stop bothering him and go motivate someone else, pick someone from your family if you must. Greedy bums!' he mumbled. 'Come, I will give you the medicine parchi. No, don't pay anything to these people. This hospital is supposed to be free. For you, I say it still is.'

For everyone else, it was not. Lieutenant Governor Krishan Chand had decreed in June that everyone would have to pay for the free medical treatment in government hospitals. Pay or produce a certificate proving that he or she had been sterilized. It was part of the family-planning programme, part of the five-point programme, and Delhi had to meet the challenge. It was already far ahead of other states in the number of sterilizations done, but it wanted to establish such a feat that even Haryana, which was coming closer and closer every day, could never touch it. Vidya Ben Shah and Ruksana Sahiba had promised to take the figure up to 3 lakh. And it was up to everyone to help them keep Delhi's prestige.

The motivation committee was highly encouraged by Sanjay's praise for it. They knew he had told these officials to cooperate with Ruksana Sahiba. He had told them that morning that the campaign needed hotting up. Things were getting into a bit of a rut. Krishan Chand had agreed that something needed to be done. DPCC leaders, including their president, Amar Nath Chawla, were stressing the need for effective implementation of the five-point programme in the capital. The order was passed from Raj Niwas. In future, free medical facilities would be available to only those who had acted on the national programme to limit families. The rest would have to pay. The proof of sterilization would be the certificate issued at the clinic and if a person did not come in the 'eligible' category, its proof would be the ration card with the names of two or more children. A side effect would be to remove 'ghost' or fictitious names from the ration card.

A copy of the lieutenant governor's orders was received in the Town Hall. The municipal corporation was required to implement the order in hospitals under its jurisdiction immediately. The corporation framed its orders; the objective was explained. The deadline was set for 8 June 1976. The notice was posted early one morning on information boards set up at the municipal corporation, Hindu Rao Hospital on the Ridge, Kasturba Gandhi Hospital in the Jama Masjid area and across scores of dispensaries, clinics and maternity centres.

> With a view to restricting the family to two children and discouraging from making another addition to their family, the municipal corporation had decided to charge Rs 5/- and

Rs 10/- per day from out-door and in-door patients in all its hospitals and dispensaries. The decision has been taken in pursuance of the policy followed by the Delhi Administration and will cover all citizens as well as the employees of the corporation, the water supply and sewage disposal undertaking, and of the Delhi Electric Supply Undertaking. All persons seeking treatment will have to produce their ration cards. Those who fail to produce the ration cards will be deemed to have more than two children and will be liable to all charges. Persons having more than two children will be entitled to free medical aid only after one spouse produces a sterilization certificate.

Another order had also been passed. This called upon the corporation officials to fulfil the quota of sterilizations from the staff and then to fulfil their quota of motivations. The health department was the hardest hit. Only in the last fortnight of April, they had to fulfil a sterilization quota of 1300, which had been set by Deputy Commissioner V.K. Chanana. In Hindu Rao Hospital, the staff started soliciting vasectomy or tubectomy cases in the long queues that still formed at the OPD windows. They set up their table and chair by the car park. And they were hurt when the senior doctor rebuked them that morning. The old man would not have lost anything with a vasectomy. It would not hurt him much. It would have helped him get some money. And helped them too. The penalty for not fulfilling the quota was strict. No salary.

So it had been for some months now. It had begun in 1975. At that time, the Delhi Administration and the Delhi Congress promised to implement wholeheartedly the four-point programme that Sanjay Gandhi had announced after his mother's broadcast of her twenty points. 'It has electrified the entire national scene. Delhi has taken a lead in implementing this programme.' The programme implementation committee set up at Rajpur Road under Bhagat took it up as one of its main programmes. 'Do Ya Teen Bas', the slogan made famous through posters and on the radio dropped the *'teen'*. It was now 'Hum Do Hamare Do'.

In September 1975, one of the first special camps was held at Kasturba Gandhi Hospital, better known as the Victoria Zanana Hospital, in the Jama Masjid area. A maternity and childcare hospital, the Kasturba Gandhi Hospital was specially patronized by the burqa-clad Muslim women of Old Delhi. Doctors performed 425 tubectomies in one stretch of fifteen days. 'This is a record,' said a press release from Raj Niwas, the lieutenant governor's official residence. Krishan Chand personally visited Kasturba Gandhi Hospital again on the day after Christmas. It was a Friday. A special camp was again being organized to break the old record of tubectomies. To get more patients, the motivators were told they would now get Rs 10 for every woman they could bring to the camp. It was quite a jump. For persuading a woman to undergo a tubectomy, a motivator would earlier get only Rs 2. All the nurses and doctors on the staff were put on the job. House surgeons and registrars were sent 'two each to each' operation theatre.

'On some days we had up to twenty-five women brought in for the operation,' said a member of the tubectomy team. 'Usually we had between seventy-five and 100 women a day. Until now most of them were eligible. They may have been only twenty-five or so, but they had two children or more. We had five operating tables in three operating rooms in all. The rooms were scrubbed clean in the mornings. The women were then prepared for the surgery in the wards; their abdomens cleaned with antiseptic. From there, they were wheeled into the operation theatre clad in a clean hospital gown. We ran out of these gowns after some time. We were then told to keep the gowns only for the women being sterilized. The other patients and those who had operations scheduled were told to put on the clothes they had been wearing before they came to the hospital.

'In the operation theatre, the doctors decided if it was to be a laparoscopy or an abdominal incision tubectomy. There would usually be one doctor and about seven to eight nurses. But later, two junior doctors were assigned to perform the surgery. An operation took about fifteen minutes, but taking the patient in and wiping the table clean took another fifteen minutes. So we were doing the operations at the rate of one every thirty minutes.

'During the operation, the only instruments needed were the scalpels, tube forceps and sufficient swabs and sponge forceps. These were cleaned and sterilized here in the morning. The surgeon would make an incision in the abdomen deep enough to enter the cavity. The fallopian tubes were then either tied off, or severed into two pieces each, with the ends then up. The incision was then closed.

'The patient would be administered local anaesthesia. They would be taken to the post-operative ward and kept there for six hours. We had thirty beds in one ward. And we always had to put two women to each bed. One woman would have her head towards the wall. The other slept with her head on the other side. Sometimes, on days when there were more than 100 women, three women were put to each bed. The only criterion was that they had to be thin women.

'Each operation would take half an hour. After one surgery, the doctor would wash his hands and change his gloves. Most of the nurses did not change their dresses. The table would be wiped clean. That's all. And then the next patient would be wheeled in. During this fortnight, sometimes the doctors and nurses had to be on their feet from nine thirty or ten thirty in the morning to six or seven in the evening.

'The women who were brought in for tubectomies were given only a superficial check. They were discharged after six days. Those who had undergone a laparoscopic operation would usually be sent home the next day.

'We had about 10 per cent of the women coming back with septic wounds. There were no deaths in the theatre. But some of the septic cases died. There were more than ten tubectomy deaths in this hospital during all the sterilization drives.'

For most nurses and doctors 1 January 1976 was a working day. In Kasturba and other hospitals, tubectomies and vasectomies were taking place on the assembly line. An unending stream of women wheeled into the operation theatres. An unending stream wheeled out into the wards. The tempo was picking up. The figures, however, were still not sufficient. 'It is good, but not good enough,' it was noted by the implementation committee. The five-point programme is to be implemented with more energy, more zest, and it is imperative that the government employees, those getting their wages from government organizations and institutions, from the corporation and the NDMC will have to take part in the programme with more vigour.

Krishan Chand set up a special motivational committee in January for family planning. The chairman was Vidya Ben Shah, who had become the first non-official president of the NDMC. Ex officio members were the family-planning commissioner in the central ministry of health at Nirman Bhawan, Municipal Commissioner Tamta, the Delhi Administration medical secretary and the director of health services and family planning.

The committee had been set up to get the top bosses of the capital's civic organizations to personally take charge of the operations. The committee, it was felt, however, needed a direct liaison with Sanjay Gandhi at 1, Akbar Road. He chose Ruksana Sultana, an attractive divorcee once married to one of the richer men in the capital, a prominent figure among the jet set in the city. On her first appearance on the capital's socio-political scene, she had introduced herself as Sanjay Gandhi's secretary and social worker. Her credentials were accepted. On 13 February 1976, Krishan Chand issued an edict: 'Shri Ruksana Singh is nominated the only non-official member of

the Motivational Committee on Family Planning in Delhi.'
The 'Shri' perhaps was intentional. Ruksana made it promptly
known that she liked being called Ruksana Sultana. The officials
started calling her Begum Ruksana Sahiba. The Muslim women
around Jama Masjid called her something else, something very
different.

The same day Executive Councillor O.P. Behl announced
that industrial workers who came for sterilization would be given
an additional cash award of Rs 50 by their employers. Industrial
employers were meanwhile learning that the programme
implementation committee wanted them to get as many of
their workers sterilized as they could. It was to their advantage
if they could get the worker to the special camp. That would
be proof that the industry owner believed wholeheartedly in
the five-point programme. It would also guarantee that there
was no hold-up in permits and delivery of materials. The camps
that fortnight were being set up in the industrial areas of Kirti
Nagar in west Delhi, the Najafgarh industrial area, the Mori
Gate in the walled city, the modern industrial estate at Okhla
on the banks of the Yamuna River and at Paharganj. The camps
were held in the dispensaries of the Employees' State Insurance
Corporation which, for an amount deducted from the month's
salary of a worker, promised to extend him and his family all the
medical care they needed.

The industrialists were also told to give special leave to
employees going to the sterilization camp. They were falling
behind in their quotas. On hundreds of shop floors, the owners
exhorted their workers to go to the camp. Or get someone else
to go. The temporary staff, the work-charged men, the khalasis
and sweepers were told: 'Go if you want your job. It is not that
we will throw you out of the job if you do not go. There may
be no job at all for anyone.'

Some workers protested in their trade union office. They
got the shock of their lives. The trade union man refused to

help them. In fact, he told them that they had better do as their employer said. They went to another union leader. He listened to them for some time and squirmed in his chair. 'I cannot help at all. I am in trouble already. If I help you, I am finished.'

The Delhi Congress was already thinking of disaffiliating their trade union front, the Indian National Trade Union Congress (INTUC). They wanted the trade union to stop approaching the INTUC. The trade union has to in future deal directly with the DPCC, it was ordered, to help in the effective implementation of the twenty-five-point programme of the nation.

Workers from Ballia, Nagpur, Sultanpur and Tihri sent their wives back to their villages. The Youth Congress men now started coming to their huts and asking them if they had any children. They told them the family was not with them. It did not matter, said the youth. 'You had better get the operation. Now you are getting Rs 150. We will give you a watch too,' said the Youth Congress worker. The men from Ballia and Sultanpur and Tihri left their jobs.

Some union leaders approached the DPCC. The workers were getting restive. Their leadership had been disgraced. They were being taunted. Bansi Lal Mehta, the DPCC general secretary in charge of the newly created DPCC labour cell, was firm. It was a national programme. The DPCC did not want to lag behind.

The administrators did not want to lag behind either. And that created tension between them and Ruksana Sultana. She had set up an organization in the Jama Masjid area. She started out with seeming innocence. The fashionable lady had gone into the dingiest, darkest hole and asked the women to throw away their burqa. She said she would teach them to sew and to read. The plump matrons just spewed a stream of red paan spittle, the bi-jis and the Bari-bis. They told the young 'chokri' to go back to her husband and children. 'Stop bothering us.'

Ruksana therefore shifted her attention to the men, and that created more problems with the women. Ultimately, she decided that the local people would have to be left alone for the time being. The family-planning camp that they had neatly worked out would have to conduct its first business with outsiders. The decisions would bring her into conflict with other authorities also prowling the streets in search of sterilization cases.

The government organizations had now started to be tough on their own employees. Nevertheless, the word in use was 'volunteer'.

At a civic hospital, more than fifty officers and men of one municipal zone offer themselves for sterilization. Tamta tells them, 'You have set an example not only for fellow employees, but for all citizens.' Dr J.C. Narang, the deputy municipal health officer, takes the commissioner into the operation theatre where a surgeon is bending over the prone figure of a man. A white sheet covers the man's torso and legs almost entirely, but for small window cut in the middle. Through it can be seen the man's genitals.

Vasectomy is child's play in the hands of an expert, the officials are told. Even a beginner can do it after a simple lesson. In fact, there is an illustrated manual on the job that has been distributed to young doctors in many hospitals so they can brush up their knowledge at home—the theoretical knowledge, that is. It is really a simple process, the patients have been told. It is really a simple process, the young doctors have been told.

'After the shaved pubic region has been cleaned with antiseptic lotion, dried and draped with a sterile sheet, one vas deferens is held firmly under the skin between the thumb, placed over the scrotum, and the index finger below. About 3 ml of 1 or 2 per cent procaine solution, Xylocaine, is injected into the skin around the grasped vas.

'A beginner may now fix the vas under the skin by a Moynihan towel clip from the front of the scrotum. A small traverse incision is then made deep enough to cut the dartos muscle. The incision is to be made over the fixed vas. With practice, you can do away with the towel clip and use just your gloved fingers for holding the vas,' informs Dr Narang. The doctor is given a choice of two alternative surgical procedures. In the second method, instead of making two antero-lateral incisions, both the vasa may be operated upon through a single paramedian incision which should be vertical so as to avoid the veins which are in plenty in the region and run vertically. The cut margins are then separated by thrusting and opening the blades of a pair of mosquito forceps. The vas, with its covering fascia, is then held inside the incision by another Moynihan towel clip or fine Allis forceps. The first towel clip that had to be used earlier is removed. A small incision is now made in the vas-covering fascia through which the glistening, pearly vas can be seen. The small part of this vas is cleaned by a few gentle strokes of a knife. The vas is pulled out by a pair of dissecting forceps. The loop formed by thrusting and opening the blade of the mosquito forceps is held and the accompanying blood vessels pushed away. Two artery forceps are applied on the cleaned part of the vas, about an inch apart, and the second towel clip and dissecting forceps removed.

Now comes the crucial moment. About half an inch of the vas is resected between the two forceps. The man is now half sterilized. The upper cut of the vas deferens is tied by a black silk thread and the artery forceps removed. The lower end of the vas is folded on itself and tied with the black silk thread. The forceps holding it are removed carefully. The threads are cut and the vas, with the surrounding tissues, is allowed to retract into the scrotum. The doctor repeats the procedure for the second vas deferens. Now the tied ends of the two vasa are pulled out of the incisions, the threads are cropped and the ends allowed to retract deep into the scrotum. The skin is closed with a pair of dissecting forceps. The doctor takes up the threaded surgical needle. One stitch to a cut. He picks up the artery forceps. The process that follows is called 'lightly crushing the margins'. A cotton swab soaked in benzoin tincture is applied to the wound. A piece of gauze and a bandage covers the area now.

The man undergoing the operation smiles wanly. The doctor tells him to put on his pyjamas after some time. Outside the theatre, the man is given a bottle of Coca-Cola by his motivator. He is told to rest for a while and then go home.

A simple procedure really, the manual says. A simple procedure, but not so for anyone with even a mild castration complex. The officials watch it with open-mouthed fascination.

Among those who witnessed these operations was Vidya Ben. The officials had hardly finished calling on their staff to volunteer when the lieutenant governor decided to take action on the suggestion that had been mooted for some months now: 'Sterilization after two children should be the official policy on the slogan "Hum Do, Hamare Do" [We are two, we have two], while the non-official slogan takes the line "Hum Dono Ek, Hamara Ek" [We two are one, we have one].'

Who took the decision to introduce compulsory sterilization? It could have been someone in the Delhi Congress which had been chided for not performing up to the mark. It could have been a personal decision by Krishan Chand on the advice of the programme implementation committee. But whoever might have been the first to take the decision, there is no doubt that the orders came from 1, Akbar Road. The orders had been accompanied by a threat. The official machinery was not as active as the Youth Congress or Ruksana Sultana; the young prince had ordained that the official machinery had better tone itself up.

Fulsome praise was heaped on Krishan Chand for his interest in family planning by Tamta who had invited the lieutenant governor to give away the prizes at a peculiar competition. He was to honour twenty-seven people whose work had been adjudged the best during the special campaign in sterilization that had begun on 26 December 1975. Tamta informed the lieutenant governor that of the 5000 sterilizations done in the special week, over 2700 were performed at the Kasturba Gandhi Hospital alone, with the Delhi Administration-run Irwin Hospital coming second, with 500 vasectomies. These 5000 operations had been done in just two months, which was startling when compared to the almost insignificant 4000 sterilizations that had been done over the course of the previous year. 'Your guidance, sir, and the cooperation of the New Delhi Municipal Committee and other agencies have been instrumental in achieving the target,' Tamta told Krishan Chand.

The lieutenant governor's address gave a preview of the things to come. He congratulated the family-planning campaigners and set for them their next task. 'We want to cover the entire city and its suburbs through concerted work.' Vidya Ben explained what this meant: 'I have fixed a target of 3 lakh people for Delhi and I hope the target will be achieved. I hope our male population will cooperate with us.' Among those who extended their support to the fulfilling of this dream was Krishan Swaroop, executive councillor in charge of health, an equivalent of Delhi's health minister. A few days earlier, in distant Badarpur on Delhi's border with Haryana, Swaroop called on residential committees and local organizations to join in the programme with vigour. 'We have so far sterilized people at the rate of 150 a day in many places. The total is 1.13 lakh. We hope to sterilize half of Delhi's population.'

The competition was on. DDA Vice Chairman Jagmohan had asked a subordinate officer to take charge of motivational work. Tikku, the officer, became an enthusiastic motivator and worked hard to get the employees to come forward for sterilization. Employees who were not on the permanent staff were told every morning, 'Operation *karalo*, you will be profiting.' The older ones were promised, 'Get yourself operated upon and we will give your son a job'. In the Delhi Administration's education department, the director of education, A. Biswas, was telling his officers, principals and workers how important it was for the department to show just how good it was. The annual examinations were approaching and it was the right time to tell the parents of students how much they stood to gain if they volunteered. Boys and girls came home from primary and higher secondary schools, telling their parents that the principals wanted to see them. Teachers started calling on homes, asking parents how many children they had. The teachers asked the parents to 'volunteer' for sterilizations.

'Get sterilized,' came the directive from Raj Niwas, the lieutenant governor's official residence where he lived and worked and where his secretary, Navin Chawla, cross-examined everyone who wanted to see him. Chawla would convey Krishan Chand's orders to officials five grades his senior in the seniority-conscious Indian Administrative Service. 'The Delhi administration,' said the notice from Raj Niwas, 'has been processing under the lieutenant governor's address several incentives and disincentive measures to lower the birth rate in the capital. This will apply both to the general public and the employees of the administration, and are likely to come into force immediately.' There were four orders for the general public, and eight for government servants, employees of local bodies, government undertakings and other autonomous institutions under the Delhi Administration. There were three orders for community organizations.[1]

The orders for the public got them at their weak spot—the search for a place to live. The DDA had nearly scrapped the 'hire' of its hire-purchase scheme for residential flats and made it almost exclusively for those who could pay up to Rs 76,000 in a lump sum. Rents were shooting up even in the suburbs and it was becoming difficult for a salaried worker to get a house for less than half his monthly wages. The order said that houses, flats, tenements, shops and plots developed by the DDA would be allotted only to those who had limited their family to two children. An eligible couple—who had only one child, and gave an undertaking not to have another, or who already had two children and one of the spouses would get sterilized—would be able to benefit from the schemes announced by the DDA. Non-eligible couples, especially those with more than two children, where neither spouse would get sterilized, would not be given houses or loans.

The lieutenant governor and the Delhi Administration had offered strong incentives to the small-scale sector in the capital. The administration, with the cooperation of bodies like the National Alliance of Young Entrepreneurs (NAYE)—which also had close ties with 1, Akbar Road—had chalked out ambitious plans for getting young graduates interested in setting up their own business to take the weight off the employment market. The response had been enthusiastic and the NAYE, with its office-bearers, had emerged as a powerful lobby controlling the interests of many a hapless body. NAYE office-bearers too had been in the vanguard of the movement to implement the five-point programme. It had been decided that efforts would pick up speed with a little help from above. The lieutenant governor's order provided this push. Krishan Chand ordered that entrepreneurs with two children would be entitled to a loan only if they got themselves sterilized and produced sterilization certificates from the notified authority. Those with more than two children, however, would not be eligible at all. But even if the couple had no child, they could get a loan only after furnishing a bond of good behaviour for the indefinite future, promising never to have a third child. Moreover, they would have to keep in touch with the administration, stating in income tax and sales tax returns the number of children they had during the year.

'Any breach,' the lieutenant governor warned, 'will entail withdrawal of the loan facilities, for future of the payment already made and recovery of the balance of land revenue arrears on the plot given by the DSIDC, the organization set up to look after industrial development of the capital under G.S. Shrivastava.'

The comprehensive gubernatorial order decreed that henceforth free medical facilities in public hospitals run by the government would be available only to those cooperating in the family-planning programme. To prove this, patients would have to produce their ration cards. Ration cards, which had earlier been the indispensable permits for food, cycle tyres and tubes, coal and kerosene, were to become health cards too. Those who failed to get the sterilization certificates would have to pay Rs 5 every time they visited the hospital, and Rs 10 for each day they remained in hospital; they would also have to pay for pathological tests. The salaried and other middle classes, including nearly 1 lakh government employees, suddenly found themselves prisoners to the sterilization slip.

The other orders made it more difficult for those in local government service to remain unsterilized. The first regulation for this group of people became operative on them even before they were employed in local administrative offices. A total of six separate forms were created to cover every stage of government employment, ranging from an applicant for a government job to an employee in long service. At the time of the interview it was announced that preference would be given to those with one or two children only. But before the appointment, the candidate would have to give an undertaking in writing that whether he was unmarried, recently married or the father of one, he would not have more than two children. The birth of a third child would be taken as a breach of faith and contract, and the employees would not be confirmed.

The lieutenant governor continued his directives on the new recruits who had more than three children. 'They will have to get themselves sterilized before they can be appointed and they will have to produce a sterilization certificate for the purpose.'

Krishan Chand was strict in his decree on the casual labourers from Rajasthan, Uttar Pradesh, Bihar and the rural outskirts of Delhi who sought employment on seasonal schemes like the anti-malaria drive and projects on flood control. 'Such employment will be given only to those who have less than two children or who produce sterilization certificates,' the Raj Niwas decree ordered.

There was also the question of those who had already been confirmed in government employment. Such an employee was beyond control, but his or her family was still vulnerable. The control tightened into a noose. The 'ineligibles', as they came to be called, who had more than two children, would not be allowed any festival allowance, housing loans, cooperative loans and advances for buying vehicles till they got themselves sterilized.

And if these families were already living in government accommodation and had another child, they would have to vacate the house unless they chose to get sterilized. For Class-IV and other low-paid staff, the lieutenant governor directed that sterilization certificates should be produced before facilities of free education and other petty allowances like those for washing clothes for sweepers and other menial workers were allowed. The government servants were totally under control. There was not a whimper out of associations and unions representing the employees. The union leaders had extended their tacit support to these measures in meetings with the authorities. The administration took the aid of infiltrations to sabotage the power of leaders who dared to dissent.

But there were many more who were not in government service. For them, the order reserved a special consideration. Village assemblies (*gaon sabhas*) and local government constituencies were given the offer of producing a minimum of 100 cases per village to get priority consideration for supply of drinking water and irrigation facilities for their fields. The elected representative who got the highest number of sterilization cases from his area would get a dole of Rs 20,000.

Krishan Chand made another offer to government employees, especially those in a position to meet and influence a number of other people. He picked doctors, nurses and teachers and directed that any employee who could get more than fifty sterilization cases from anywhere in the capital would be rewarded with an increment to his salary. The person who procured the maximum number would get an honorarium of Rs 100 for the next year. Each government employee was encouraged to become a procurer of cases for sterilization. In government hospitals, staff set up their own motivation offices and their scouts roamed the dispensary and outpatient queues hunting for someone who looked remotely virile. They did not always look very closely. They had caught the old man in the OPD queue at Hindu Rao Hospital. 'These people have gone absolutely crazy. They have forgotten that they too have been put under so many restrictions. They are busy hunting for more victims,' said a doctor of Hindu Rao Hospital. In wards, patients slept in makeshift beds on the floor and in corridors. A viral epidemic was suspected. A senior doctor entered a ward and found it strangely empty of medical staff, doctors or nurses. 'Where is everyone?' the doctor asked. He knew the answer himself. The staff had decamped to the family-planning camp to earn their Rs 2. Later, many people, including teachers, would be forced to spend half a month's salary to get a case of sterilization. Some would spend up to Rs 1000 to get cases so they could get their salaries the next month.

A different crisis was brewing in the campaign. Ruksana Sahiba, as the lieutenant governor and other members of the programme implementation and family-planning motivation committees called her, was converting her sewing classes for old women into sterilization camps. She chose Dujana House, the 'new' enclave in the hoary Muslim-dominated

Jama Masjid–Turkman Gate area. Ruksana set up a shamiana and called on the local people to come for sterilization which would be performed in the basement of one of the tenement houses. No one came. Ruksana used all her charm on the women of Dujana House. She tromped around the lanes of Chitli Kabar and Matia Mahal, but to no avail.

Workers, meanwhile, had come to Dujana House with hammers and wood and huge sheets of asbestos. The lieutenant governor was to inaugurate the camp on 15 April, and still there was no response. Ruksana complained to Krishan Chand that his officers were trying to sabotage her good work and wanted all the credit for themselves. She would not tolerate it. He pulled up his officers. They started cooperating by the time he inaugurated the camp. The women in Dujana House saw the police arrive in large numbers for the bandobast for the governor sahib. He gave his speech and went away. The police remained.

From behind curtained windows, the women of the Dujana House complex saw trucks drive in and come to rest in front of the basement. Men got down from them—men they had seen roaming on the streets perhaps in Daryaganj or Kashmiri Gate. There were labourers wearing Rajasthani attire. 'Bagris', they called them. And many others. Most of them were filthy, their clothes were dirty. They looked like beggars picked off the streets. The policemen watched. There were many men who now sat on the ground. They did not want to go into the room. They did not want to collect their slip and go for the operation. Ruksana came out to cajole them. There was no response. The policemen used their lathis. The men moved slowly. The women behind the curtains shivered. What if this supply of men ran out? Their husbands would be next.

There was a hitch. On 19 April 1976, the Turkman Gate and Dujana House area exploded with a violence not seen in four major communal riots in thirty years, a violence neither seen nor even heard of for generations. The state was succeeding in entering the most intimate privacy of a citizen's life, into the folds of his family. One social structure, one cultural entity had resisted the attempt. That had sparked off the explosion.

But the echoes of police firing and the rumble of the bulldozers had not stopped reverberating from the walls of Dujana House when the state moved in again. The lieutenant governor issued a warning that drastic action would be taken against anyone found hindering the pace of the Dujana House sterilization camp. 'Ruksana Sultana Sahiba and Mrs Vidya Ben Shah have been working persistently. Already in the four days of its operation, the camp has seen 300 people sterilized. This is only the beginning,' said Krishan Chand. With his personal reference to Ruksana Sultana, the race was joined. From 15 April, each department of Delhi would be on its toes.

Already the municipal corporation had geared itself up. So had the DDA and the NDMC. The NDMC, which looked after the central portion of New Delhi, was perhaps the most active. Its president, Vidya Ben, had become the first woman and the first non-official president of the committee in its history. She was also the chairman of the committee set up by the lieutenant governor to motivate people for family planning. She had given strict instructions to her officials to help motivate as many as possible from amongst her staff and the NDMC area. It would be a matter of concern if New Delhi lagged behind. Member Secretary Ailawadi and Education Officer T.N. Bhatt were preparing to carry out her instructions. The campaign would start in earnest when schools reopened after the summer vacations. Camps were meanwhile organized for the employees. At one such camp, Vidya Ben turned to a man standing near her and asked him, 'Why don't you also get yourself vasectomized?' Without waiting for his answer, she announced over the public address system, 'This gentleman has just volunteered.' The audience of officials applauded.

In the municipal corporation, orders were passed to all department heads, assistant commissioners and drawing and disbursing officers for 'strict compliance' to make the programme a success. The orders, signed by Deputy Commissioner Chanana decreed that the sterilization certificate was a must before the recruitment and promotion of any employee in any category. The most bizarre in the long list of orders was that no maternity or abortion leave was to be granted to female employees who found themselves pregnant and already had two children. In his orders, the official did not explain what was to be done in those cases where women employees were about to deliver their third or fourth child. All they said was that they would not be given paid maternity leave. And because another order had directed that no employee was to be given leave except on medical grounds, confusion prevailed for some time, especially in the lower category of employees. Later some of them were unofficially told that the order meant their salaries would be deducted for the period they were absent and that they could even be dismissed if they did not get themselves sterilized.

The women were now afraid to go to government hospitals to deliver their second or third children. Some even refused to go to a hospital for the first delivery fearing that the doctors who had been ordered to get as many cases as possible, would perform sterilization operations on them soon after delivering the babies. To those who found the fears all too real, no amount of persuasion by even the senior doctors could make them change their mind. Neighbourhood clinics reported an increase in business.

Chanana continued to give further instructions. The corporation required all staff to give the model undertaking prescribed by the Delhi Administration. The undertaking was that they would restrict the size of their families and keep the government informed of it every year.

A fifteen-day target was fixed for a more difficult task. The corporation bosses were now fixing quotas for their various departments and were entrusting the department heads with fulfilling them. The total target for the corporation for the period between 14 and 30 April 1976 was 7100. The maximum sterilization cases were demanded from the health department which had on its rolls a large number of workers dealing with the fight against mosquitoes and the parthenium weed that was proliferating all over the city, spreading a dangerous rash. The health department was ordered to get 1300 cases of sterilization from among its men and women. In the engineering department, which employs a large number of workers, and in the education department with its nearly 20,000 teaching and non-teaching employees, the target set was 1000 each. The garden department had to get 500 cases, the independent DESU and the water supply undertaking 1000 each, the property department 100, the city terminal tax office 100 and the urban community development department 300. The fire brigade, which was under the corporation's water department, was required to dispatch fifty of its firefighters for sterilization.

Tamta was soon in a position to say that the corporation had achieved its target with 100 per cent success. All eligible employees had been sterilized, he said.

Summer of 1976: With the advancing days and the soaring heat, the higher officials mounted the pressure. 'Get the quotas. Get the figures. The need is dire.' The junior officials turned the screw further down. The *jamedar* in charge of the contract labour told the workers, 'No advances till you get vasectomies. No advances and no more jobs.'

On 15 May 1976, the lieutenant governor's order was repeated in a codified form by Reva Nayyar, the medical secretary to the Delhi Administration. The order was forwarded to all departments. Meanwhile, the officials held special meetings with their subordinate officers and exhorted them to fulfil the quotas. The education department which had been active during the April examinations in asking parents to volunteer had not been very successful. The teachers had asked the students to call their parents. The parents told the teachers that if they got vasectomized, it would be to get their own salaries, not to help the teacher with his. They needed the motivation slip themselves. In primary schools, the efforts met with slight success. This was because in the rural areas and in some of the colonies of Shahdara, parents agreed to do it for the good of their children, especially if the child happened to be in Class X and the only way to get him promoted to Class XI was this. This time, Class XI was particularly important because it was the last year of the three-year higher secondary course. From next year, the 10 plus 2 scheme would be in place, and if the child failed in Class X, he would have to waste not one but two years before he could get out of school.

The teachers drew a blank when they approached the sons and daughters of labourers. Promises of making them pass in exams did not help. The labourers had already been caught in the vast vasectomy net spread all over the city, particularly in the poor labour colonies.

The search for cases among employees had not yet begun. The heat was now on for their own sterilization. In various departments the meetings continued. In the police, the superintendents were being exhorted at the meetings with the inspector general to espouse the national programme. At official meetings the SPs (superintendents) were reminded that the task had to be done. Suddenly, the Delhi Police, which had so far been almost exempt from becoming the target of any concerted drive of family planning found itself in the midst of the general excitement.

Earlier, the thinking had been that the policeman was too vital a unit of the State apparatus to be antagonized by such an obvious attempt to bring him down to the same level as the ordinary citizen or the government employee in the degrading routine of compulsory sterilization. There had also been the fear that if driven with the same whip, the Delhi Police as a body might rebel at a time when there was a dire need for its services. Buttressing the argument was the thought that the average Delhi policeman in the ranks came from a people especially sensitive to the castration connotations of vasectomy. The Jat, Ahir, Gujjar, Rajput, the farmer and the son of the martial race, all of them held male virility to be sacred. To them virility made the man. There was only scorn for the impotent male. More so, if the male wore a uniform of authority and had pretensions of being an alpha male. But reason had taken a back seat in those strange times. The decision had been taken. The Delhi Police were in for 'voluntary' sterilization. By 20 July 1976, over 1100 policemen and officers had undergone vasectomy, it was announced. In a tree plantation ceremony just a fortnight later, the Inspector General of Police Bhawanimal announced that the number was now 2000, 'including three superintendents of police'.

That this wave of sterilization was not voluntary was quite obvious. There was tremendous dissent, particularly among the lower ranks of the police. This dissent threatened to become a full-scale rebellion in the traffic police unit when they heard the story of the gruesome death of a traffic head constable after he contracted an infection following a sterilization operation.

The story which was repeated from barrack to barrack in New and Old Police Lines was indeed horrendous. The traffic head constable had, like so many other policemen, been forced to get sterilized. A few days later, he noticed there was an infection. So he went to his superior officer and asked him for medical leave. The constable, however, was refused leave as his superior thought that if the news leaked that there had been a case of infection, no other traffic policeman would be willing to get sterilized. The constable was told that it was a minor thing and no leave was possible. The infection, however, worsened with every passing day. The head constable's testicles had within a week swollen up to enormous balloons.

Finally, in pain and desperation, the head constable went to the chief of Delhi Traffic Police. There, in the office of his chief, the constable took off his trousers and showed the superintendent his ghastly state. Aghast, the superintendent telephoned for an ambulance. The head constable was admitted to hospital but died two days later.

The story had created such a furore among traffic policemen that sterilization had to be called off among their ranks. Reports of the death of three other policemen after they had been sterilized also reached the police barracks. One of the dead policemen was a head constable in the East District Police.

Bhawanimal, who was in the forefront of the sterilization campaign among the police, had a taste of the policemen's anger when he was gheraoed at Old Police Lines. He had gone there to give a call for more enthusiastic participation by the police in the family-planning programme, but instead of a response, he found resentment.

'If I have one more child, shoot me, sir. But please don't sterilize me,' pleaded a constable, the father of two children. The IGP was furious. 'Shut up! Who is talking of shooting? We are talking of a national programme,' he shouted.

But the IGP was again cornered by another constable. 'I am a Brahmin, sir, I have to take my holy bath every day. If I have my bath after getting operated, I will catch an infection, sir,' the constable said. 'Take the man away,' the IGP ordered. 'We will have everybody pleading that he is a Brahmin.'

In the departments of civic bodies like the corporation, the DDA and the NDMC, in electricity departments and the water supply undertaking, peculiar cases were happening. Endless lines of aggrieved people waited on the senior officers with long lists of complaints. The complaints at this stage were that the officers who had asked them to volunteer to get sterilized were no longer keeping their promises. There were also complaints that those who had undergone sterilization had been totally forgotten since they could not get sterilized again. The officers just pushed them into a corner. One man who had just undergone a vasectomy and had been told by the doctor not to cycle or walk long distances, had been transferred to a place 20 kilometres from his house. The bus fare took up a sizeable portion of his salary. The man was in a dilemma. He could not cycle, given his condition.

A woman sweeper was in a worse situation. She had been tubectomized in a camp. The wound refused to heal. She had run out of leave, and then taken a few more days off. Now she needed leave again. She had been coming to the head office every day for a week to meet the establishment officer but in vain. One day, as she was climbing the stairs, she collapsed, bleeding.

The senior officials, the politicians and the peculiar breed of politician-officials and official-politicians who constituted the various implementation committees were now totally united in their aim of fulfilling this one out of the five points. They differed from each other only in their capacity to mobilize the maximum number of people.

It was not mere competition for most of them. It was survival. A senior officer in the rat race recounts how the proceedings at meetings took on the shape of public auctions, with various people bidding for the highest number. 'I promise to get 1000 industrial cases,' one would say; 'I can get 1000 from the shopkeepers,' another would claim.

In the DPCC, it became a race to power. Sanjay Gandhi was judging men on the number of vasectomies they had facilitated. Sober and venerable public men forced their families into sitting at motivation camps that were sprouting all over the city. Chief Executive Councillor Raman's aged wife, Kaushalya, who could hardly walk straight, was named chief motivator for a family-planning motivation camp that had been set up in the most desirable location in the capital. The spot was near Race Course Road, a prime location because it was a kilometre away from Sanjay Gandhi's residence. In decreasing order of seniority, the others took up positions.

It was July, and it was around this time that the Youth Congress entered the family-planning scene with a vengeance. Their task was to saturate the capital, reaching all sections, from industrialists and traders to shopkeepers and owners of cinema houses. The Youth Congress was directly coordinating with Sanjay Gandhi and, through him, had got the local official machinery to act as their backup organizations to implement their blackmail and threats which were to become the main tool of getting ever-increasing numbers of men for vasectomies. Acting as their local liaison agent with the Delhi Administration was Ruksana Sultana who was, by July 1976, recognized as the motivator-in-chief for the capital region. As the monsoon progressed, the youth took up the five-point programme in right earnest, seemingly refreshed after their long vacations. Along major streets and even minor lanes, shamianas came up, complete with two sets each of loudspeakers, a record-playing turntable and a stack of catchy Hindi film records. A disc of Mohammad Rafi, the famed playback singer, exhorted people to keep the children in check. The Youth Congress's dalliance with the film world would culminate later in mammoth musical evenings organized with the help of Information Minister Shukla.

The Youth Congress had chosen to concentrate on tree planting and sterilization. The DPCC elders had agreed to the priorities. The officials had agreed to the targets. The stage was set. Each day from now on would see two or three or even a dozen major functions held at various places in the capital—from primary schools to colleges, industrial establishments and of course the police headquarters and the lines. At one of the first functions after schools reopened, Raman, who held the education portfolio, presided. This marked the second thrust of the tree plantation programme of the Delhi Administration, involving more than 5 lakh students of nearly 980 schools in the city and the suburbs. Present along with Raman was Biswas, the director of education, who was being absorbed into the prestigious Indian Administrative Service much to the jealous anxiety of most of his non-cadre colleagues.

After planting trees, Raman focused on sterilization. He called a meeting of various industrial associations representing a wide range of industries from all over the capital. Also at the meeting was Executive Councillor Swaroop (there were four executive councillors for Delhi, including the chief executive councillor, Raman, the others being Swaroop for medical, Behl for food and civil supplies and Hira Singh for development) who called upon the representatives of the industrial associations to motivate the people they employed for sterilization. Raman was not sure if the hint had been taken. He elaborated, 'The Delhi Administration has activized its various departments and agencies to implement family planning and achieve the target of cent per cent coverage by the end of March 1977. Therefore the industrialists should not lag behind in helping the administration to achieve the target.' Raman also asked industrialists in the capital to give additional incentives to the workers to persuade them to get sterilized.

The industrialists took the hint. Union Minister of State for Health Choudhry Ram Sewak inaugurated a camp at Wazirpur industrial enclave organized by the industrial employers with whom Raman had had a talk. Behl was in the chair. The employers had promised to make it worthwhile for their workers to undergo the vasectomies. The threat of electricity cuts and taxation raids and the risk of being at odds with the powerful programme implementation committee were too great.

Business houses and industries were approached again by the administration. Cyclostyled forms were sent to them, seeking information on their employees—how many children each had and how many were eligible for sterilization. The employers were told to get the forms filled before the next month's wages were paid. They were called upon to get their employees to go for sterilization and to offer them leave and additional facilities. The employers bent over backwards to do this. The workers were offered additional increments and ex gratia payment. They were offered new uniforms and alarm clocks.

The programme implementation committee was now strengthening its campaign against shopkeepers and other traders. The objective was threefold. Shopkeepers survived on daily business. The municipal corporation's beautification drives launched in the various zones had resulted in the loss of thousands of rupees when their shop projections were removed. The Delhi Administration's price control order was now being vigorously enforced. Squads of personnel tasked with enforcing the order roamed the bazaars to check each item and pounce on the occasional bottle or box or bag which did not have the price tag. Youth Congress volunteers formed themselves into committees to see if the order was being enforced. All the shops in all the markets promptly put up Congress flags as they had first done in June 1975. Only this time, the flags were being sold by the Youth Congress volunteers. Ruksana Sultana had been approached by many youth associations and local groups. She told them that the only way they could participate in the national development programme was by joining the Youth Congress and taking part in its activities.

The traders decided to join in the national programme in a big way. The competition started. Each market desired to be the one with the biggest family-planning camp. The traders joined hands with the Youth Congress volunteers. Shamianas were erected in every market. Each shamiana was festooned with posters and placards. Every shamiana shaded tables loaded with colourful pyramids of tins of vegetable ghee, called vanaspati, sold at a premium of Rs 2 per kg in the market because of its additional demand in the family-planning campaign. The shortage of vanaspati made the pile of tins all the more attractive. Next to the tins were placed rows and rows of clocks. And behind the table sat the motivators, the sons of the shopkeepers who had joined the Youth Congress and the local leaders of the party. In their hands they held a sheaf of papers. The megaphone invited passers-by to come and collect their registration slips. They could collect the slip and go to the nearest clinic for vasectomy. They could then produce the vasectomy certificate and collect Rs 300, a vanaspati tin and a clock. Metropolitan Councillor Brij Lal Goswami asked the chief executive councillor to inaugurate his camp. Raman and Swaroop jointly went to unveil the camp set up in commercial Karol Bagh, all spruced up after the municipal corporation's cleanliness drive in the area. Raman expressed satisfaction at the speed at which the family-planning crusade was being carried out. He repeated what he had said on earlier occasions, 'Delhi has been the pacesetter in implementing the five-point programme of Shri Sanjay Gandhi.' Swaroop told the traders of Shadipur while inaugurating their camp that they should make the programme a grand success. 'The Delhi Administration is keen,' he said 'to achieve the target by the year-end.'

The biggest function was held in Lajpat Rai market. The two Lajpat Rai markets had been in the race a long time. The old Lajpat Rai market had won the first round. It had set up two huge 10-foot by 10-foot paintings of Indira Gandhi and her son. The new Lajpat Rai market on the Jama Masjid side displayed a hoarding 100 feet long and about 4 feet high. It called for the traders' support for the programme of national reconstruction. Their family-planning motivation camp was by the DTC office making monthly travel passes for the students. There, Raman gave his sternest call yet, 'Family planning workers should approach their task with a do or die spirit.' A do or die spirit was necessary to stem the rising tide of population. The chief executive councillor reminded the traders of their role. He pointed out to the traders of Lajpat Rai market that their brethren all over the capital were contributing generously towards the additional incentives offered to those agreeing to be sterilized. 'I hope the traders of Lajpat Rai market will not lag behind.'

Quick to take the hint were those engaged in the very sensitive entertainment trade. A cinema house came under the local administration not only for its buildings, taxes and entertainment taxes but also for electricity and sanitation certificates. The information minister had just announced his new modalities which called for stricter censoring of films. He had also warned against any disobedience and called upon the industry to cooperate wholeheartedly with the government. In Delhi, five cinemas suddenly found themselves prosecuted. Only a few days earlier, cinemas had been told to discontinue their daily advertisements to the *Patriot* and the *Indian Express*. The two dailies and the *Statesman* had been the only papers in Delhi which had challenged the methods used to implement the five-point programme and the building up of the personality of their progenitor. The cinema owners were forced to issue a circular cutting off advertisements to these papers. Members were tacitly told that advertisements would in future have to be given to the *National Herald,* the pro-government newspaper. The cinema advertisers were also tacitly told that the earlier rules on how much advertising could be given by a particular producer or theatre had been suspended in the case of advertisements to the *National Herald.* While previously the standard advertisement for a new film would be a 5-centimetre spread over two columns, now a 20-centimetre spread over four columns was allowed, and after some time, became the norm. The theatre owners had no choice. They had the example of the Shiela theatre before them.

A posh cinema house in the heart of the town, Shiela was one of the first in India to come up with the widescreen equipment needed for modern films, especially those from Hollywood. It was also one of the best-maintained halls and its cleanliness was acknowledged by competing theatre owners. Shiela fell foul of the authorities. The municipal corporation, which had a long-standing dispute with it on taxes, now decided to act.

The cinema was sealed for some days. But before it was sealed, there was an hour of high drama. An officer came to the theatre with a work gang just as the last show ended. They asked the staff for the keys. The staff demurred. The government men entered the toilets forcibly, spread cans of filth over the floor and dumped sand and stones into the sinks and the toilet bowls. They smashed sanitaryware and put their lock and seal on the main doors. The theatre was then challaned for being dirty and for contravening sanitation regulations. The owners of the theatre begged the prime minister to intervene. It was days before the theatre opened again.

The film industry had the noisiest motivation camp in the capital. It had to be the loudest because it was situated bang in the middle of the noisiest street of the capital—the busy Chandni Chowk. Movie posters, vanaspati tins and the latest music from the newest films competed with each other to catch the attention of the passer-by.

It was now out in the open. A regulation would be passed and a new set of traders or businessmen or other professionals would come and join the family-planning programme. The DDA had persuaded other local authorities like the municipal corporation to help it dispose of the costly business flats it had in the Nehru Place commercial complex. To begin with, companies were reluctant to shift there. Also, the DDA was developing some very costly plots in posh areas and earmarking them for clinics and nursing homes. The authorities directed that all business concerns, including doctors' clinics and nursing homes, would have to shift to places earmarked for them. They could not do business in residential areas. They would have to pay high penalties for every month they continued at their old location.

On 21 July, the medical executive councillor reported that all seventy-five nursing homes in the capital had started undertaking sterilization operations free of charge. The doctors said they would be willing to go to the villages to perform sterilization surgeries. Swaroop then called upon all other doctors doing private practice to join the campaign more vigorously. That launched the doctors on a search for cases. By the end of July, different sections of the Delhi social strata had joined the mad race for sterilization.

This included trade union leaders of various hues and controlling diverse worker interests. Trade union activity had all but ceased during the first twelve months with widespread arrests of political leaders, some of whom were patrons of the trade unions. More trade unionists lay low for fear of arrests. Meetings and processions had been banned. And even for an indoor general body meeting of an association, the rule required that prior permission be taken. Behl, who was in charge of labour in the local administration, repeatedly called on the workers and the trade unions to participate in the programme more enthusiastically. Union Labour Minister Raghunath Reddy stressed the same thing at a meeting of workers. He said the trade unions should work in complete cooperation with the others to motivate the labour class.

As the established trade unions and their leaders took time off to think about it, in government and private establishments, the Youth Congress and its supporters moved in to take over the trade unions. They succeeded in many cases. One of the most glaring instances was the taking over of a section of the New Delhi Municipal Committee Employees Union by Arjan Das, the metropolitan councillor who had started out as a motor mechanic and helpmate of Sanjay Gandhi when that young man first dabbled in the manufacture of motor cars at Das's Roshanara Road garage. Das became the patron of all New Delhi municipal employees, and the guardian of all businessmen in south Delhi. With him and others like him heading the trade union organizations, the other trade union leaders were forced into hibernation. When the workers found their old leaders no longer useful in getting them a better deal they, especially the ones in the smaller institutions, accepted the leadership of these new figures. In the big industries, the management sided with the Youth Congress nominees to sabotage the trade unions that had been the bane of their existence over the years.

The effect of this was that the trade union leaders also started talking of family-planning motivations. The workers found themselves trapped. The managers were insisting that the worker get himself vasectomized. They were willing to pay him five times what the government booty was because they themselves had to meet the targets imposed on them. The worker found that the trade union was no longer listening to him when he complained that he was being chargesheeted or sacked for not agreeing to a sterilization operation. A large number of workers, including highly trained technicians, found it safer to leave their factories and work somewhere else. Even at the industrial workers' health centre run by the Employees' State Insurance Corporation, the worker was harangued to get himself vasectomized. The ESI hospital at its peak was doing eighty sterilization procedures a day.

At this juncture the DDA stepped in to increase the pressure. Already the Delhi Administration had passed its decree on housing loans: they were to be given only to eligible persons. Among the victims of the large-scale demolition taking place all over the city were workers of all types. From Class-IV government employees to casual labour, all of them found themselves in need of a sterilization certificate if they wanted to construct a home.

For some time, therefore, the many camps organized by the Youth Congress to motivate people and by various other groups to sterilize them saw unprecedented crowds. 'These camps were peculiar places, full of noise and people, laughing and crying,' said a medico on duty. 'We were working for long hours standing at tables covered with a blanket and a wax-cloth. We were performing up to seventy or eighty operations in these structures, school buildings, even tents. And we ran out of instruments, ran out of gauze and lint. A number of forceps were required in tubectomy and vasectomy operations and they had to be sterilized in bulk in the morning because there were no facilities at these outposts for continuous sterilization of a high standard. There were cases where the instruments were cleaned in hot water and reused.'

With such large crowds, overworked doctors and motivators running all over the place, the men and women undergoing sterilization were not given the thorough medical examination that the doctors knew to be necessary. 'It is incumbent on the operating doctor to convince himself that the case is a suitable one for operation,' the operating manual said, 'and the doctor should satisfy himself that the case has been prepared mentally and emotionally.' The doctor was also required to satisfy himself on points of selection of the patient. The first was that the man to be operated upon should be married and his wife should be in the reproductive age of fifteen to forty-two years. Generally speaking, the regulation said, 'the age of the husband should not be less than 24 and that of the wife not less than 20 years'. The second requirement was that 'not only should the couple have two living children, the age of the youngest child should be less than three years'. The third point was that 'the person to be operated on should be stable in mind and be convinced of the efficacy of the method. His fears, anxieties and doubts, if any, should be removed before he undergoes the operation.'

The special points that doctors ought to remember, the manual said, pertained to the health of the person. Those with high blood pressure, diabetes, fever and severe anaemia should be first treated for the diseases and then considered for operation. The scrotum and adjacent part of the thigh should be free from ulcers or any other infection. And, of course, persons with a history of epilepsy, fainting spells, unusual bleeding after injury, hydrocele, varicocele and hernia should be operated upon in hospitals where advanced facilities are available.

Hard-pressed doctors busy meeting the demand of the quotas admitted to having disregarded many of these common rules. In the madness of the sterilization camps, the special regulations for post-operative care were also sidetracked, and the follow-up action was ultimately scrapped for want of time. This important step envisaged that every sterilization case would be examined by paramedical staff on the second or third day after the operation to inquire about his welfare and to reassure him. The patient was to be contacted once every month as the success of the programme was dependent on the patient being totally satisfied. It was also desirable that as far as possible, a seminal examination be done after three months to make sure there were no sperms in the ejaculate, and only after this could the patient be advised to stop the use of traditional contraceptives.

In practice, during the height of the family-planning drive, these regulations were totally forgotten. Many of the Class-IV workers of government departments, who were vasectomized at the ESI and other government clinics, said their testicles were enlarged after the vasectomy, but when they brought it to the doctor's notice, they were told it was nothing serious. No care was taken either of the excessive bleeding over prolonged periods. Women employees of the DDA and the municipal corporation, especially those whose jobs involved lifting of heavy objects, said they had to report to work too soon after the operation, and the strain had turned their abdominal incisions into running sores.

Meanwhile, with Ruksana Sultana confining her activity to only the walled city, the implementation members felt that there was an urgent need to involve more people of other communities. A group of Christians called upon people to work towards the implementation of the youth programme, as did some Muslim leaders. Mir Mustaq inaugurated a camp that Begum Zorra Mushir had organized for the slum resettlement colony of Seelampur which was one of the few suburban areas with a Muslim character. Seelampur had been settled with the people who had been evicted during a redevelopment project a decade ago.

The beginning of the monsoon, and the reopening of schools after a long summer vacation of two months, saw the activity reach frenetic heights in the capital. It was keeping pace with the tree planting programme that was also being carried out. At most places the two were combined, and a sort of proportion was worked out between the trees to be planted and the people to be vasectomized. The programme was launched at the Old Secretariat headquarters of the local administration on 17 August when, after an Independence Day celebration function, Krishan Chand planted an ashoka sapling. The second sapling was planted by Vidya Ben Shah. The lieutenant governor felt that all these programmes should be carried out by everyone. Hira Singh said the target for trees was 9.6 lakh, of which 50 per cent had been met. Raman did not beat about the bush. While the others had so far refrained from naming Sanjay Gandhi in their speech, Raman took pleasure in pointing out that 'Delhi has been a pace-setter in implementing the five-point programme of Sanjay Gandhi' and the twenty-point programme of his mother.

The pressure was kept up continuously. While the Youth Congress reactivized its camps, which had become less active in the June heat, the departments again took note of the lag in the implementation of the programme. In September, Hira Singh called a meeting of all officials to expedite the pace of the family-planning campaign. From his talk followed a decision that senior officials were to be personally held responsible for their departmental quotas. They would also be responsible for getting as many cases as possible from members of the public who came in contact with their departments in an official capacity. For example, the deputy registrar of cooperatives whose department had control over thousands of cooperative societies in the capital, informed his subordinates that 'it will be your personal responsibility to stress on the staff the dire need of achieving the target. You may also personally go to the field and contact the concerned office-bearers of societies for that purpose. A special drive needs to be carried out in right earnest for that purpose.' The officer did not mince his words about what would happen to those who did not follow these orders: 'I may make it very clear that adverse notice is likely to be taken in case you and your staff do not meet the expectations in achieving the target.' He also wanted, with immediate effect, a daily report on the progress made in the case of these special drives.

What form these special drives took was seen in the case of the gigantic education directorate with its representative departments in the local civic organization. In the Delhi Administration, where Biswas was the head of the education directorate, orders were issued for strict compliance. All teachers were to motivate up to five people. The Class-IV employees of the department in July 1976 started a move that was strongly reminiscent of Aesop's fable of the hungry lion in the jungle. The wanton lion was killing more animals than he needed for food. The animals of the jungle therefore held counsel and decided that instead of the lion picking them, they would rather get some of their own to volunteer and go to the lion to be eaten so that other animals were not unnecessarily killed.

On 27 July, the Class-IV employees of the education directorate decided that they would send five volunteers from among themselves every day for sterilization. The employees announced this at a special family-planning camp held at the Old Secretariat itself. Raman reported on 30 August that 'although Delhi has exceeded its target of 29,000 sterilizations by achieving a record number of 70,000 sterilizations so far, yet we must achieve our self-imposed target of 1 lakh operations. For this we must all bend our energies so that the target can be met within the year.' At about the same time, the administration announced it had planted 1.8 lakh saplings with the target at 2.5 lakh for the year.

Exhortations within the department were becoming routine. Each day would begin with another appeal by the director or the principals to get more cases. The continuous record of the NDMC education department under Education Officer Bhatt gave a fair example of the inside happenings. On 9 August 1976 the education officer issued a circular for an urgent meeting of the heads of the NDMC nursery, primary, middle and higher secondary schools. The heads were asked to bring a range of information. Important among them was 'the family planning figures in respect of cases motivated from outside the school, including the name of the teacher who has motivated the cases and their number; employees of the school sterilized so far; names of employees with one child and with two children; and with three children and above separately in each category'. It may be clearly indicated whether they are sterilized or not, the circular added.

It also asked the headmasters to bring with them the list of employees eligible for sterilization, including those with three daughters or more who had not been sterilized. Also find the reasons for non-sterilization, the teachers were asked. The result of that meeting can be seen from the record of one school, the Nagar Palika Boys Higher Secondary School at Mandir Marg. The minutes of the staff association meetings read:

21.8.76, Subject: Special meeting on family planning: NDMC vigilance officer held special meeting on family planning. The vigilance officer read out the message of the member secretary of the NDMC, Ailawadi, that all staff members had to prove their competence and get more and more cases for sterilization. It was first suggested that the teachers should first motivate themselves and their family members. A drive for a family planning fund was proposed. Minutes confirmed by Principal J.N. Labroo.

24.8.76, The Principal today held a special one-hour meeting on family planning. It was suggested that a form be distributed to get the correct situation on family planning. The students should be given these forms to give to their parents. The parents should declare whether they are sterilized or not. New office-bearers of staff association were chosen. Treasurer chosen of family planning fund.

26.8.76, Education officer of Delhi administration held meetings with principals some time ago. Principal Mr Labroo briefed teachers on that meeting. The meeting lasted two hours. The Principal asked the teachers to be more vigilant in their work and should give the highest priority to family planning work. The teachers assured they would get sterilization case before 30 August.

27.8.76, Principal held special staff meeting on family planning. The Principal asked each teacher individually about what he or she was doing about it and how successful they had been so far. The Principal also reads out the order calling for a daily report on the progress of family planning.

28.8.76, Special meeting on family planning: Principal held consultations on the drive. Today four teachers got themselves sterilized. It was announced that a list of employees eligible for sterilizations was ready.

30.8.76, Principal called special staff meeting to find the progress of the family planning drive. Each teacher asked if he had sent for the eligible parents of the students. The principal collected figures from each teacher. The total was 125. Principal Labroo announced that two more persons in the school had been sterilized today and four more will be ready by tomorrow.

13.9.76, Principal Labroo called a special staff meeting on family planning. He exhorted the teachers to motivate as many people as they can.

Driven out of their senses by the daily harangue and the unwritten threats, the teachers announced they were willing to 'buy' their cases for up to Rs 500. Some unmarried girls were specially married. They too were compelled to bring five cases the first month and one every following month or their salary would not be paid. The orders withholding salaries were conveyed to the cashier by word of mouth, so that there was no written record. Those who could get the cases even after four months were paid their salaries, but they had to sign the old dates of all the previous four dates. That took care of the staff. The exceptional written directive was given in the case of a teacher who has been on a deputation to another school. He came to his parent school to collect his salary only to have the cashier advance him a slip from the principal:

Pay of Sh. P.S. Yadav will be released on production of a motivation slip of a family planning case as a general policy in this respect. He may collect his pay as soon as the case's motivation slip is deposited with the undersigned. Signed by Shri Niwas, Headmaster, Nagar Palika Middle School, Medical Institute.

Teachers tried desperately to persuade people to have a second vasectomy if possible, or better still, to get both the spouses sterilized. That would make for two motivation slips!

The sterilization drive was at fever pitch in schools. Suddenly, a different crisis exploded. Municipal health officers had been busy in the post-monsoon months with a widespread inoculation and vaccination programme against communicable diseases. But this time they were not vaccinating the children on the arm or the forearm. The vaccine was being administered on the thumbs or palms of the students. Although the Emergency was in full force, a rumour spread like wildfire that the children were being vaccinated to sterilize them for life. Within hours, many schools shut as parents rushed to take their children home. In some schools the angry parents caught hold of the teachers. Parents demonstrated against the principals. The vaccination staff was told they would be lynched if they were seen anywhere near the children.

The authorities and the politicians were caught napping. The intensity of the protest scared them into prompt action. Immediately the vaccinations were stopped. A publicity campaign was launched to counter the rumours. But by then the people had developed more faith in the rumours, and no one believed him when Municipal Commissioner Tamta announced that the vaccinations were genuine and had nothing to do with sterilization of the children. Schools in many parts of the city saw thin attendance as most of their students were held back at home. The Delhi Administration's director of health services, Dr O.P. Sharma, and the municipal health officer, Colonel Kewal Krishna, repeated the claim that no inoculation was ever given on the thumb, sole or palm. Still no one believed them. In desperation, an angry Town Hall decreed that while it was immediately stopping all free inoculation and vaccinations, in future parents would have to pay a Re 1 fee for every vaccination or inoculation given to their children in the epidemic months.

Meanwhile, the Delhi Administration and the local Congress congratulated themselves on a coup. Sanjay Gandhi was now a busy national leader, but they had managed to get him to spare some time to inaugurate on 2 October, Mahatma Gandhi's birth anniversary, a special rural development week launched by them to focus attention on the twenty-five-point programme. During the week 5000 saplings would be planted and mass sterilization done in all rural blocks of the capital.

The day dawned to a strong police bandobast at the Narela township deep in the rural Alipur block of the capital. The villagers went to the city every day, but they had never seen so many policemen before. At 9.30 a.m. Sanjay Gandhi drove in with Hira Singh. 'Sanjay Gandhi zindabad!' shouted the crowd; 'Sanjay Gandhi zindabad!' shouted the young men scattered in the audience. Sanjay inaugurated a 1-mile road and told the people, 'Talk less, work more. Plant more trees. Motivate more people for sterilization.' The leaders clapped. It was one of Sanjay Gandhi's last public appearances in Delhi. The police officers saluted as Sanjay Gandhi drove off.

chapter five

THE DINOSAURS . . .

~

It was around 10.30 a.m. when the black Ambassador drove in through the gates of the JNU campus. Young Prabir Purkayastha watched it lazily as he lounged on the grass outside the School of Languages. He was busy talking to the three girl students who sat around him. The Ambassador came closer. It seemed to be coming towards him. Yes, it was heading straight for him. The Ambassador was almost upon the students when it screeched to a halt. Prabir Purkayastha's trauma was just beginning.

Four burly men got out of the car. There was something familiar yet peculiar in their gait and manner. The clothes that hung limply on their erect frames looked almost like uniforms.

But Prabir had little time for these details. The men came up to him. 'Are you Devi Prasad Tripathi?' one of them asked. Prabir's heart gave a sudden leap.

There was no reason to be afraid, Prabir thought. He was sitting in his own university campus among his own friends; all he had to do was to answer, No, he was not Devi Prasad Tripathi, the president of the students' union. He was Prabir Purkayastha, the solitary student of the School of Computer

Science. And yet his heart gave a leap. There was something menacing about the four men. Their query held a veiled threat. It was this nervousness that made Prabir hesitate before he answered no. His hesitation cost him his freedom. 'Don't lie!' one of the men shouted at him as he caught him by the collar and started dragging him towards the car.

Two of the girls shrieked; then watched in stunned silence as Prabir was being dragged into the car, their reflexes numbed by shock and fear. But now they sprang up and tried to extricate their friend from the grip of the men. It did not make much of a difference. The men brushed the girls aside and pulled Prabir into the car.

The car started moving even before Prabir was fully inside it. With a sudden burst of energy, Prabir managed to wrench free and fell out of the moving car.

It immediately came to a halt and the men got out again. This time two of them got a firm grip on Prabir who was picked up bodily and thrown into the car.

By this time, the girls' cries had attracted scores of students who came running to the spot. But before they could get to Prabir, the car had already reached the gates and, though it had to leave two of the men behind in the melee, the black Ambassador with Prabir in it vanished from sight.

The two men made a dash for it. One just about made it out of the gates but the other was caught by the students. Before they could start his interrogation, another vehicle zoomed in through the gates. This time, it was a jeep full of armed policemen. The students fell back as guns pointed at them, and the fourth man clambered into the jeep. The jeep zoomed away.

The Emergency was exactly three months old.

Back in the black Ambassador, Prabir tried to communicate to his captors that he was an innocent student of the university. But they had kept silent. The car had driven to the R.K. Puram police station. Seeing the police station, Prabir had been somewhat relieved. After all, he came from a respectable family and had absolutely no criminal record. He would prove his bona fides in no time.

Yes, he had been able to convince the police that he was Prabir Purkayastha. But they seemed to be in no hurry to release him. They just kept on making phone calls.

'Yes, sir,' the inspector had muttered. 'The damn fool CID man has made a mistake again. This boy is definitely not Tripathi. We do not even have his name on the list.' Curses and abuse from the other side.

'Now what do we do with him, sir?' asks the inspector. 'Do we release him?'

No, he was told. Find out more about him and see if some charge can be slapped on him.

Finally, after many more phone calls, the police found out that Prabir's fiancée happened to be Ashoklata Jain, the girl who had been expelled from JNU for alleged 'anti-university' activities. The students of the university had in fact been picketing the campus for the last three days in solidarity with Ashoklata.

That was enough for the police. An hour later, a shocked Prabir was presented with a MISA arrest warrant. It would keep him behind bars and out of the university for a whole year.

The clumsy kidnapping of Prabir Purkayastha and his consequent arrest showed the pattern of police operations throughout the Emergency. There was no discrimination in those nineteen months. Students, clerks, politicians or labourers were equally arbitrarily, and often without any specific cause, rounded up and put behind bars.

Coupled with the clumsy and ham-handed way in which the police went about terrorizing the populace was also the mysterious and conspiratorial air that they built around the arrests. The press being gagged, there could be no news published about the arrests. In fact, the censors had rung up newspapers on the day of the JNU kidnapping and told them that 'there was no trouble today at the Jawaharlal Nehru University and no report should be given about it'.

Delhi Police had been an inefficient force even before the Emergency. It had been castigated time and again in the press and the courts for using unnecessary force not only with criminals but also with innocent citizens. Now, armed with Emergency powers, the police force had a clear field for bungling.

The universities were the first to feel the wild arm of the law during the Emergency. Less than three months before Prabir's kidnapping and just thirteen days after the Emergency was declared, the police had first come to the JNU campus.

In the early hours of the morning of 1 July 1975, inmates of the JNU students' hostel were rudely woken up by the sound of police sirens. Looking out of their windows, they found that a vast army of more than 1000 men of the Delhi Police and the Central Reserve Police Force had besieged the hostel.

Then a group of police officers went from room to room in the hostel, consulting a long list. About fifty students were rounded up from their rooms by the police. Protests and imprecations by the students fell on deaf ears.

The students were taken to the Hauz Khas police station where they were made to stand in a line while a man behind a wire mesh identified some of them. After the identification parade was over, the police released thirty of the students. Soon after, there was another identification parade. This time a man with a red mask pointed out ten of the twenty remaining students. The police served the DIR on those pointed out, while the rest were released. The police had deployed more than 1000 personnel and put in days of planning to arrest just ten students. It later turned out that of those arrested, half were innocent. A number of political activists had managed to pass the parade.

The police came even earlier to DU. Here the main target seemed to be the teachers. The arrests started on the night the Emergency was declared. In one swoop on the night of 25 June, the police rounded up 110 teachers of the university from their homes. In the dragnet were caught all the teachers of the Sanskrit department which had to, as a consequence, close down for there was nobody to teach Sanskrit. Later the university managed to cajole the police to release a few of them so that classes would not be affected.

This was just the beginning. From outdated police files and sketchy CID reports on university gossip, the police prepared a long list of suspects. Half of these unfortunate people presented not even a remote threat to the State and the number of those who could have actually brewed some trouble on the campus could be counted on the fingers of one's hand. One by one the suspects were hounded out. The number of teachers arrested during those nineteen months totalled as many as 200—the largest number of teaching staff to be arrested from any university in the country at that time.

The atmosphere in the university had changed overnight. Teachers and students whispered rumours of arrests to each other. They wondered who among them were police informants. If one were to believe the rumours, almost all the senior teachers of the university out of jail had been passing information to the police about each other in some way or the other. State pressure on the university was considerable.

Krishan Chand himself had attended a function at the university and asked the staff, including the vice chancellor, to 'attune themselves more to reality'. After asking the teachers not to merely contain themselves in a cerebral existence but to come down and join the family-planning programme of Ruksana Sultana, the lieutenant governor had suddenly whirled round and pointed an accusing finger at the vice chancellor, R.C. Mehrotra.

'I know that underground activities are continuing in this university,' he told the vice chancellor who shrank in his chair.

'If the university cannot put its house in order, then I am afraid the administration will have to step in.'

Under this sort of pressure, many in the academic community cracked. Devendra Kumar, the acting president of the Delhi University Teachers' Association (the association president, Om Prakash Kohli, was behind bars), had faithfully handed over at regular intervals a list of 'suspicious' teachers to Sanjay Gandhi. These lists were as unverified and as inaccurate as the CID lists. Personal dislike often played a large role in ascertaining whose name would be on the list. Such an avid supporter of the Emergency as the president of the Congress National Forum of Teachers, V.P. Dutt, a member of Parliament, was also reported to be on the blacklist. Goaded by the administration and fed by such inaccurate information, the police became an object of terror for all and sundry on the campus.

If the academic community was trampled under police boots during the Emergency, far worse was the fate of the poorer and less educated sections of the capital's population who had little or no protection against the law-and-order machinery. By far the most vulnerable were the rehriwalas, tangawalas, payment hawkers and other casual labourers. They had been at the mercy of the beat constable even before the Emergency. Now their lives became a constant nightmare. For them, meeting a police constable on the road after 9 p.m. would almost certainly end up in arrest, a severe beating, extortion of as much money as they could give and a possible prison sentence.

With the start of the sterilization campaign in the capital, the police had another threat to dangle over the head of the poor. Woe to the man who was stopped by the police at night. He would first be taken to the police chowki and locked up for the night. In the morning he would be taken to the nearest family-planning camp and forcibly made to undergo sterilization. This served the double purpose of not only increasing the number of sterilization cases but also keeping the public in a state of terror.

The labourer was used to the occasional beating up by a cop but he dreaded losing what he considered his manhood. In a city where many slept out on the pavements on summer nights, there was hardly a soul to be found on the streets after 9 p.m. in the summer of 1976.

Yet, what was even more indicative of the tremendous powers given to the police during the Emergency was the fact that they had scant regard for even the middle class and the upper middle class.

Amit was a DU student and stayed in his college hostel on the campus. It was usual for students to spend some time late at night over a lassi in front of the Khyber Pass row of restaurants. Amit was sitting with a friend and two girl students drinking lassi at Khyber Pass when two constables walked up to him and asked what they were doing there at that time of the night.

The students answered that they were drinking lassi as the police could well see. 'You better come with us,' the constables told them and in spite of their protestations forced them to come along with them.

'Where are you taking us?' Amit asked the policemen as they walked down Mall Road. 'To do your medical,' replied the constable mysteriously.

Amit's heart sank. Medical in the new parlance could mean only one thing—sterilization.

Amit tried to flatter the police constables by calling them 'Inspector Sa'ab'. But this was of no use. The constables were determined to take them along.

Finally, at 2 a.m., the students and the constables reached the Roshanara police station. There, Amit made a last-ditch effort with the station house officer (SHO). The SHO seemed to be more amenable than the constables. The students were made to sit for at least two hours of interrogation, and released after they gave a written statement that they would not drink lassi at Khyber Pass at night any more.

Twenty-four-year-old Ravi Kumar was not so lucky. It was May 1976, the height of the Emergency. Ravi lived on Lawrence Road and was in love with a twenty-year-old girl who lived in a neighbouring house. Though the girl's family was against the marriage as Ravi was a Christian, the couple went ahead with their wedding. After filing intent to marry on court-notarized affidavits, the boy and the girl were married at a largely attended religious ceremony. Hardly had the newly married couple spent their nuptial night, when next morning the girl's family filed a complaint at the local police post that their minor girl had been kidnapped by four men in a vehicle the night before.

The next night the young couple and two of Ravi's friends were kidnapped by the police and taken to the chowki. There Ravi, his young wife and his two friends were severely beaten up by policemen. Helping the cops were the girl's relatives who were also present at the police station.

After a good beating, the girl was taken away by her family even though she said she wanted to stay with her husband. The three boys were made to stand outside in the scorching heat and were repeatedly beaten with fists and lathis till one of them, an epileptic, passed out. Frightened by this, the police released the boys that night.

The case probably would have been buried like so many others during the Emergency had it not been for the fact that Ravi's family had good contacts with some VIPs.

However, because of persistent representations to Inspector General Bhawanimal an inquiry was ordered. The inquiry immediately ran into obstacles. Firstly, not only was there no evidence of the boys' arrests available at the police post, but the complaint against them by the girl's family of abduction had not even been entered in the FIR or police diary. The persons who were helping in the inquiry were the two sub-inspectors who had beaten up Ravi and his friends in the first place. The deputy superintendent who was in charge of the inquiry seemed to not mind it.

The family again made representations to Bhawanimal but with not much effect. The inquiry was carried on in its usual rambling fashion. The odds were too great against Ravi. He had chosen the wrong girl to marry. The girl's relative happened to be a policeman.

In Delhi, matters soon reached such a pass that even journalists were falling prey to the whims of the police. The journalist, particularly the press reporter, has traditionally been a powerful man in Delhi. Before the Emergency, even the inspector general of police talked politely to the press, often going out of his way to placate journalists. All this changed overnight with the imposition of the Emergency. Let alone the IGP, even the most junior constable treated reporters in a shoddy manner. Soon it became difficult for reporters to cover any programme concerning a government leader, particularly the prime minister, without being humiliated at the hands of the security men. In fact, some policemen and officers took great pleasure in getting back at those reporters who had criticized them in their earlier days of freedom. A well-known and well-liked reporter of a noted national daily published from the capital found out just how much. In October 1975, the Commonwealth Parliamentary Conference was held in the capital. The day after the conference, the foreign delegates were given a reception at the Red Fort. This reporter had gone to cover the function. Just before the programme was to begin, a group of demonstrators had suddenly appeared on the scene, shouting slogans criticizing the Emergency and the murder of parliamentary democracy in the country. The demonstrators started distributing pamphlets. Good reporter that he was, the journalist had rushed to the spot and picked up a pamphlet. Meanwhile, scores of policemen grabbed the demonstrators and were dragging them away. In the melee suddenly appeared Ambika Soni, a Youth Congress leader who later became the Youth Congress president, and asked the reporter to hand over the pamphlet. This he refused to do.

'You better give it, or you will be in for trouble,' Soni said.[1] The reporter was, however, adamant. Before he knew what was happening, even as other reporters watched helplessly, he had been whisked away into the police van. A few hours later, the reporter had been arrested under the DIR. He was released on bail after a few days but was rearrested within a week, this time under the dreaded MISA. Just one altercation with a Youth Congress leader had cost the reporter nearly one full year in jail.

With the press gagged and intimidated, the police reeled out a series of fancy figures and statistics showing that one of the 'boons' of the Emergency was the drop in the crime rate. On 2 September 1975, the DIG (Range) Bhinder said at a press conference that there had been in the last three months a drop of as much as 52 per cent in heinous crimes such as dacoities, murders and robberies. 'With the promulgation of Emergency the capital is now free from rallies, processions and demonstrations and consequently the Delhi Police have been able to give its uninterrupted attention to crimes and criminals,' Bhinder said to pressmen.

Bhinder held another press conference seven months later on 3 April 1976 at which he announced the fall of a further 27 per cent in the crime rate. He said that cases of attempt to murder had declined by 50 per cent, robbery and snatching by 45 per cent, dacoity by 83 per cent and rioting by 89.5 per cent.

The reason for the decline in the crime rate, as Bhinder put it, was that the Emergency made it possible to have more vigilance and better attention towards law and order besides general awareness to control crime. The MISA was another factor which had brought down crime, the DIG added. Bhinder's only complaint at the press conference was that the police force available at the moment was too small to contain the population of Delhi.

The third press conference announcing a further dip in the crime rate was by Bhawanimal who said that it had fallen by another 15 per cent.

Giving the usual graphic details of the city's plummeting crime graph, Bhawanimal attributed it to the Emergency and 'greater discipline' in the capital.

Newsmen at these press conferences exchanged knowing glances but most kept their lips sealed. It was not the time to try and find out the actual details of the crime rate in the capital. If the IGP said that the crime rate was zero, they had better believe it was zero.

Most of them knew that the crime rate had hardly gone down and that there was now no free registration and free reporting of crimes. As the police bulletin dwindled in size day by day except for long-drawn-out news about tree plantation and sterilization activities by the IGP, the crime reporters (the very word had become an anachronism now since there was no crime to report) had no way out but to publicize police figures and rest content.

That was why the reporters found it extremely intriguing when the police began to publicize the exploits of Sunder, a dacoit who seemed to be clever enough to elude the all-reaching hands of the Emergency State.

The only dacoities or murders publicized by the Delhi Police during the Emergency were those of Sunder who went from one audacious feat to other. The first dacoity which Sunder was supposed to have committed in Delhi was in February 1976 and the very acknowledgement of this fact by the police was highly mysterious. Hardly had a month gone by, when Sunder struck again. This time in the East District, a sprawling area of filthy slums and a den of all sorts of criminal activities. Interstate dacoits usually used to operate across the East District as it was right on the UP border. This time Sunder's offence was even more serious. Two murders in one month, and that too by a dacoit who had committed a robbery just a month ago. On the last day of March 1976, the police claimed to have got to Sunder and two of his associates at Faridabad. The two associates were said to have been shot down by the police party. Sunder had somehow managed to escape, leaving behind a huge cache of arms, including an assortment of firearms. There was, however, a small complication for the Delhi police in Faridabad regarding the death of the two associates of Sunder. The Haryana police insisted that the two men had not been shot down in an encounter but at point-blank range. In fact, a case of murder was registered by the local police against the Delhi police team. The Haryana police had later withdrawn the allegation on orders from higher-ups. This part of the story had of course not been publicized by the Delhi Police. They had merely narrated the hair-raising chase of Sunder and his associates by the police: the shoot-out and finally the escape of Sunder despite the best efforts of the police. Sunder had emerged out of the police story a bigger and blacker villain than ever before. Crime reporters in the capital were even more intrigued. It was not often that the Delhi Police chose to build up the image of a criminal.

Sunder was back in action a month later, when on 10 May his car was stopped by the Delhi Police on Tilak Marg. But again, Sunder, who was increasingly becoming the Indian version of the Scarlet Pimpernel, managed to escape. This time, he left behind a car in which two hand grenades, one revolver and ninety-two self-loading rifle rounds were found. Sunder seemed to be having a regular ammunition dump, according to the Delhi Police's descriptions.

Finally, in September came Sunder's most daring feat. On 10 August 1976, around 9.30 p.m., Constable Sultan Singh of the anti-dacoity patrol police on duty near Wazirabad in East District spotted a suspicious-looking man. The constable asked him for his identity, whereupon Sunder pulled out a revolver and shot him three times at point-blank range. Sultan Singh died on the spot. The other members of the patrol party fired at the fleeing dacoit but the culprit managed to escape. Bhawanimal announced dramatically at a press conference held on 12 September that Sunder had 'of late become desperate after persistent police pressure'. He added, 'The task of apprehending this notorious dacoit has thrown a challenge to Delhi's police force and the death of Constable Sultan Singh will be avenged.'

In five months, Sunder had become the sole challenge under the Emergency to the Delhi Police. What was more surprising than the story which the police told were the reasons why they said it at all. Every story the police publicized about the escapades made the Delhi Police look a bigger fool than ever before. And why had the prime minister or the home minister not criticized the police till now for having been continually outwitted by Sunder? The story told by the Delhi Police about the dacoit toying with the foolish cops was getting curiouser and curiouser.

And then finally, the cops got together and nabbed the ace dacoit. At least this was the undertone in the story of Sunder's dramatic arrest by the Rajasthan police on 3 September in Jaipur, in Bhawanimal's own home state. As Haryana Inspector General of Police S.S. Bajwa put it, 'It was the brilliant coordination among the police forces of Haryana, Delhi and Rajasthan which made the police dragnet close on Sunder.'

Sunder was brought within a few days to Delhi and imprisoned in Tihar Jail. Meanwhile, there was an interesting episode at his identification parade. The parade took place, strangely enough, the day after a photograph of Sunder had been prominently displayed in an evening daily. Anyway, Sunder was identified as Sunder and if there were a few doubts among some reporters, the police evidently had none.

Hardly had the Sunder hullabaloo died down in the next two months when the police revived it again on 26 November to announce that the notorious dacoit was dead. The story that the police told about the death of Sunder would probably rank as the most absurd and ridiculous tale that has ever been told by the police to the people.

The story put out by the police said: A police party headed by a deputy superintendent was bringing Sunder back from Tughlakabad where he had been taken to make a recovery of arms for which he had given a tip-off. However, the car in which the police party was travelling got a puncture and stopped near the pontoon bridge over the River Yamuna in Gandhi Nagar. While the police personnel got down to help the driver change the tyre by the roadside, Sunder asked for permission to relieve himself. As soon as one of his hands was released from the handcuffs, Sunder snapped himself free and jumped into the river. The police chased him and opened fire but missed their mark and Sunder managed to escape. The Scarlet Pimpernel had done it again. But not quite.

The police report said that about four hours later, 'a police officer spotted a piece of cloth floating in midstream in the river. When they reached the spot, they found a man who was identified as Sunder.' The story of the life and death of Sunder, the greatest dacoit of our times, as told by the Delhi Police is a flamboyant one that would have put any Bollywood film to shame. The most absurd part of the story was about the sub-inspector and the constable who were escorting Sunder and who had, according to the police story, opened one of his handcuffs. 'Sub-inspector R.P. Gautam and constable Paras Ram received injuries while chasing the dacoit. The constable has been admitted to the hospital. Both the policemen have also been placed under suspension and a magisterial inquiry ordered,' the police story said.

Baffled by how two policemen could be injured while chasing an unarmed, handcuffed man, crime reporters in the capital did not know whether to laugh or to cry!

Who was the dacoit Sunder? Why were his adventures so extensively publicized by the Delhi Police? And what were the circumstances of his death in police custody? During the Emergency, these questions could only be asked. The answer to them was perhaps the most closely guarded secret of the nineteen months.

As the police would have it, Sunder was an ex-army man who went rogue after his dismissal from the army in 1961. His first crime was said to be an attempt on the life of the SHO of Dadri in Uttar Pradesh. That was the first of many attempts that Sunder would make on the lives of policemen. From different accounts of the exploits of Sunder one common characteristic emerged. He had a consuming hatred for all uniformed policemen. The reason for this is said to be the fact that Sunder's sister had been raped by a few police officers and men in a police station in Haryana. It is said that this incident had turned Sunder against the police.

The exact details of the rise of Sunder as a dacoit were hidden by the myths that the police as well as the man on the street had made up about him. If the flights of fantasy and romance that the police tale spun about him seemed mysterious, the Sunder myth among people in general was quite natural. He was the only person they were hearing about during the Emergency who had stood up to the police and constantly hoodwinked them. The common man took a great deal of vicarious pleasure in the daredevil exploits of Sunder. The oppressive State machinery might have cowed people's minds but not their imagination. And so the Sunder myth grew.

The myth-making reached a peak when the name of the most dazzling star of the Emergency firmament, Sanjay Gandhi, was associated with Sunder. The myth had now reached epic proportions. Sunder versus Sanjay. This was the epic battle discussed on almost every street corner. There was something in this battle which appealed deep down in the common man's heart. On one side was arrayed the forces of the establishment, the tyrant prince and his cohorts. On the other was the Robin Hood of the people. The Emergency had at last thrown up a hero they could identify themselves with in true Hindi-film style.

There was also an angle of caste to the Sunder myth. Sunder came from the Gujjar community and the Gujjar colonies like Kotla Mubarakpur in south Delhi worshipped him like a god. Even the police admitted that Sunder was liked by the people in these colonies.

There were varying accounts of Sanjay's association with Sunder. One account held that the young prince and Sunder used to be friends but had fallen out over a girl. According to that version, Sunder was the girl's 'dharambhai' and had sworn that he would kill Sanjay.

Another story was that Sunder had been hired by a prominent businessman to annihilate Sanjay after the young prince had refused to marry the businessman's daughter. The businessman who had invested crores of rupees in Sanjay Gandhi's Maruti car project had withdrawn his money.

The publicizing of Sunder's dramatic escapes had added to the romanticization of the man among the people. In an atmosphere of wholesale mass arrests, there was something consoling about a man who could not be touched by the police time and again. The day the dramatic arrest of Sunder was announced, gloom descended on the people of Delhi, particularly in the poorer and middle-class colonies. The prince had won. Now there was nobody left to fight against the State. But the Sunder story refused to die so tamely. The police brought out the final instalment of their Sunder thriller, describing his escape and consequent drowning in the Yamuna.

There were, however, few takers for the story. There were just too many loopholes in it. Apart from the absurdity of the two policemen getting hurt while chasing the unarmed, handcuffed Sunder, there was the question of the disposal of his body. Sunder's body was not handed over to his relatives or his wife. It was cremated within twenty-four hours of his death, though it is customary to wait at least two days in such deaths.

If the police had expected to capitalize on the people's imagination, they did not meet with much success. The death of Sunder had sobered people down considerably. A far more brutal story was emerging. A story which had not only gained currency among the people but was also being whispered among police personnel.

The name of Sanjay Gandhi figured in the story. It was he who had called a meeting late on a November night of the three most senior police officers—Inspector General Bhawanimal, DIG (Security) Mander and Sanjay's own man DIG (Range) Bhinder. The young prince was blunt at the meeting. He did not want to go through long court proceedings to get rid of Sunder. He wanted the police to dispose of him right now.

Bhawanimal and Mander had anticipated a few difficulties in undertaking such an unprecedented operation. Sunder had been publicized too much. Nobody would believe that he had just passed away in police custody. Only Bhinder, known to be close to the young prince, agreed to do his bidding, the story went. Bhinder had much experience in such incidents before, in Bansi Lal's Haryana. He was not afraid. So the IGP and the DIG (Security) had been told to go on leave for a few days and Bhinder had taken over under the specific orders of Sanjay Gandhi.

The story varies in the matter of the exact location where Sunder was bumped off. Some versions say it was near the Yamuna, while others maintain it was at the Gandhi Nagar police station. It also varies in the method used to murder Sunder.

One account holds that Sunder was first shot in the head and then thrown into the Yamuna, but another and probably more accurate account is that Sunder's head was forcibly held down in water till he suffocated to death.

This was the story that did the rounds in almost every corner of the capital and even outside it. But like all other stories of the Emergency, it could never be totally corroborated or confirmed. Both in life and in death Sunder remained a mystery. Yet there was still his ghost to contend with. It seemed to haunt the Delhi Police, particularly the Gandhi Nagar police station where Sunder was said to have been done away with.

Taxi driver Surjit Pal was in no way as romantic a figure as Sunder had been. So when a police jeep picked him up from his village home in Bawana late at night on 31 January 1977, only his relatives got upset. There was no sign of Pal for sixteen days, and his relatives and friends ran around desperately to find out which jail he was in. They were lucky, in that by February 1977, the Emergency climate had changed somewhat. With the elections due to be held in March, the authorities were more amenable and the gag on the press had been loosened. Nearly three weeks had passed since Pal's disappearance in the police jeep when a report appeared in one of the daily newspapers about the incident. The report also expressed doubts about whether Pal was alive or not. The next day, another newspaper took it up and then followed it up with a week-long intensive campaign which not only exposed the inside story of the Surjit Pal case but also indicated that his was not the first of its sort in the East District, particularly the Gandhi Nagar police sub-division under Deputy Superintendent Sukhdev Singh. The police force that had kept mum about it for the whole three weeks was suddenly galvanized into action. It first arrested Devi Chand, inspector of the Gandhi Nagar police station, and then for a week continued to arrest every day at least one policeman of the area, including DSP Sukhdev Singh, the first DSP to be arrested in the history of the Delhi Police.

The arrest of ten policemen, three on charges of murder and the rest for criminal conspiracy and kidnapping, revealed a startling story of brutal police torture and connivance of high police officials to hush up the cases. The Crime Branch which was handling the cases had a strange story to tell after a month-long interrogation of the arrested policemen.

According to the charge sheet, under directions from Sukhdev Singh, a police party comprising Inspectors Devi Chand and Krishan Chand, Sub-inspector R.P. Gautam and Head Constable Harbir Singh, Constables Gurdev Ram, Rattan Lal and Hari Parsad went to Bawana village in the small hours of 31 January 1977 to arrest Pal who was allegedly involved in a car theft. The policemen wanted to interrogate him in connection with the theft.

They brought Pal to the Gandhi Nagar police station, and he was produced before Sukhdev Singh. The SHO, Som Prakash, was also present. Pal was beaten up by Devi Chand, Sukhdev Singh and Som Prakash with lathis and fists. On the afternoon of 6 February, Pal was taken to a Shahdara nursing home with his face swollen. He was in a precarious condition. He was given treatment but in vain; he died of his injuries.

The body of Pal was taken to Garh Ganga, just across the border in a black Ambassador car. The car was escorted by Sukhdev Singh who was in his jeep driven by constable Sahi Ram. Sub-inspector Sita Ram was at the wheel of the car.

The body was thrown into the Ganga at Brijghat under the supervision of Sukhdev Singh, the charge sheet alleged.

The intriguing feature about the Surjit Pal murder case is that Sub-inspector Gautam who arrested Surjit was the same sub-inspector who had escorted Sunder when he managed to 'escape'. He had then received 'injuries' while trying to chase the dacoit and was finally suspended for the incident. The sub-inspector was indeed a man of action.

The case of the missing man from Bawana became the catalyst for a holocaust among the Delhi Police. After twenty long months, the bubble had burst. The IGP was profuse in his apologies about the Surjit Pal case. A controversy raged in the police quarters over which senior officials were involved in the case. The superintendent of East District, Gurcharan Singh Anand, had been hurriedly banished to the New Police Lines, but rumour had it that the involvement went higher up. The name of Bhinder figured prominently in the rumours.

chapter six

. . . AND THE PRIMEVAL SLUSH

~

Officers of the Union Territories cadre of the Indian Police
Service (IPS) posted in Delhi met in a secret conclave one evening
in January 1975—long before the Emergency was declared.
One of them, a superintendent, had connections at the prime
minister's residence and had come to know that an officer of the
Haryana cadre, a man called Pritam Singh Bhinder, was being
brought to Delhi to take over as the deputy inspector general of
police. The IPS officers were told by their 1, Safdarjung Road
contact that it was Sanjay Gandhi's idea. Bhinder and Sanjay had
become friends when the former was the senior superintendent
of Gurgaon in Haryana. The Maruti complex was on the Delhi–
Gurgaon road and Bhinder had been ordered by Haryana Chief
Minister Bansi Lal to ensure that things went smoothly with
Maruti. Bhinder was a diligent officer. Sanjay wanted him to
be brought in as the Range deputy inspector general of police
for Delhi.

These were bad times for the Delhi Police, and for its
officers. But the IPS Union Territories cadre that met that
evening could not hide its anger at the news. The officers had
been castigated, criticized in Parliament and ridiculed at public

forums in the preceding months when a rapidly rising crime wave had been topped by Delhi's most vicious communal riot in the Sadar Bazaar area on 4 May 1974. The news about Bhinder was the last straw. The IPS officers, many of them belonging to families of the ruling circles, mounted a high-pressure campaign to sabotage Bhinder's transfer.

The officers canvassed support. Newspaper reporters covering the police assignment were approached one evening and requested to write against Bhinder's posting to Delhi. Bhinder, the Delhi officers said, was much too junior to be allowed charge of the DIG Range which was the number two position in the Delhi Police. The DIG Range controlled most of the functional area in the capital. Bhinder, they said, had only recently been just a senior superintendent of police at Gurgaon and had then been sent to Ambala as DIG. Bhinder had no executive experience of managing a big metropolis with its peculiar problems. This posting would hurt Delhi. And it would hurt even more the morale of the police force, which was at its lowest ebb since the subordinate policemen had gone on an unprecedented strike in 1967.

The Delhi officers carried on their campaign for a week. But in vain. Bhinder came to the capital and took charge of the range administration from Ved P. Marwah. The contrast between the personalities of these two officers was tremendous. And it was reflected in the nature of their functioning. Marwah had been a cool, sophisticated officer with social graces. Bhinder was gruff, direct and abrasive. His shabby uniform, the belt often slipping way down his waist, belied his high rank. His voice had a harsh edge to it, and when he spoke to his subordinates, he chose to address them in the direct lingo of the village.

But within two months of his transfer to the capital, the cop from the ultra-rural state of Haryana had taken over the police in Delhi with a completeness that was unprecedented. In these months he successfully smashed to splinters the semblance of unity that was in the covenanted IPS cadres. He succeeded in pushing officers of his own rank so far into the background that for the next two years they would cease to matter altogether. Bhinder also identified at first glance the cliques that existed in the ranks of the officers and the men. He also perceived the deep unrest in a particular section of the officer class—the deputy superintendents of police who nursed a strong distrust of their superiors in the service. He knew of the inefficiency of various sections of the police structure. Coming from Haryana, Bhinder could also understand the mentality and psychology of the rural constables and the Punjabi sub-inspectors who constituted the bulk of the Delhi police force. With a shrewdness belying his hick reputation, Bhinder struck.

He used the standard ploy of reward and punishment—but with a difference. For the critical posts, Bhinder carefully chose men he could trust. No one found it surprising that the men he chose were to an extent almost like him. Before him, most of them had routine careers without any particular burst of brilliance. He had them transferred to sensitive posts. The district superintendents, the police station chief officers and, within police stations, the anchormen sub-inspectors were all Bhinder men very soon. And willingly so, as was evident from a liquor party Bhinder threw for local newspaper reporters at his official residence. The party was a rare occasion. Bhinder had never displayed any anxiety about fraternizing with reporters. Not a believer in letting anyone know what was afoot, Bhinder as DIG Police would acknowledge the presence of reporters only when it became necessary for reasons of publicity. And yet he sought to have closer relations with some of them. He called them to his house for a drink. Helping Bhinder play host was a powerful deputy superintendent of police recently promoted to the rank. The DSP made the drinks and passed the glasses to the reporters. He beamed when Bhinder smiled. Bhinder revelled in such a display of loyalty from his officers.

Secure in the loyalty of the key men of the force, Bhinder effectively created a situation where IGP Bhawanimal—also an outsider, and brought in from his parent state of Rajasthan to take over from P.R. Rajgopal after the Sadar Bazaar riots of 1974—was somewhat pushed to the background. In the months of the Emergency, it would be Bhinder who would make the vital decisions, pass the crucial orders. His orders were obeyed, because it was common knowledge that he spoke on behalf of Sanjay Gandhi. This was to create problems for the police and the public. It was only when the major part of the Emergency was over that the IGP could oust Bhinder from his supreme position. In a matter of weeks, in August 1976, the transition was made. Bhinder was no longer hogging the limelight, with the IGP reduced to a faint shadow in the background. How Bhawanimal managed to oust his subordinate is still not known. But the sterling work done by Bhawanimal to promote family planning among the police was said to be a major factor. The young prince had been pleased.

The immediate and clear parallel to this was the tussle between the DDA's Jagmohan and the municipal corporation's Tamta. The difference was that they controlled separate organizations. In the case of the two police officers, the contenders were within the same force. In this strife, the inefficiency of the Delhi Police itself became an instrument of terror in the peculiar atmosphere of the Emergency. And the latent criminality of the Delhi policemen, highlighted in the past in psychological studies and testimonies before investigating tribunals, was encouraged and exploited by its new mentor.

The crisis in the police force had first become public in 1967. Modelled on the lines of the colonial police, the force had not been able to grow past its pre-independence roots where a staff of white officers had controlled a mob of local men to enforce the dictates of the Crown on the masses. After Independence, the white officers left, but the chasm between the Indian officers who took their place and the men subordinate to them was never bridged. Neither did the rules change significantly to bring about a character change in the force, in its purpose of functioning and its methods. While such a situation may have prevailed in the police force across the country, the peculiar situation in Delhi aggravated the problem.

The officers and men of the Delhi Police belonged to vastly different classes. They had nothing in common. They belonged to different strata of society and were even trained differently. In fact, till the late 1960s, there was a clear pattern in the recruitment of the constabulary from a narrow band of socio-ethnic groups. There had been two main sources for the recruitment of men to the Delhi Police. The smaller of the two was the manpower pool created in the wake of the partition of India in 1947. The refugees who had come from Pakistan and their sons who could get some education found in the police just the sort of a career they could be successful in. It did not entail long, wasteful years of higher education which was necessary for a clerical job. The proverbial corruption of the police was just the additional perquisite that made the whole thing attractive. The major source of the constabulary, however, was the peasantry of rural Delhi which had a contiguous ethnic contact with the neighbouring states of Haryana, Uttar Pradesh and Punjab. To the Jat, Ahir and Gujjar youth, coming from the backward classes of the same villages, the semi-martial character of the police force offered just the right combination of monetary benefits and prestige to make the profession one of the most desirable in the capital. Even today the police is a prime target for job-hunting rural youth. The continuance of this pattern of recruitment over the years gave the subordinate police force a unique character which was totally at variance with that of the officers who governed it.

The force was controlled by two sets of officers. The senior ranks belonged to the all-India cadre of the IPS. The subordinate chain of command was with the inspectors and sub-inspectors, the best of whom were promoted to the gazetted officer rank of a deputy superintendent of police. The IPS officers were selected together with other all-India services through nationwide examinations conducted by the Union Public Service Commission. The IPS ranked third in importance after the prestigious Indian Foreign Service and the coveted Indian Administrative Service. The gazetted officers were also recruited in another manner. This was an inferior service called the Class II police cadre and was to become one of the persistent abscesses in the Delhi Police constitution, sapping its morale.

These officers were given a broad-based training, part of which they shared with the other administrators. The administrators too were in turn familiarized with the police service, because after graduation, the IAS boys were to become the controllers of the district police, a situation that was the gift of the British and a testimonial to their well-founded distrust of the police if it were given absolute powers. The magistracy of the IAS was supposed to take the final decisions and supervise the police in its district activity. The magistracy was empowered to sign arrest warrants and other warrants that authorized the police to take action. The IPS training, while it had been criticized for its colonial content in many quarters, did turn out officers who possessed a distinct stamp, and who had been indoctrinated, at least enough for a working knowledge, in the more scientific aspects of police functioning. It was the cadre which resisted most strongly the ham-handed ways of Bhinder under the Emergency.

The training of the constables on the other hand was of a primitive standard. The result was that the constabulary very specifically took on the appearance of a rural force with a mental framework that made it unfit for the extra-special demands imposed on it because of the cosmopolitan nature of the big capital city, its range of people and the complexity and diversity of its crime.

The gulf between them and their officers therefore became more apparent, and with it came a sense of alienation for both. The officer chose to take the least possible interest in the constable. Constables were therefore reduced to impersonal digital entities significant only in numbers to be deployed for the task at hand.

Between the officers and the men were the sub-inspectors who successfully managed to combine in themselves the worst aspects of both. The inspector was the highest non-gazetted rank, and the immediate agency for police functioning as he was in charge of the precinct police stations and police posts known as thanas and chowkis. In investigating as well as in law-and-order functions, he was again the immediate superior heading the team of constables. The sub-inspector enjoyed the delegated powers of the inspector and but for the fact that he was under the overall command of an inspector, there was little or no difference in his and the inspector's functioning. This buffer rank too had suffered because of the closed-end nature of the posting. The inspectors had only rare chances of ever being promoted to the gazetted levels. The ensuing frustration created a vested interest in the perpetration of corruption which radiated from these ranks in the two directions of the constables and the officers. In cases exposed in the past, the rank of the non-gazetted junior officers emerged as the vital link in the corruption chain. It was these frustrated junior officers who knew that they had little or no chance of further promotions whom Bhinder cultivated under the Emergency. In the days of the Emergency, this move was to save Bhinder time and again from the machinations of other senior officers who wanted to oust him.

Working under this double set of officers of the IPS and the subordinate services, the constabulary became susceptible to extreme frustration, a shattered morale and a serious grouse that the government and its police administration were giving them a raw deal. The overworked constable revolted in 1967 in one of the rarest displays of labour unity in a uniformed force. The strike was declared illegal and the leadership of the constabulary arrested and jailed. The government took pains to see that the backbone of the resistance in the police was shattered with a completeness that would ensure it never again posed a threat to the State. This was important to the government not only to keep its control over the police absolute, but also to see that the policeman could never make common cause with fellow workers in the country. The government had used the policeman in a very routine fashion to handle labour unrest and to break up strikes, with violence if necessary. It would not do to have the police joining them, or even actively sympathizing with them.

But it did him some good. It forced the government to appoint a high-powered judicial committee to investigate the causes of unrest among the police, to study the police structure and functioning, and to recommend measures to improve them so that the events that led to the police strike would never again be repeated. The Justice Khosla Committee report was to become one of the most damning documents against the Delhi Police till the report of the R. Prasad one-man committee ordered an investigation into the causes of the Sadar Bazaar communal riots of May 1974. That many of the suggestions made by Justice Khosla were found not to have been implemented even when the second report was submitted in 1975, was evidence of the government's attitude towards the police. The government, however, immediately implemented some measures to satisfy the police.

One of the recommendations not implemented was to give the Delhi Police a manual and regulations of its own. For years the Delhi Police had been operating on manuals designed for different types of state police. The methodology of police functioning that the other states followed was dictated by their own peculiar circumstances and often bore little or no relation to the special situation in the capital. Neither did the regulations. Within the police department, these regulations were necessary to streamline management and discipline. But these too were imported. The Delhi Police faithfully dispatched a police officer to the office of the superintendent of police for the manual, but it had still to make its appearance. A peculiar condition arose because of these lacunae. The officers and men of the Delhi Police generally followed the rules of the Punjab force for their functioning. But the inspectors general of police and the deputy inspectors general who came to Delhi followed different rules. Because the Delhi and Union Territories cadres of the IPS did not have officers of a seniority sufficient to take command as independent inspectors general, the practice had been to get the inspector general from other states with large stagnant pools of senior officers, or from the Intelligence Bureau at the central government headquarters, and lastly, from the central paramilitary forces like the BSF.

These officers were schooled in the rules of their own organizations. Some of them had little experience of managing a cosmopolitan city. They tried to impose a tougher style of functioning on the Delhi Police structure, which tried its best to obey, but if the gap between the rules and methods it knew and the new orders was too wide, the police force went into a crisis. The chasm between the senior officers and the main implementing officers of the rank of superintendents increased. Work suffered. To offset this, it had become a practice for the visiting inspector general to bring men of his own from their parent states when Bhinder came to Delhi to take charge. This of course immediately sparked off the formation of a new set of coteries, intrigue groups and pressure units. A new set of favourites and blue-eyed boys emerged. The morale of the force plummeted even further. Bhinder's coterie of favourites was not the first of its sort. The advantage, however, of Bhinder and his men over the previous coteries was that they enjoyed the backing of the two people who mattered most—Bansi Lal and Sanjay Gandhi—in the days of the Emergency.

Inspector General Rajgopal had taken over in such a situation. A competent officer of the BSF, Rajgopal found that he too needed men he had known and worked with to help him in the Delhi Police. With him came DIG Yusuf Rahim and SP Ashok Patel, an intelligence officer from the BSF who had been active in the counter-espionage cell; both came from Madhya Pradesh, Rajgopal's parent state of allotment. The three were to make one of the most successful teams in the history of the Delhi Police. With Rajgopal at the top and Rahim in overall charge of the crime and security wings, Patel ran up a series of spectacular successes, solving some of the most sensational crimes in the capital. Among them was the attempt by a band of youths to rob a bank van. They had killed the driver and the guard of the van and made off with a Rs 6-lakh loot. Patel caught them. In the sensational Vidya Jain murder case, Patel headed the team that exposed the conspiracy to kill the socialite wife of N.S. Jain, a famous city eye surgeon. Convicted in the case were the doctor himself, his one-time secretary and paramour Chandresh Sharma and a host of others.

Such triumphs created problems of their own. Jealous fellow officers in the Union Territory cadre launched a systematic campaign against Rahim and Patel, a campaign whose viciousness increased with every success racked up by the group. The morale plummeted further, as did the integrity of the force. And that was among the reasons that the police force lost whatever edge its vigilance and intelligence units possessed. While the new wave of scheming was to reduce the campaign strength of the officer corps to the level that they could do precious little to prevent Bhinder from coming or to stop him from doing things as he wanted, the real failure of the intelligence set-up was when the police were caught napping on 4 May 1974, when a minor dispute between three persons in a marketplace flared up into a communal riot of frightening intensity. The Delhi Police was exposed as an organization nursing a deep rot within it.

The Prasad investigating commission also unearthed other skeletons in the cupboard. The more sinister among them served as evidence during the commission's hearings of communal tendencies in the police and their colouring of its functioning. There was also the exposure of the acute distrust felt in the Delhi Police that its prosecutions were influenced not so much by the facts of the case as extraneous influences and pressures.

On the communal aspect, the commission had discovered that the minority communities did not have a fair representation in the force, and that the people of those communities therefore felt that the Delhi Police could not consider their interests with the desired impartiality. The utter barbarity shown by the police at Turkman Gate during the Emergency was not without its reason.

There was another reason for loss of faith, Prasad was to find:

> In the course of evidence, I have been struck by the near unanimity of the witnesses in expressing doubt about the impartiality of the police and the authorities in conducting investigations and charging cases before the courts. There seems to be a widespread belief that law and order authorities and particularly the police officers are subjected to the pulls and pressures from outside, especially from political parties and influential persons and that they do not have a free hand in dealing with matters in their own right. Respectable witnesses have spoken of officers of the administration being humiliated and browbeaten in the discharge of their duties.

The police were displaying other types of bias, often to hide their inefficiency. A classic case was their offensive against the Sansis, a tribe of nomads who had once during the British regime provoked the government into listing them in its abhorred list of criminal tribes. Long after they had been denotified by more enlightened state governments, the police were still using them as one of the stock excuses for explaining away the rise in crime in various areas. The police had of late conducted no research of its own to revaluate the socio-anthropological phenomena which could affect crime.

The police had to find ways out of its dilemmas because its own specialized departments were finding the going tough. The semi-secret CID and the special staff did their cloak-and-dagger business with a naivety that was startling. The process continued, with the result that the Delhi Police was virtually always in the dark about the activities in town. Its spies fed it with half-truths, concocted information and facts of such a trivial nature that they were not worth collecting at all. The police chiefs in fact got more information from newspaper reports than from their own sleuths because the sleuths—more so those who were detailed to keep tabs on political activity, students, youth and trade unions—themselves depended on newspaper sources for primary information. It was not uncommon to find that undercover police agents would walk up to their target, tell him point-blank that they were from the police and ask them if they could provide some information about their day's programme so that the policeman could make the proper report to his superiors. Another form of vigilance kept was at press conferences where semi-educated spies kept vigil and begged reporters returning from press conferences to spare them a copy of the press statements released by the organizers. Sometimes the CID man just asked the reporters what was the latest thing in town, and for reasons wide and varying, reporters generally obliged such of the cops as made no bones about their mission. The most pitiable case was of those policemen who pretended to be something other than policemen. At press conferences they pretended to be journalists. In mills, they thought they looked like the workers and in the university, the Delhi police got them admitted to various courses so they could be right in the centre of wherever things were happening. And always, the policeman stuck out like a sore thumb. At press conferences, he was the man with the folded newspaper and the writing pad. He was the man with the four pens sticking out his pocket, with the sheepskin cap in winter and the bush shirt in summer. He was the man who wore shoes without socks, and whose trousers were generally khaki, his crew cut an instant giveaway. 'Look carefully and on every CID man, you will find at least one piece of his uniform,' was the dictum followed by political leaders to spot the cop.

The subversion of its intelligence wing made the police more barbaric. If it could not get the right information, it had to act on more general measures. This fact explains why, when the political arrests during the Emergency came, they did not have any logic attributed to them. A large number of fictitious files had been built up on some people for the flimsiest of reasons. And even in the genuine files, a sizeable amount of poppycock was forced to masquerade as classified facts.

The day-to-day functioning of the police was done at the precinct or thana level where an inspector kept control of a section of the district. The thanas developed vested interests in the regions in which they were located. The commercial aspects of the area and the political leadership of the zone helped the police to cultivate a strongly entrenched system of thana-level corruption. The corruption was born of an open protection racket indulged in by the policemen with the connivance of the local political boss. For traders, the protection racket meant the payment of a weekly charge for police immunity from repeated prosecutions on the minor infringements that were so much a part of normal business. From petty traders and big businesses, from the local smuggler and the neighbourhood pickpocket, the police collected its 'toll' with the promise that it would look the other way.

This caused a gradation in the list of thanas based on their earning capacity. The ones in market areas and the big bazaars were the most sought after by sub-inspectors and policemen. Upwards, the district with the most market thanas became the prime posting. Its contribution to corruption among the police was tremendous. Not only were the policemen taking from the people, they were collecting money from other policemen as well. Some years ago, *Hindustan Times* in an investigative report exposed how the policemen and sub-inspectors paid heavily to get a desired transfer to the thana of their choice. In the same exposé, it was also disclosed that at the recruitment stage, the eligible candidates paid up to Rs 10,000 for a job as sub-inspector.[1]

But more than corruption, it was the criminality in the police force that was to matter subsequently. An expert committee in the home ministry[2] investigating the quality of manpower coming forward for police recruitment found in them a high percentage of latent criminality. Even in those who were selected, the latent criminality was evident. The report discovered that not only did policemen commit crimes of passion, like murders and assaults, but they also took part in organized crime and were sometimes found guilty of rape and molestation. The report found that men of the force who do not live with their wives (the average constable's wife lives in the village) in the Police Lines were more prone to sexual crimes.

Sources in the Delhi Police[3] revealed that in organized crime some policemen had been found to be involved with bands of robbers and pickpockets. They had connived in large robberies and in the business of stolen automobiles. And mostly, they had shielded criminals, leaked information to them, and saved many a smuggler from a prison term by warning him in the nick of time. This became evident in one of the first drives launched under MISA, enacted by the Indira Gandhi government in 1971, giving the police special powers to arrest those involved in organized crime such as smuggling. Despite the high publicity around the drive, sources in the Delhi police revealed that of the fifteen smugglers who were on the original list to be arrested, the police managed to nab only three. Significantly, many of the smugglers who had eluded the police net had done so with just minutes to spare.

The day Bhinder walked into the Delhi Police, the cumulative crisis of the force was coming to a head. The Class-IV employees, including the servitors, batmen, cooks and other menials, were grumbling at the apathy shown to them. The sub-inspectors were consolidating their position on the long-overdue promotions. The most immediate crisis was in the senior ranks of the deputy superintendents. The officers, some of them promoted from the ranks of inspectors and others appointed directly through a competitive examination, were slowly getting into a rebellious mood against what they said was a conspiracy to deny them their rights. In the previous year and a half, the DSPs had approached the IGP to get him to look into their demands which now included a protest that they were being humiliated by the IPS officers. The DSPs also made efforts to move the central ministry of home affairs, but their efforts again ended in failure. They requested that they be allowed to form an association. But their request was firmly rejected, even though the Delhi wing of the IPS cadre had an association that acted as a pressure group and had been active in taking care of the interests of its own members. The association chose not to take notice of the cause of the DSPs.

The frustration found an outlet elsewhere. Many police drives to check the soaring crime rates in 1974–75 met with failure, and sabotage was suspected.

The DSPs complain that though they were the backbone of the Delhi Police structure and formed the direct link between the policy planners at the top and the lower-order implementation machinery, the authorities had not changed the heartless promotion policy followed for them in which a DSP with over twelve years' experience in the service was routinely superseded by an IPS entrant with less than four years' service for the post of superintendent. The promotion rules contributed to the creation of a caste system in the police, and the DSPs who numbered about 100 found their position humiliating. In fact, they were contemplating further action when the Emergency was declared.

Bhinder found the Delhi Police frustrated with their lot. The things that were criticized as weaknesses—the strife, the intrigues and the corruption—could be turned into assets that could be extremely useful to him. He set about this task with a singular dedication under the Emergency. In the first phase, he succeeded in creating a coterie owing loyalty to him. It was easy for him to do so. An outsider, he was not party to the intrigues of the police officers in Delhi. He did not have to bother about any sensibilities. He started choosing his men, making his selection from the senior ranks of the superintendents down to the lowliest head constable, sometimes even the constable.

Within a short span of time, the rest of the officers and the constabulary knew who Bhinder's own men were. The yardstick was simple. The cushiest job, the sensitive job—each had to have on it someone Bhinder could command implicitly.

The rewards were big enough to guarantee this loyalty. Sub-inspectors who were with the 'in' group found themselves promoted within the shortest time possible. Inspectors far down on the seniority list were ordered to take charge as SHOs. A large number of them had vigilance and judicial inquiries against them. Bhinder's obvious motives behind these moves forced Bhawanimal to sit up and take notice. A running war started between the two, with Bhinder striving to get the transfers and promotions through and Bhawanimal staying the proceedings. In one instance, a long list of transfers was ordered by Bhinder when the IGP was away on leave. The IGP returned to find that the transfers he had been stalling for so long had been pushed through by his subordinate.

According to a Delhi Police source,[4] a vigilance inquiry had been ordered into widespread allegations that the confidential records of subordinate officers and men which were deposited in the special section had been withdrawn and changes made in them. The tampering was proved in the vigilance inquiry, but its findings were hushed up.

Towards the end of the first year of the Emergency, Bhinder had reached the pinnacle of his power. The district police all over the capital were firmly in his grasp and he was offering his private army to the municipal corporation and the DDA for their clearance and family-planning drives.

The IGP had meanwhile developed differences with the lieutenant governor. Only the principals involved knew what the precise reason was. But they were exposed to public view in the most dramatic circumstances when the IGP invited Krishan Chand to the New Police Lines at Kingsway Camp for the special Vanamahotsava drive that the police force was organizing in Delhi. Bhawanimal in his welcome address assured the lieutenant governor that the police force was always eager to take part in national programmes. Then came the lieutenant governor's turn. Krishan Chand stood up, looked around and spoke. He hailed the twenty-point programme, and the unprecedented wave of enthusiasm in the capital and the country. And then came the bombshell. Without preface, Krishan Chand said, 'The Delhi Police believes that only that governor is good who signs whatever paper the inspector general of police sends to him. The inspector general of police must be angry with me.' The top officers of the Delhi Police and the Delhi Administration, and the special invitees looked at each other to figure out what was going on. That something big was afoot had become obvious. The strain in the atmosphere had become a tangible presence.

Soon thereafter, Bhawanimal made a concerted effort to reassert his supremacy vis-à-vis Bhinder. The opportune time came with the inauguration of the family-planning drive among the police. Bhawanimal and his wife took a personal interest in the matter and the public relations department was soon eulogizing their services to the cause.

The Youth Congress involvement with the police had in fact started much earlier. When the police set up its Civil Voluntary Force (CVF) early in 1974, the idea was to involve the local public in the keeping of law and order and the prevention of crime. Within months, however, it became obvious that the CVF had legitimized to a considerable extent the interference of local politicians in the working of the thana police. Whereas earlier, politicians had to be content with exercising their powers through the obliging policeman, now they did so in their own right. It also became clear that the organization which was created to offer representation to the local people to play a part in the affairs of their community was being infiltrated by the bully and the extortionist—in fact, the same elements that gave to the Youth Congress its special flavour during the Emergency. The CVF had all but ceased to be an effective entity in the management of law and order when the Emergency revived it with a fresh dose of entrants. Only now they were called the lieutenant governor's Law and Order Thana-level Committees. They were again meant to help consolidate the gains of the Emergency and keep the peace in mohallas.

Most of the members of these committees were usually the local rich people, the local Congress councillors and members of the Youth Congress. They offered the thana police political patronage in exchange for generally accepting their commands. This was an ideal situation for the local bully. As a member of the Youth Congress, he could move the local police to take action on his requests. His ability to get the police whenever he wanted gave him just the extra leverage that made all the difference to the various fund-collecting drives that the members launched. It was no longer necessary to bother the higher-ups in the Youth

Congress or the programme implementation committee. Nor was it necessary to invoke the powerful names.

If these members got some people arrested, they also got others released. In many police stations, a telephone call or visit from such a person was enough to get the police to revise charges. Discussions during meetings of these members of the law-and-order committees often superseded the original findings of the investigating policeman himself.

chapter seven

THE DENOUEMENT

~

Prime Minister Indira Gandhi surveyed with satisfaction the massive crowd milling on the Boat Club lawns. She had been a little tense about this rally. Shashi Bhushan and other local Congress leaders had assured her that they would arrange for the numbers; crowds were no problem during the Emergency, they had assured her. Hadn't they got hundreds of people to come and support her outside her residence post the Allahabad Court judgment, before the Emergency was imposed? Yet she was apprehensive.

Next to the prime minister on the dais was Bhushan. He was an expert crowd gatherer. It was easy for him to arrange for truckloads of people to attend rallies like this one. A little money here, a little pressure there, and the crowds would come wherever required. Bhushan had been ignored during the Emergency by the prime minister.

The officials of the NDMC had come in the morning and inspected the dais and the arrangements for the rally. So had the prime minister's security men. And so had most of the local political leaders of the Congress, from ageing Executive Councillor Raman to Youth Congress leader Jagdish Tytler. This was a crucial rally.

The security arrangements were extensive. Rows and rows of Delhi Police and CRPF personnel stood by watchfully under the personal supervision of Bhinder. They did not expect any trouble. The gathering seemed harmless.

In the rectangular enclosures that the Boat Club lawns had been divided into by steel pipes sat what the officials and politicians called the crowd. It was a huge crowd. But its size was not the most significant thing about it. There was something inherently different in this throng from any other that had assembled in the past nineteen months.

The difference perhaps was not apparent from the dais. From up there, it was just a sea of black heads, a swarm of flies on a gigantic saucer. The large semicircle, empty but for some security men separating the dais from the cubicles, lay like a mile-long chasm. But down below, inside the enclosures, one could tell that every face bore a distinctive expression, and yet the faces complemented each other as they looked up at the dais. The expressions exuded a strange rebelliousness.

The assembly consisted mostly of government employees. This was their lunch break, but with a difference. This was not just a one-hour lunch break. The employees were free to come back to work any time they wanted in the afternoon. The employees had quite a few of these lunch breaks during the Emergency, depending on when the prime minister or her son had to address a rally and crowds were needed.

Their officers would have been shocked if they saw the employees now. This was not the cheer group that was the norm for such rallies. These people weren't clapping or shouting slogans. They were just laughing and joking among themselves as they sat under the sun. They were in a festive mood today. But not far beneath their laughter lay a strange mocking arrogance.

The trucks that were parked in a distant corner of the Boat Club had brought a paid 'cheergroup' from the far-off resettlement colonies. Five rupees and meals for the day—Who could resist this bait in the resettlement colonies! But there was no applause or sloganeering from this group either, as the people sat in separate enclosures. The rally meant no more than money and meals to them. They would do the barest minimum to earn that.

It was only a handful of Congress workers who could be seen clapping and cheering and they weren't particularly enthusiastic either. The workers weren't too happy about the rally. It meant too much hard work.

Bhushan was having second thoughts about the crowd.

'Why isn't there any clapping or slogan shouting?' he asked irritably to a Congress worker.

'We tried to get them to shout slogans and clap, Shashi Bhushanji but they just laughed at us,' replied a haggard worker.

Bhushan rose to address the crowd.

'Friends! First, I want you to clap and shout slogans to greet our beloved prime minister who has come to address you today,' he began.

There were signs of turbulence in the sea of black heads. The people seemed to be raising their hands and saying something. Bhushan could clearly see from the dais that the people were shaking their hands in the air.

'What is the matter? Can't you hear me?' he asked.

No answer. The hands kept waving up and down.

'Perhaps the loudspeakers aren't working,' suggested Raman standing beside him.

That could be it. Bhushan felt relieved.

'Okay, okay, I am getting the loudspeakers repaired this minute,' he told the crowd and, turning to a worker, instructed him to fix the speakers. But the worker returned within a few minutes and informed Bhushan that the loudspeakers were perfectly all right.

'The loudspeakers are working, aren't they? What is the matter now?' he asked the crowd. Still no answer. Only hands moving up and down.

'I think they want to hear you speak,' Bhushan turned to the prime minister and smiled weakly.

Down below, the men and women who had assembled for the rally were having the time of their lives. The moment Bhushan tried to speak, they raised their hands and started waving. His desperate instructions to the Congress workers about repairing the loudspeakers had been heard clearly and elicited much laughter in the enclosures. The crowd seemed to take deliberate pleasure in shooing Bhushan off the dais.

Mrs Gandhi fought off her tension and panic as she rose to address the crowd. She was too clever not to see through Bhushan's lie. The crowd was turning hostile, without any doubt.

As she rose, she stumbled on the wire of a mike, and a wave of jeers and laughter swept through the cubicles. What was happening to this crowd? Never in her eleven-year span as prime minister had she been treated like this by the people of Delhi.

'Brothers and sisters,' Mrs Gandhi began, 'I have come to you not as the prime minister but as your sister who is being attacked by reactionaries and vested interests.'

There were a few moments of hushed silence as the crowd stopped its laughter to hear the prime minister. Then a chant rose from one corner of the crowd. It was immediately taken up by another section and within a minute had spread throughout the cubicles all over the Boat Club lawns. The chant was getting louder and louder.

She stopped her address.

'What are they saying?' she asked the Congress leaders on the dais. Nobody had the courage to reply. But there was no need for an answer. Mrs Gandhi herself could now hear quite clearly what the crowd was saying.

'We want DA! We want DA!' the government employees were shouting. 'No DA, no vote!' they were chanting. Mrs Gandhi's words were unintelligible in the din.

There was a great deal of commotion among the rows of policemen standing beside the enclosures. 'Shut up!' bellowed a police officer. 'Won't shut up, what will you do?' the employees retorted. The officer shut up.

There was no restraining the crowd now. New slogans were added to the one about dearness allowance. 'Give us two sterilization cases and we will give you our vote,' they shouted. Some of them were on their feet now, waving their fists at the dais.

'Where is your son? Where are you hiding him?' they asked the prime minister.

'The cow is here but where is the calf?' jeered another group.

On the dais there was pandemonium. Raman and the others shrank back in a corner. They avoided looking at the crowd and the prime minister. Bhushan was like a madman. The rally was his responsibility, as he was the candidate for New Delhi.

'Go and stop them!' he ranted to his workers. But there were few Congress workers in sight. The few who were there tried their best not to be seen. One would have to be insane to try and stop this crowd.

Bhinder fumed: If only he were free to deal with the troublemakers! But his instructions had been clear: leave the crowd alone.

The prime minister was numb with rage. She had never been so openly rejected by the people of Delhi. But like the fighter that she was, she went on with her speech.

'I know that many of you are angry with what happened during the last nineteen months. I know that there were some excesses done on you,' she said, and for the first time in the meeting there was applause from the crowd.

'And these excesses were done not only by officials but also politicians,' the prime minister added with an emphasis that made the politicians on the stage shrink back farther. She would never forgive them for her humiliation today.

'But still, you must take a balanced view of the Emergency. There have been many good things that have been achieved during the last nineteen months and . . .' the prime minister stopped abruptly.

The swarm of flies was no longer sitting on the saucer. They had grown legs and were walking away. The crowd was walking out on the prime minister.

'I know that your lunchtime is over and you have to be back in your offices,' Mrs Gandhi made one last try. 'But remember, before you go, to vote for the Congress.' Her voice was almost broken. It was no use. The prime minister was talking to people who were walking away. Walking away after mocking her, she brooded darkly as she got into her car later, shaking with anger.

The first rally in New Delhi by Prime Minister Gandhi for the Lok Sabha election of 1977 at the Boat Club lawns on 1 March was over. It showed, as she had correctly presumed earlier, you could never tell with the people.

The denouement had started exactly a month earlier. On 2 February 1977, a bombshell had shaken the seeming monolith of the State: Jagjivan Ram, H.N. Bahuguna and a host of other Congressmen had resigned from the party and formed the Congress for Democracy. But since this had occurred in the capital, its impact was felt more immediately in Delhi than in other places. The elections had been announced less than two weeks ago, and though it had taken most officials and politicians of the capital by surprise, they had been confident at the outset.

There had not been a particularly mad scramble for seats. The State had grown too powerful during the Emergency to allow for much commotion. The people who had grown to be the most effective implementers of the whims of the State had been chosen as candidates and the few old Congressmen who still held fond hopes of sitting in Parliament had been told firmly what they could do with their hopes.

The first list of candidates had been full of the now all too familiar faces of the Emergency. Begum Ruksana Sultana of course found a prominent place in the list. She was standing from Chandni Chowk constituency where residents of Turkman Gate and Dujana House would have the privilege of voting for her. The Coca-Cola magnate, Charanjit Singh, had got the New Delhi constituency, DPCC President A.N. Chawla from Sadar, Youth Congress firebrand Jagdish Tytler from South Delhi, Executive Councillor Krishan Swaroop and H.K.L. Bhagat, the old faithful servant of the young prince, had got the Karol Bagh and East Delhi constituencies respectively. The elections would put a parliamentary seal to the new faces that had risen during the Emergency.

All this changed with the explosion of the 'J-Bomb' on 2 February 1977. The first list vanished. In its place came a new one which, though retaining a few of the old names, dropped such vital names as Ruksana Sultana, Tytler and Swaroop. Charanjit Singh, the shrewd business magnate, retained his nomination with a burst of generosity to the Congress party.

But the Begum Sahiba was heartbroken. 'The people of Jama Masjid would feel let down if I don't stand from there,' she had sobbed to one of the senior official admirers. 'See if you don't need my help in campaigning there,' she had challenged, brushing away a tear. The new candidate was the once-discarded Subhadra Joshi brought in to fight for the third time from the constituency. It would be third time unlucky for Joshi.

But the impact of Jagjivan Ram's resignation had been far greater on the people of Delhi than on the politicians. The day the bombshell burst, the public erupted in joy and enthusiasm. Never before had newspaper supplements been read so avidly as when they announced the resignation.

The enthusiasm had steadily mounted day by day. This was evident in the contrast between the size and quality of the crowds at rallies of the Congress and of the Janata Party.

Congressmen in Delhi were surprised at the utter hostility of the people of the capital when they went to address election meetings. Bhagat was garlanded with shoes when he went to speak at a meeting at Shahdara, while a second venture with Sanjay Gandhi to Khichripur was even more unfortunate. The car in which the two were travelling was surrounded on the way and they barely managed to escape the mob fury and come back. No wonder Sanjay Gandhi stayed pointedly away from Delhi during the pre-election campaigning.

Worse still, people refused to turn up for most of the Congress meetings.

On one such occasion, Bhushan was addressing an election meeting at Nizamuddin attended by exactly fifteen people, when two among them got up.

'See those people walking away from the meeting. They are RSS fascist workers. They are trying to sabotage the meeting,' Bhushan screamed as he saw them walking away.

The two men stopped. They turned to Bhushan and politely told him that they were not RSS reactionaries and that they were not going away. In fact, they had got up merely to ease themselves. Amidst the Homeric laughter that followed, the meeting was dissolved. The Congressmen were slowly becoming paranoid.

Rallies by the Janata Party on the other hand drew giant crowds, the size and scale of which Delhi had never seen before. People would throng every square inch of space available at the venues and many even clambered on to the dais and press galleries. There were no security men to keep the people away at the Janata Party rallies. None were needed.

Faced with this growing hostility, the officialdom hurriedly announced massive concessions to the people. Suddenly, the State was bending over backwards to accommodate the people's demands. Withdrawal of family-planning incentives, regularization of unauthorized colonies, release of dearness allowance and pay hikes were only a few of the concessions given by the government as pre-election sops to the people.

But the nineteen months had made the people clever enough not to believe promises by the government.

'Take the note from the Congress, and give the vote to the Janata,' became one of the most common slogans seen on the walls of the capital as reports spread of Congress campaigners distributing 100-rupee notes to voters.

In its desperation, the Congress used intimidation to stop more and more people going over to the Janata camp. But this plan also boomeranged. After a series of engineered incidents of fighting, serious violence erupted on the afternoon of 13 March 1977, at Gali Niarian in Farah Khana, less than 2 kilometres from Turkman Gate.

The Janata Party office situated deep inside Gali Niarian was attacked. In the melee about ten Janata Party workers were seriously injured, while a police sub-inspector died.[1]

The death of the sub-inspector was, strangely enough, hushed up by the police themselves. In normal times, and particularly during the Emergency, the death of a sub-inspector would spark off hundreds of arrests and beatings. But on 13 March, it figured only as a small news item in the police bulletin, which said the sub-inspector had died of a heart attack. With elections only three days away, the State was lying low.

Election day at Turkman Gate, 16 March 1977. Since morning, long queues of men and burqa-clad women lined up to cast their votes. By 3.30 p.m., a polling booth in Turkman Gate had recorded 856 votes; of that, only fifteen had gone to the Congress. The figures were known to the officer at the booth because the voters had told him, 'Look, we don't know how to put the vote in the ballot box. So why don't you put it in? We are all voting Janata, it's no secret.' The amazed presiding officer had done the people's bidding.

At the resettlement colonies, the election turnout was fantastic. After a long time so much enthusiasm was seen among these broken hutments. For one day, the people of the wilderness decided to forget about the daily race for survival. They voted en masse against the bulldozers that had sent them here.

Counting day, 21 March 1977. From 1 p.m. to midnight, few of the capital's 7 million people slept. Till late at night hundreds of people lined up in front of the counting centres and newspaper election boards, while others kept their ears glued to their transistors. The results they heard and saw cancelled out the nineteen-month-old State with unbelievable ease.

The results were:

The Congress Loses All Seven Seats.

Atal Behari Vajpayee of Janata Party beat Shashi Bhushan of Congress by 80,294 votes in New Delhi.

T.N. Sarsunia of Janata Party beat T. Sohan Lal of Congress by 65,000 votes in Karol Bagh.

V.K. Malhotra of Janata Party beat Charanjit Singh of Congress by 1.07 lakh votes in South Delhi.

Kanwar Lal Gupta of Janata Party beat A.N. Chawla of Congress by 79,871 votes in Sadar.

Choudhry Brahm Prakash of Janata Party beat Choudhry Dilip Singh of Congress by 1.04 lakh votes in Outer Delhi.

Kishore Lal of Congress for Democracy fighting on Janata symbol defeated H.K.L. Bhagat of Congress by 1.33 lakh votes in East Delhi.

And

Sikandar Bakht of the Janata Party defeated Subhadra Joshi of the Congress by 1.5 lakh votes in Chandni Chowk.

Turkman Gate is in the Chandni Chowk parliamentary constituency.

AFTERMATH

~

The Politicians:

Sanjay Gandhi, second son of Mrs Indira Gandhi, prime
minister of India. Imprisoned by the Janata government
for two months but still managed to craft Mrs Gandhi's
comeback in the 1980 elections. Hailed by the Congress
as the successor to Mrs Gandhi. He, however, died a few
months later, on 23 June 1980, after the plane he was flying
crashed near Safdarjung Airport, New Delhi.

V.C. Shukla, information and broadcasting minister. Imprisoned
along with Sanjay Gandhi by the Janata government, he
became a minister when Indira Gandhi came back to
power and again in the government of Rajiv Gandhi but
joined in the revolt against him by V.P. Singh and other
Congress leaders in the late 1980s. He became a minister in
the short-lived Janata Dal government and then switched
his loyalties to the even briefer Chandrasekhar regime.
He returned to the Congress, holding ministerial berths
in the Narasimha Rao government in the 1990s but later
shifted to the breakaway National Congress Party from
where he defected to the BJP. From there, he returned
to the Congress some years later. After his many political
perambulations, Shukla died a gruesome death at the age

of eighty-three in a Chhattisgarh forest, shot dead by Naxalites.

Bansi Lal, defence minister, formerly chief minister of Haryana. He became chief minister of Haryana again twice, first when Rajiv Gandhi was in power and later in 1996 after he broke away from the Congress, forming his own Haryana Vikas Party and winning power in the state. He died in March 2006 after a protracted illness.

H.K.L. Bhagat, Congress MP from Shahdara and Union minister of state for works and housing. Chairman of the Programme Implementation Committee, Delhi. Although he helped Indira Gandhi to come back in 1980 and win the local elections in 1983, Bhagat became a controversial figure for his role in the 1984 anti-Sikh riots after Mrs Gandhi's assassination. He was indicted by the Nanavati Commission for his involvement in the anti-Sikh riots but the government declined to prosecute him because of his poor health. He died in 2005 after a protracted illness.

Jagdish Tytler, president, Delhi Youth Congress. After Indira Gandhi's comeback, he became central minister in several governments, including that of Rajiv Gandhi and Narasimha Rao. He was charged along with Bhagat for his role in the 1984 anti-Sikh riots and the Nanavati Commission found 'credible evidence' against him for being involved indirectly in the violence, although the government did not prosecute him for 'lack of concrete evidence'. The CBI gave him a clean chit in 2009, provoking protests by Sikhs which forced the Congress high command not to give him a ticket for the parliamentary polls. In 2013, the Supreme Court rejected the CBI clean chit to Tytler and asked investigations to be reopened against him.

Om Mehta, minister of state for home. Accepted full personal responsibility for all decisions taken by his ministry during the Emergency while appearing before the Shah Commission investigating Emergency excesses. He did not participate in active politics after the Congress was defeated in 1977, and died in February 1995.

Ambika Soni, Youth Congress president and Rajya Sabha member. She held several senior party and ministerial posts in subsequent Congress governments.

Shashi Bhushan, member of Parliament and ace crowd collector for the Congress. He faded away in politics after the defeat of the Congress in 1977 and focused on social work. Bhushan was awarded the Padma Bhushan in 2006 for promoting communal harmony by the Manmohan Singh–led UPA government. He died in 2011.

Radha Raman, chief executive councillor and Congress Election Campaign Committee chief in Delhi. Announced he would not seek election to the Metropolitan Council after the defeat of the Congress and died a few years later.

Vidyaben Shah, president, NDMC. Stayed away from politics and promoted social welfare, education and culture over several decades.

Charanjit Singh, vice president, NDMC, owner of Coca-Cola franchise. Lost in his electoral debut in the 1977 polls but won three years later when Indira Gandhi made her comeback. He, however, did not pursue his political career, choosing instead to concentrate on his soft drinks empire and the hotel industry.

Arjan Das, motor-mechanic friend and confidant of Sanjay Gandhi. He was a member of the Delhi Metropolitan Council but his political career never took off because of Sanjay Gandhi's death in a plane crash shortly after the Congress came back to power in 1980. Das, who was charged by Sikh civil liberties groups for instigating the 1984 anti-Sikh riots, was assassinated by Sikh militants in his office on 5 September 1985.

Ruksana Singh/Sultana, glamorous socialite friend of Sanjay, who was involved in the sterilization drive in the Muslim

ghettos of the walled city in Delhi. With her political
ambitions thwarted by the defeat of the Congress in 1977
and the death of her mentor in 1980, she faded away from
public life and went back to selling boutique jewellery.

The officials:

Jagmohan, vice chairman of the DDA responsible for the
demolition drive against slums in Delhi and moving their
residents to rehabilitation settlements on the outskirts
of the city. He was promoted to lieutenant governor of
Delhi after the Congress regained power in 1980 and later
made Governor of Jammu and Kashmir where he raised
controversy by dismissing the Farooq Abdullah government
in the summer of 1984. He later joined the BJP and
served as a minister in the Atal Behari Vajpayee–led NDA
government, winning several parliamentary elections from
Delhi. Now retired from politics.

Krishan Chand, ICS (Retd), lieutenant governor and
administrator, Union Territory of Delhi. Resigned after
the Lok Sabha elections in 1977. Although he claimed in
front of the Shah Commission investigating Emergency
excesses that he had only followed orders, Chand was
blamed by other members of the Emergency coterie for
being responsible. After several months of being grilled
by the Shah Commission, the former lieutenant governor
committed suicide under mysterious circumstances, walking
out of his South Delhi residence on the night of 9 July 1978
and jumping into an abandoned well.

Navin Chawla, IAS, Secretary to the lieutenant governor, with
special magisterial powers. Transferred to the Lakshadweep
Islands in the Arabian Sea after the defeat of the Emergency
regime. He was rehabilitated later and, after serving in several
senior bureaucratic posts, was appointed the chief election

commissioner of India by the Manmohan Singh–led UPA government. He also wrote a biography of Mother Teresa.

B.R. Tamta, IAS, MCD commissioner. Transferred to the Andaman and Nicobar Islands in the Bay of Bengal after the defeat of the Emergency regime. He turned approver during the Shah Commission hearings and implicated Sanjay Gandhi in Emergency excesses. He later tried to start a regional party that failed to take off. Tamta also wrote a book on the Andaman and Nicobar Islands.

Sushil Kumar, IAS, chief secretary of the Delhi Administration, former deputy commissioner and district magistrate of Delhi. Reverted to his service cadre home state Andhra Pradesh where he served in several bureaucratic posts.

V.S. Ailawadi, IAS, member secretary, NDMC. Served in several bureaucratic posts in his service cadre home state Haryana and after retirement was posted as chairman of the Haryana Electricity Regulatory Commission.

The Police:

Bhawanimal, IPS, inspector general of police. Retired as chairman of Rajasthan State Road Transport Corporation.

Pritam Singh Bhinder, IPS, deputy inspector general of police (range). After the fall of the Emergency regime, arrested in the Sunder dacoit murder case but acquitted by the court for lack of evidence. After the Congress returned to power in 1980, Bhinder was promoted over several other more senior Delhi Police officials to become the all-powerful police chief of the national capital. However, he lost his clout after the death of his mentor, Sanjay Gandhi, and was shunted out of Delhi. He was later inspector general of police in Punjab and director general of police in Haryana. His wife, Sukhbans Kaur Bhinder, was a Congress member of Parliament for several terms from Punjab.

Gurcharan Singh, IPS, superintendent of police, East District. Arrested along with his boss Bhinder in the Sunder dacoit murder case, he was acquitted along with him. He subsequently served in several posts in the Delhi Police and home ministry.

Sukhdev Singh, DSP, sub-divisional police officer, Gandhi Nagar. Arrested in the Sunder dacoit murder case, he was acquitted and returned to the Delhi Police.

Others:

Syed Abdullah Bukhari, shahi imam of Jama Masjid, Delhi. Because of his role in mobilizing Muslims against the Emergency regime, particularly the sterilization campaign, he became very influential after the Janata government came to power. Prime Minister Morarji Desai is said to have even offered him the job of India's vice president which he turned down. With the return of the Congress in 1980, his power waned but he once again became influential after the V.P. Singh government was formed in 1989. In 2000, he handed over his clerical post to his son, Syed Ahmed Bukhari, and died in 2009 at the age of eighty-seven.

GLOSSARY

~

Burqa	A veil to cover the body of Muslim women in purdah
Chowdhry	Honorific for local elder, clan chief or former landlord; also caste name
Chowk	Crossing or square
Chowki	Police post, or sub-police station
Lathis	Batons of varying sizes used by police forces; made of cane, often covered with leather and sometimes tipped with brass
Masjid	Mosque
Namaz	Muslim prayers, said five times a day
Nasbandi	Sterilizations, especially vasectomy
Randi	Whore
Rehriwala	Hand-cart puller
Sambal	Heavy iron or steel pick used in demolition
Tangawala	Driver of a horse-driven two-wheeled carriage used as popular transport in older and poorer sections of the city
Tasla	A steel hood or plate for removing slurry or debris
Thana	Police station

Ranks in the Police

Gazetted officers (in descending order)
Inspector general (IGP)
Deputy inspector general (DIG)
Senior superintendent (SSP)
Superintendent (SP)
Assistant/Deputy superintendent of police (DSP)

Senior subordinate officers
Inspector
Sub-inspector (SI)
Assistant sub-inspector (ASI)

Other ranks
Head constable
Constable/jawan (for BSF and CRPF)

APPENDIX I

~

RAJ NIWAS DELHI

PRESS NOTE

The Lt. Governor, Shri Krishan Chand, has been laying a great deal of stress on Family Planning on December 26, 1975 he inaugurated a special camp in Kasturba Hospital. A noteworthy feature of this camp is that the financial incentive was raised 5 times in the case of motivators. Hitherto, motivators were paid Rs 2/- per case. On the special camp motivators were paid Rs 10/-. In a special Camp held in September 1975 as many as 425 operations had been performed within a fortnight. This was considered a record. A second camp was organized in the same area from December 26, 1975. In a fortnight about 1000 operations were performed.

In addition to various camps which are going on in different parts of the city including the Badarpur and Shahdara area, the Delhi Administration, under the Lt. Governor's directions, has been processing several incentive and disincentive measure to lower the birth rate in the Union Territory of Delhi.

It has now been decided that incentives and dis-incentives will apply both to the general public and the employees of

Delhi Administration. The measures which are likely to come
into force almost immediately are as follow:

(A) *For the General Public*
(i) Allotment of houses, flats, tenements, shops and plots in
all groups i.e. Janta, Lower, Middle and other income groups
will be made to only those who have limited their family
to two children. An eligible couple will be open to hire
purchase and instalment basis facilities. Those couples that
are not eligible would have to pay for all such houses etc on
lumpsum basis. (An eligible couple for the provision of these
facilities means a couple who has less than two children and
has given the prescribed undertaking, or a couple having two
or more children who get either spouse sterilised).

(ii) Non-eligible couples will not be eligible to houses,
buildings loans. (An eligible couple for the provision of this
facility means a couple who has less than two children and has
given the prescribed undertaking, or a couple having two or
more children who get either spouse sterilised).

(iii) Entrepreneurs having two children coming forward
for establishment of a small scale industry will be entitled
to loan only if they get themselves sterilized and produce a
sterilization certificate from the authority prescribed. Those
having more than two children will not be eligible at all. Those
having no/one child they will be entitled to loan only on
furnishing and undertaking that they will restrict their family
to two children only. They will have, further, to furnish an
yearly declaration about the number of children and will also
be bound to inform the department of any addition in the
family. Any breach of the undertaking will entail withdrawal
of loan facilities, forfeiture of the payment already made and
recovery of the balance as arrears of land revenue.

(iv) Only individuals who have been able to show by their
ration cards that they have two or less than two children will

be allowed free medical coverage in Government hospitals. Those having more than two children will receive this free coverage only after producing a sterilisation certificate from the authority prescribed in respect of the husband. Those who have failed to obtain this sterilisation certificate will have to pay a minimum of Rs 5/- per visit for the OPD, and Rs 10/- for the indoor.

(B) *Government Servants, Employees of Local Bodies, Government Undertakings etc. | Autonomous Institutions Under Delhi Administration.*

(i) *Recruitment Stage:* At the time of interview individuals having two or less than two children will get due weightage.

(ii) Before appointment, unmarried/recently married/ those having less than two children will have to give an undertaking that they will limit their family to two children. Breach of the undertaking will dis-entitle the employed member from confirmation.

(iii) Such individuals who have more than two children, within two months of the issue of this order will have to get sterilised before they can be appointed and produce a sterilisation certificate from the authority prescribed.

(iv) Employment of daily wages/seasonal basis e.g. Malaria Workers will be only available to such individuals who have two or less than two children or who have obtained sterilisation certificates from the authority prescribed.

In Service Personnel

(i) Those having more than two children shall not be entitled to festival advance, housing loan, car/scooter advance, cooperative loan, allotment of scooter on priority basis till they get themselves sterilised or until they give the prescribed undertaking. In the case of such personnel already having more than two children, they will not be entitled to these facilities until they get sterilised and produce a sterilisation certificate from the prescribed authority.

(ii) Those having more than two children will not be entitled to government accommodation if they do not get sterilised or if they fail to give a written undertaking that they will limit their family to two children. Those in occupation of Government accommodation will become dis-entitled as soon as there is a child added to the family beyond two children. In the case of such employees who are already in occupation of Government accommodation and have already more than two children, they shall be entitled to retain the Government accommodation only after getting sterilised and producing a sterilisation certificate from the authority prescribed.

(iii) All freeships, provision of free book grants, children education allowance, uniform allowance, washing allowance and similar other allowances which the lower income group amongst the Government servants enjoy today, will be available only to the employed members from amongst eligible couples.

(iv) Such Government servants who limit their families to one will be entitled to out of turn allotment of plots, houses, tenements from Delhi Development Authority. For this purpose a special quota will be reserved.

(C) *Community Incentives*

(i) Gaon Sabhas in the rural sector who produce the maximum number of sterilisation cases in one financial year (minimum 100 cases) will be entitled to drinking water and irrigation water facilities on a priority basis.

(ii) A metropolitan constituency which produced the maximum number of cases will be entitled to a certain community incentive like beautification, additional schools, health benefits and similar services. The elected representative of such a constituency will get an incentive of Rs 20,000/- to be used for the betterment of his constituency.

(iii) Such Government servants especially who are opinion leaders in their areas e.g. doctors, nurses, paramedical staff teacher who set 50 or more than 50 sterilisation done in a year will be entitled to a letter of commendation and an extra increment. A Government servant who tops in this performance (family workers excluded) will in addition receive an honorarium of Rs 100/- per month the following year.

APPENDIX II

~

LIEUTENANT GOVERNOR'S SECTT.
DELHI

PRESS RELEASE
DELHI, APRIL 19, 1976

The Lt. Governor, Shri Krishan Chand, has issued the following statement to the press:

'Certain reports are reaching the Administration that some interested persons are bent on creating conditions in which the work of family planning can not be carried in an orderly manner.

The facts are that as a result of the persistent efforts of the Motivational Committee on Family Planning headed by Smt. Vidyaben Shah, President, NDMC, and of Ruksana Sultana Saheba, 15,000 persons male and female have offered themselves voluntarily for measures which will check the reproduction of unwanted children permanently. The people are motivated because large families, particularly in the city areas, live in very trying conditions of housing, education and incomes generally.

There are certain vested interests who for their own reasons want to impede the process of this vital social programme. Family planning constitutes the core of national re-construction on which the nation has embarked. It is the duty of every citizen to give full co-operation in this stupendous task. By restricting the size of families, the living standards will go up. The economic gains conserved and a new era of prosperity ushered. I am confident that the small groups with vested interests will not be allowed to operate to the determent of the vast sections of our people.

I want to make it clear beyond doubt that if any obstruction is caused to the doctors, the nurses or the personnel and the workers engaged in promoting the family planning programme, very drastic action will be taken against the offending persons.

Today itself in Dujana House, where a family planning camp was opened only four days ago, over 300 cases have already been treated. I am certain that this momentum will gather in strength. We are at the beginning of the work and by no means it is the end of it. It is necessary to have the co-operation of all right thinking persons so that this stupendous programme can be successfully executed.

It is the duty of the Delhi Administration that all incentives disincentives are offered for carrying on the work successfully. Some of the measures already taken have been announced and the public will be kept fully informed of further measures and facilities to be provided from time to time.

APPENDIX III

~

MUNICIPAL CORPORATION OF DELHI
CENTRAL ESTABLISHMENT SECTION

No. 15/CES/HCIV   Dated: 15.4.76

OFFICE ORDER

In continuation of this circular No. 14/CES (HCIV) dated
6.4.76 and the instructions issued by the Health Deptt. vide
their circular No. HD/MSCW/76-481, dated 1.4.1976,
the following further/instructions are issued to all heads of
the Deptts./ZACs/Drawing & disbursing officers for strict
compliance to make the programme of family planning a real
success:

(i) No recruitment or promotion, efficiency bar,
increments or confirmation of any staff member of any
category be done till he/she produces sterilization certificate
if he/she has more than two children.

(ii) All muster roll employees and daily wages may be
allowed to get six days leave with full pay after vasectomy
operation and 14 days leave with pay after tubectomy
operation.

(iii) A municipal employee will be entitled to get municipal accommodation only if he/she produces sterilization certificate in case he/she has more than two children. *Those already in possession of accommodation have either to produce the certificate within one month of issue of these instructions or penal rent will be charged from them.*

(iv) No loans or advances from provident fund etc. be sanctioned to any employee till sterilization certificate is produced if he/she has more than two children.

(v) No earned leave or any other long leave sanctioned to the employee except on medical grounds unless sterilization certificate is produced if he/she has more than two children.

(vi) No reimbursement of the cost of medicines be allowed till sterilization certificate is produced if he/she has more than two children.

(vii) No maternity or abortion leave be granted to a female employee who already has two children.

(viii) No fellowships in India or abroad will be granted to any official having more than two children unless he/she produced a certificate that he/she has undergone sterilization.

2. All heads of the Deptts./RACs/ drawing & disbursing officers may please get information filed up in the enclosed proforma (A) within 4 days of the receipt of this order or by 30th April, 1976 whichever is earlier, in respect of each officer/ working under them and ensure that aforesaid instructions are fully enforced in respect of officers/officials having more than two children and those having two children are made to give an undertaking in the following form:-

UNDERTAKING

'I hereby declare that I have at present------children only and I hereby undertake to restrict my family to two children only.

In the event of breach of this undertaking, I understand that I get exposed to any penalty that may be prescribed by the competent authority'.

'I further undertake to furnish yearly declaration about the number of children and to immediately inform the administration about any addition to the family. Failure to inform the Government in time would also mean breach of undertaking.'

3. Unless the concerned officer/official furnishes the above information his salary be not released.

4. In proforma 'B' of this circular is enclosed department wise targets of sterilization which have to be achieved by each Deptt. by 30th April, 1976. ZACs will make department wise break up for their respective zones so that the zonal target is achieved by them.

Sd/-

(V.K. CHANANA)

DY. COMMISSIONER (C)

To All Concerned

ANNEXURE 'B'

Sterilisation Targets for April 14 to 30, 1976

Health Department	1300
Engineering	1000
Education	1000
Garden	500
Water & Sewage	1000
D.E.S.U.	1000
Assessment & Collection	100
Terminal Tax	100
Urban Community Development	300
C.E.S.	400
C.A.	100
Labour Welfare	100
Licensing & Enforcement	100
Law Office	50
Vigilance	
Fire	50
Total:	7100

N.B.:
ZACS to implement and see that the Zonal break up of the targets by various departments is achieved.

APPENDIX IV

~

MUNICIPAL CORPORATION OF DELHI
CIVIL LINE ZONE

No. 124/D/G/7/CIZ   Dated: 26.4.76

It has been ordered by the Commissioner that all Muster Roll Employees as well as temporary employees eligible for sterilization should produce a certificate of sterilization by 30th April, 1976 or else they will lose their job in the corporation. This fact should be clearly made home to all the employees under you.

He has also directed that if other officers/officials of the Corporation eligible for sterilization get themselves sterilized before 30.4.76, they may be transferred to the place of their choice in addition to incentives already communicated to them earlier while those who although eligible but do not get themselves sterilized by 30.4.76 will have to be shifted to unimportant place of posting in addition to the disincentives already communicated to them earlier. In this way the employees on outdoor duties will be shifted to indoor duties.

I would again emphasize upon you all that the commissioner has desired in unequivocal terms that employees eligible for sterilization showing reluctance for sterilization will have to be dealt with very severely. It should also be noted that target date for oneself getting sterilized is 30.4.76. Please inform me by 9 A.M. tomorrow that the contents of this order have been communicated by you to each and every member of the staff working under you.

You will all be meeting me daily at 9 A.M. in my office in this connection with the figures of achievements.

Sd/-
Zonal Asstt. Commissioner (CLZ)

All Heads of Deptt. and Ward Officers,
Civil Line Zone

NOTES

~

Introduction to the 2018 Edition

1. Omar Rashid, 'Uttar Pradesh's Encounters: 1,000 and Counting', *The Hindu*, 31 March 2018, http://www.thehindu.com/news/national/ups-encounters-1000-counting/article23404224.ece. See also, 'A Chronicle of the Crime Fiction That Is Adityanath's Encounter Raj', Wire.in, 24 February 2018, https://thewire.in/rights/chronicle-crime-fiction-adityanaths-encounter-raj

Prologue: Bioscope

1. 'Most Important Out Today' is the nomenclature given to a very important category of order issued by the Delhi Administration.
2. The order quoted above is verbatim. The language may be difficult to understand to the layman, but it is intelligible to those who have to carry it out.
3. 'Shri Ruksana Singh' mentioned in the press note is Begum Ruksana Sultana.
4. DDA Vice Chairman Jagmohan's quote attributed by Chowdhry Kaimuddin, resident of Turkman Gate and member of delegation that went to see Jagmohan to stop the DDA demolition in the area. This is from a direct quote in the chapter 'The Story of Turkman Gate', by Kaimuddin, interviewed by the authors at Turkman

Gate in April 1977. In his book, *Island of Truth*, Jagmohan denied he had said this.

5. Direct quote from speech on 1 March 1977 by Syed Abdullah Bukhari, shahi imam of Jama Masjid, at midnight meeting at Jama Masjid.

Chapter One: The Story of Turkman Gate

1. In his book, *Island of Truth*, Jagmohan denied he had said this.

Chapter Two: The Bulldozers

1. Quote from a senior official of the Delhi Administration who could not be named because he was a source.

Chapter Four: The Days of the Long Knives

1. All orders on sterilization by the office of Delhi Lt Gov. Krishan Chand quoted in the book are reproduced verbatim from a press note issued by the Raj Niwas Delhi on 26 December 1975. The authors have a copy of the press note.

Chapter Five: The Dinosaurs . . .

1. The quote of Ambika Soni was attributed by Virender Kapoor, the reporter concerned, who was interviewed by the authors. The authors have the notes.

Chapter Six: . . . And the Primeval Slush

1. From a report by Chand Joshi in *Hindustan Times* on 17 May 1971.
2. From an expert committee set up by the home ministry in 1973 to prepare an internal report to help police recruitment. The contents of the report were shared on condition of anonymity

by an individual expert with John Dayal, in his capacity as crime reporter of the *Patriot*. This was subsequently carried in a report in the *Patriot*.

3. Based on information given by sources in the Delhi Police to John Dayal, in his capacity as crime reporter. They were carried in reports in the *Patriot*. The information was gathered from Delhi Police sources between 1972 and 1975 by Dayal when he was crime reporter for the *Patriot*.

4. Details of the vigilance inquiry were revealed by a Delhi Police source to John Dayal.

Chapter Seven: The Denouement

1. The clash on 13 March 1977 between Congress and Janata Party workers at the Turkman Gate Janata Party camp was reported in all the Delhi newspapers the next day, 14 March 1977.